Praise Fo

"HISTORY WILL N
ment to the cause of fr

—*President Ronald Reagan*

"Bill Casey, with his intelligence, courage, wit and zest, contributed enormously to his family, his country, his President, and his friends."

—*The Honorable Jeane F. Kirkpatrick,*
former U.S. Ambassador to the United Nations

"From his extraordinary achievements in OSS through a productive private career . . . down through his dynamic leadership of the CIA, Bill Casey was a far-sighted and patriotic public servant. In the secret intelligence world, history will record him as a sophisticated analyst of geopolitical conflict and a fearless activist trying to protect the security of our vulnerable democratic society."

—*Dr. Ray S. Cline, Chairman of*
The United States Global Strategy Council and
former Director of Intelligence at the State Department

"No one is better qualified to discuss this aspect of OSS history."

—*Ambassador Richard Helms, former Director*
of Central Intelligence and a former OSS officer

WILLIAM CASEY was Chief of the London OSS headquarters during World War II, and Chief of Secret Intelligence for General Dwight D. Eisenhower's European operations. He was awarded the Bronze Star. In 1981 Mr. Casey became Director of the CIA. He died May 6, 1987.

THE SECRET WAR AGAINST HITLER

WILLIAM CASEY

BERKLEY BOOKS, NEW YORK

This Berkley book contains the abridged
text of the original hardcover edition.
It has been completely reset in a typeface
designed for easy reading and was printed
from new film.

THE SECRET WAR AGAINST HITLER

A Berkley Book / published by arrangement with
Regnery Gateway

PRINTING HISTORY
Regnery Gateway edition published 1988
Berkley edition / June 1989

ISBN: 0-425-11615-8

A BERKLEY BOOK ® TM 757,375
Berkley Books are published by The Berkley Publishing Group,
200 Madison Avenue, New York, New York 10016.
The name "BERKLEY" and the "B" logo
are trademarks belonging to Berkley Publishing Corporation.

PRINTED IN THE UNITED STATES OF AMERICA

10 9 8 7 6 5 4 3 2

Acknowledgments

The publishers wish to acknowledge the assistance of John E. Taylor, Professor Arthur L. Funk, Thomas Troy, Al Graham, Edward Mark, Robert Haslach, Lawrence H. MacDonald, Timothy Mulligan, Richard J. Summers, and Betty Murphy in the preparation of this book.

Contents

Foreword

IT IS EASY, too easy, to blame Bill Casey for anything that went wrong with American intelligence towards the close of the Reagan presidency. In December 1986, while Director of the Central Intelligence Agency, Casey had a severe stroke, due to a brain tumour; he died in the following May. Since then, as he can neither answer back nor sue for libel, he has become everybody's whipping-boy. He was denounced, for instance, on the authority of Bob Woodward, as "the man who broke the rules" in the London *Observer* on 27 September 1987. Yet he remains a significant figure in current American history; and those who believe him guilty of improper conduct of the nation's secret affairs will be as interested as those who think him innocent in the account that follows, of how his views on the role of intelligence were originally formed.

He learned in a tough and practical school, during a world war. This book shows how he progressed, in little over two years, from a posting to run David Bruce's office for him in

London—where Bruce then headed the Office of Strategic
Services' mission: it was long before he became ambassador—to becoming the chief of secret intelligence for the European theater of operations. That is, he moved from being
a senior clerk to being—at the age of thirty-one—a force that
could help decide the fate of nations.

He explains how, step by step, the OSS found its own feet,
first in northwest Africa, then in northwest and central Europe. He shares General Donovan's opinion that the initial
debt the Americans owed to the British, in the fields of clandestine activity, was huge; he shows also how fast the Americans learned, and how competent they were at escaping from
British tutelage when they needed to do so. Their experiences
before, during, and after operation "Torch," the Anglo-
American landings in Morocco and Algeria in November
1942, gave them plenty to think about, and from their western
Mediterranean bases they were able to provide operation
"Dragoon," the landing on the French Riviera coast in mid-
August 1944, with a wealth of intelligence and subsequent
resistance support. He goes into some fascinating details both
about "Dragoon" and about "Overlord," the earlier landing
in Normandy. He shows too how the Germans' rear areas in
France were permeated and controlled by resistance forces,
which were part spontaneous, part communist-inspired, part
inspired by de Gaulle; advised by the British Special Operations Executive and the American OSS, and armed by the
two countries' air forces.

The British instructed the Americans that the Gestapo's
hold on Germany itself was so tight that the country was
pretty well impenetrable to agents. Casey, alerted by the apparent intelligence failure to predict the failed German offensive in the Ardennes—popularly known as the Battle of the
Bulge—was able in the last few months of the war to send
several highly successful agents into the Reich itself. He
throws some new light on the circumstances of the war's end,
both in Europe and in the Far East: required reading for diplomatic historians as well as intelligence buffs and those who
want to comprehend the world we live in now.

During his brief years with OSS, he learned the value of

close analysis, picked up the art of asking the incisive instead of the ordinary question, discovered the value of the spy on the spot as well as the value of the academic blessed with a talent for decipherment, and studied the intricacies of secret radio. He has some almost lyrical passages on the portable radio set the OSS nicknamed Joan Eleanor, a big advance on SOE's bulky S-phone, with which agents could safely pass their findings straight out to a passing aircraft, as easily as if by telephone.

Rank does not count for much in this sort of work. For a time, in Britain's SOE, a three-star general and a two-star admiral took orders quite calmly from a squadron-leader (the equal of an air force major). Nevertheless, Casey was a shade concerned lest, with no higher standing than that of a reserve lieutenant in the United States Navy, he might not be able to hold his own with general officers in the United States Army. The way round was easy: he was "put on inactive duty," dressed thereafter in plain clothes, and carried his points by force of personality. His obituary in the London *Times* on 7 May 1987 noted his chill grey eyes as well as his affable manner; he was able to combine both with effect.

His book lacks a final chapter, which only he could have written, to point out its main lesson. This is, that in any fight against tyranny—with or without a formal declaration of war— any free society needs to possess a deadly secret, deadly efficient body to equip it both with intelligence about the enemy and—if need be—with the means of covert action. Necessarily such a body must come under the control of a freely elected authority. There are some in the United States, both among politicians and among journalists, who oppose the existence of any such force, on the ground that it is unconstitutional. Yet the words that come next in the American Constitution after the President's oath of office are: "The President shall be Commander-in-Chief." For Casey, a devoted American and a devoted lover of freedom, that was authority enough.

MRDF

London, 21 January 1988

Preface

DURING THE First World War, Winston Churchill wrote:

> *"Battles are won by slaughter and manoeuvre. The greater the general the more he contributes in manoeuvre, the less he demands in slaughter."*

In the Second World War that Churchillian insight was implemented on a scale unprecedented in history. Ten days into D-Day, the Allied invasion of Europe, 500,000 men were crowded into a beachhead that was, on the average, ten miles wide. Still, as large as that force was, if deception had not succeeded in keeping 15 of Hitler's best divisions 100 miles away on the other side of the Seine waiting for a second invasion by a phantom army; if resistance forces had not engaged infantry divisions behind the German lines and along with our air forces delayed four Panzer divisions from reaching the Normandy beachhead; if railroad lines to the front had not been sabotaged not once but over a thousand times;

if the guns and defenses, the order of battle, and even the operational orders of German generals had not been laid out cold for Allied commanders—who can say that half a million men crowded into a slender beachhead would not have been slaughtered and rolled back into the sea?

The thrust and cutting edge that intelligence, deception, and psychological and irregular warfare can give to troops in battle cannot be conjured up overnight. The foundations of the covert war against Hitler were built by the British when they stood alone. The organization that William J. Donovan created in the United States, the Office of Strategic Services, had to be taught and trained and built on the organization and professional expertise that had been built in Britain—and in France and Poland, Belgium and Holland, Scandinavia and Czechoslovakia.

I've written this book because I believe that it is important today to understand how clandestine intelligence, covert action, and organized resistance, saved blood and treasure in defeating Hitler. These capabilities may be more important than missiles and satellites in meeting crises yet to come, and point to the potential for dissident action against the control centers and lines of communication of a totalitarian power.

The experiences of the OSS also carry important lessons and reminders of:

- *the need for close observation and sustained analysis by trained minds to obtain and piece together fragments of information and interpret their meaning and implications.*

- *the danger of deception, for which cameras in the sky and listening devices of all kinds can be a target.*

- *the importance of remaining alert and receptive to assistance from forces from within the ranks of our enemies.*

- *the need for continuing scrutiny of new technologies and accurate information and evaluations of new weapons systems in order to take timely action as well as to avoid over-reaction.*

This book comes in part from my own experience and observation, in part from discussions over the years with others who were involved in these activities during World War II, and in part from research in archives in America and Europe.

During 1943 and 1944, I was a staff officer to General William J. Donovan and David Bruce, commanders of the Office of Strategic Services in Washington and in London, respectively. However, it should be emphasized that in these activities one does not have and does not want access to secret information unless one's duties require it. For that reason, and because so many of the more important clandestine operations were British, I did not, at that time, have more than general knowledge of many covert activities. During the last six months of the war, as a civilian, I had command of the first fully independent American effort to send large numbers of clandestine intelligence agents into enemy territory.

From the fall of 1946, when I spent several weeks on a committee advising on America's peacetime intelligence needs, I had no contact with our intelligence apparatus until 1969 when I became a consumer of national intelligence—first, as a member of the General Advisory Committee on Arms Control, and later as Under Secretary of State. During 1974–75, I worked on the Commission of the Organization for the Conduct of Foreign Policy, and in 1976, President Ford appointed me to the President's Foreign Intelligence Advisory Board. Under President Reagan, I was fortunate enough to be named Director of the Central Intelligence Agency.

I have updated and rounded out my intelligence knowledge and experience with talks and visits to wartime colleagues in America and Britain and all the countries of western Europe. Over the years I've had the opportunity to discuss these events with General Donovan, General Colin Gubbins, Chief of British Special Operations Executive, Allen Dulles, David Bruce, Russ Forgan, and Ed Gamble, all deceased, and with Otto Doering, Henry Hyde, Bill Quinn, John Haskell, John Bross, Hans Tofte, Frank Canfield, Ken Downs, Lyman Kirkpatrick, Bob Alcorn, Paul van der Stricht, Ed Mason, Harry Rositzke, Charles Kindelberger, Bill Grell, and Joe Dasher, all wartime colleagues. Prime movers in the covert war of 1941–45 have been kind enough to read relevant portions of my manuscript and criticize it. For this I am indebted to André Dewavrin, known as Col. Passy when he headed de Gaulle's intelligence and resistance activity in London; Col. John Bevan, Sir John Masterman, and Roger Hesketh, organizers of Allied deception; Commanders Dunderdale and Kenneth Cohen, and Dr. R. V. Jones of British Intelligence; Maurice Buckmaster and Vera Atkins who sent hundreds of British agents to the French resistance; M. R. D. Foot, fighter in the SAS and official historian of the SOE in France; Stefan Mayer and Thaddeus Lisicki of Polish Intelligence; Joachim Ronneberg and Knut Haukelid, who led the attack on the heavy water plant in Norway; Svend Truelsen and Flemming Juncker, leaders in Danish intelligence and resistance work; Pat O'Leary, now Count Albert Guérisse, organizer of escape chains; and Col. Le Page, chief of Belgian intelligence in World War II. I have benefited from talks with the leading historians of intelligence and resistance groups: Harry Hinsley, Michael Howard, and Hugh Trevor-Roper in England; Louis de Jong in Holland, Jorgen Haestrup in Denmark; and General Bernard in Belgium. Their guidance has been invaluable and their encouragement and my admiration for them have done much to sustain the effort required for this work. Chapter 18, on the penetration of Germany, relies, in part, on the information supplied by the *War Report: Office of Strategic Services* prepared by the War Department and edited by Kermit Roosevelt in 1946, which was released (with deletions) to the public in 1976. The responsibility for the information in that chapter and throughout the book, however, is mine.

1. Washington

ON A bright day in the early spring of 1943 I sauntered up the steps of the marble-pillared Administration building in the National Health complex at 25th and E streets NW. It was a small building with only two stories and perhaps thirty offices, but it was stylish and elegant and looked a fitting home for General Donovan's still embattled Office of Strategic Services, not yet two years old and already regarded as the most exciting place in Washington. Just turned 30, I wore—still uncomfortably—the khaki uniform of a Naval lieutenant junior grade which I had donned only a few months earlier. I was due at a job interview with Colonel Charles Vanderblue who was charged with finding someone to establish and run a secretariat in London for Colonel David K. E. Bruce, the commander of OSS operations in Europe.

I knew little about the OSS beyond the common grist of Washington's rumor mills. Certainly, it sounded more exciting and more worthwhile than what I had been doing. Armed with the brashness of youth I had little doubt that I could accomplish whatever the job required. After all, I was an old Washington hand by then, having spent the last 18 months or so in the capital and having learned its highways and byways pretty well. Leo Cherne had sent me to Washington shortly before Pearl Harbor to open an office for the Research Institute of America, a private business advisory service that stayed far ahead of the press when it came to information on the coming mobilization of American resources for the war. I prepared and directed studies and analyses on price controls, production requirements and priorities, manpower controls, excess profits, taxation, etc. Our material circulated widely. As a result, I was often asked by the government to undertake special jobs, such as simplifying the immensely complex plan establishing government control over the materials and production facilities needed for war production. That particular project was useful preparation for the OSS because it gave me my first taste of battling entrenched bureaucracy.

It was also the kind of work that gave me the broadest contacts within the wartime Washington community. I knew journalists, politicians, government officials, and senior military officers.

As Chairman of the Board of Editors at the Research Institute, I was a man of some consequence, enough at any rate for Cherne to write golden letters insisting I was too valuable to the war effort to be drafted.

That, however, was an opinion I could not share. I longed for action and did not want to sit out the war as a civilian. Wrangling a Navy commission proved easy, getting into action did not. The Navy was not about to waste my Washington experience on a ship. There was other work for someone who had been analyzing industrial mobilization and who had been serving as a consultant to the Board of Economic Warfare, pinpointing Hitler's economic jugular and investigating how it could be squeezed by blockade, pre-emptive buying, and other economic warfare. Accordingly, I was put into Jack Small's office, helping him break bottlenecks in the production of landing craft. It was an interesting place. Small, in civilian life President of Publicer Alcohol and a high-powered business executive, had been commissioned as a captain in the Navy and assigned a bright staff to increase the production of landing craft and other Navy necessities. But sailing a desk in the old Navy building on Constitution Avenue was not my idea of helping to win the war. I itched for action and the OSS seemed the best place to get it. Surprisingly, Small was sympathetic and put no obstacles in my way. I began to look for leads. Jerry Doran, with whom I had parked cars at Jones Beach and practiced law on Long Island, was in Donovan's law firm, Donovan, Leisure, Newton & Lombard. He introduced me to Otto Doering and Ned Putzell, partners in the firm who had followed Donovan to Washington and into the OSS. Doering, then a Lt. Colonel and the OSS executive officer, arranged for an interview with Colonel Vanderblue, a New York shoe manufacturer turned OSS recruiting agent in London.

It was an easy interview. Vanderblue was encouraging. Given the fact that I would have to write my own job description in London—no one had ever run an OSS secretariat there—my lack of specific experience was more advantage than handicap. And of course I had no idea what I was letting myself in for. It all went smoothly. I was to spend several months in Washington learning Donovan's ropes and then would go to London. Weeks later I sat behind a desk in Ned Putzell's office on the same corridor as Donovan, his deputy Ned Buxton, Charlie Cheston, a Philadelphia investment banker who was number three, and Doering. Doering and Putzell ran Donovan's secretariat. For about four months, until I went to London, I had an unobstructed seat from which to watch Donovan in action and study the OSS's hectic present and, for all its brief existence, already turbulent past.

You had only to be around the OSS a few days in the summer of 1943 to realize how embattled an organization it was, even after its mettle had been tested and proved in the crucible of the North African campaign. It is no exaggeration to say that Donovan created the OSS against the fiercest kind of opposition from everybody—the Army, Navy, and State Departments, the Joint Chiefs of Staff, regular army brass, the whole Pentagon bureaucracy, and, perhaps most devastatingly, the White House staff.

When I came aboard, the OSS still had not won a final government charter setting out its functions and authority. Donovan, Doering, and Putzell were spending an inordinate amount of time fighting a legal and bureaucratic battle for survival. They drafted paper after paper setting forth why the OSS needed complete organizational independence and the broadest possible turf for intelligence activities. At the same time they were on a tiresome merry-go-round handling countless requests and debates over OSS authority. Donovan would submit a request for manpower slots to the Joint Psychological Warfare Committee. The Committee was made up of representatives of the Army, Navy, State Department, Board of Economic Warfare, Office of War Information, and OSS. Donovan was Chairman but such deliberations bored him and he rarely attended. So after hearings, his request would be passed on to the Joint Staff Planners who would pass it on to the Joint Chiefs of Staff where it would go back to the Joint Psychological Warfare Board for further hearing. It was the kind of grinding opposition calculated to wear down anyone with the kind of imagination and lust for action that Donovan had. But nothing could alter Donovan's vision of the role intelligence had to play in a successful American war effort.

Roosevelt had made Donovan Coordinator of Information in the summer of 1941 after using him for a year as a special roving ambassador to Britain, the Balkans, and the Middle East. On returning from a 22,000 mile mission in the spring of 1941 Donovan decided to put some of his ideas on intelligence into a memo to FDR. The U.S., he knew, had at best a skeleton intelligence apparatus brightened only by the genius of William F. Friedman, who broke the Japanese diplomatic cipher before Pearl Harbor, and a handful of other cryptographers working out of the Munitions Building. The Army had a total of 80 people—officers, enlisted men, and civilians—on intelligence duty in Washington and perhaps 30 attachés doing intelligence work at overseas missions. It was a pitiful apparatus for putting together the torrent of information that began to flood into Washington during the war.

"Although we are facing imminent peril, we are lacking in effective service for analyzing, comprehending, and appraising such information as we might obtain (or in some cases have obtained) relative to the intentions of potential enemies and the limit of the economic and military resources of those enemies," Donovan wrote to FDR.

"We have, scattered throughout the various departments of our government, documents and memoranda concerning military and naval and air and economic potentials of the Axis, which, if gathered together and studied in detail by carefully selected trained minds, with a knowledge both of the related languages and techniques, would yield valuable and often decisive results."

Roosevelt scrawled OK on the Donovan memorandum and shot it along to Ben Cohen, his all-purpose legislative draftsman, to put into a directive. Cohen's first draft suggested that Donovan be named Coordinator of Strategic Information and that he be commissioned as a Major General (he had risen to command of the 165th Regiment in World War I and had been awarded the Distinguished Service Cross in 1918, the Distinguished Service Medal in 1922, and the Medal of Honor in 1923). He was to be given authority to recruit a staff able to roam broadly across intelligence related functions—propaganda, subversion, espionage, clandestine operations, research, and analysis.

The draft had no sooner been circulated through the Administration before a collective bureaucratic howl went up. Fierce opposition flamed in virtually every corridor of power. The Army and Navy wanted no part of such an operation, arguing it would usurp functions assigned each branch of the service. Secretary of War Henry L. Stimson, whose distaste for intelligence was summed up in the now classic phrase that "gentlemen don't read other people's mail," tried to tempt Donovan out of his new post by offering him command of the 44th Division. Donovan, always the man of action, almost bit. And, finally, when he didn't, he asked for another crack at the bait—after he got the Coordinator's office established. Still, Stimson carried off something in this first engagement. He succeeded in changing Donovan's title to

Coordinator of Information and insisted that Donovan run his new outfit as a civilian, not as a Major General on active duty. It was the first skirmish in a running battle.

As bureaucratic shells whistled round his head, Donovan set to work. By Pearl Harbor he had assembled a staff of nearly 600, and was recruiting in the most unlikely places— the halls of academe, Madison Avenue advertising agencies, the big New York and Chicago law firms, newspaper and wire service offices (he had a predilection for young journalists and lawyers), and was fishing in the great American melting pot for men with the physical stamina and linguistic ability to undertake missions behind enemy lines. Before he was finished he collected what was certainly the most sweeping array of talents, disciplines, and experiences ever assembled anywhere in so short a period of time—bankers and tycoons, safecrackers and forgers, printers and playwrights, athletes and circusmen.

His methods, however, appalled established brass who from the beginning were afraid of "Donovan's private army" and did everything they could to kill it, including, paradoxically enough, trying to dismember it and pick up the pieces for their own use. Thus G-2 was forever trying to grab Donovan's scholars away from him and put them into the humdrum activities of conventional and narrowly-focused military intelligence work.

The months before Pearl Harbor showed the bureaucratic problems Donovan would encounter. As the Japanese storm began to gather force in the Pacific, the most private communications between the Japanese government and its ambassadors in Washington, Berlin, Rome and other major capitals were being read in Washington. Army and Navy cryptographers having broken the Japanese diplomatic cipher, were reading messages that foretold the attack. The British had sent word that a Japanese fleet was steaming east toward Hawaii.

Among those not reading the intercepts was Donovan, President Roosevelt's Coordinator of Information. The military had confined the priceless intercepts to a handful of people too busy to interpret them. Small wonder that Friedman cried out in despair on hearing of the attack on Pearl Harbor, "But they knew. They knew." The fact is that Friedman knew, but those with the responsibility and power to act had received only an accumulation of raw intercepts. No one had put the pieces together for them and told them of their momentous implications. Great power that we had become, arsenal of democracy and beacon of freedom, we still lacked an organized intelligence service.

Distribution of intelligence intercepts was strictly limited to the President, the Secretaries of State, War, and Navy, and a few ranking military officers. Moreover, secrecy was so tight that even those who did see the intercepts saw them only for moments, certainly not long enough for any detailed analysis of their content. One set of these messages was hand-carried to the President and the Navy, a second to the War and State Departments. After they had been shown to the selected few, each of the separately distributed copies was destroyed. The Army and the Navy kept one master copy, each. Also, each service had one, and only one, Far Eastern specialist who was allowed to see the Japanese intercepts.

Even worse, no one conducted long-term analyses of messages to check trends and make estimates and comparisons. General Marshall summed up the top-level mood when he told a Congressional inquiry on Pearl Harbor in 1946: "If I'm supposed to have the final responsibility of the reading of all Magic [the broken code] messages I would have ceased to be Chief of Staff in every other respect."

The problem was that the role of military intelligence was seen in the narrowest of terms, and had strict limits put on its use. Army intelligence, for example, did produce situation estimates for the Chief of Staff but not for field commanders. Only static information like size and location of armies was sent out. Judgments and projections about enemy intentions were withheld from the front lines. The Navy was even more rigid. Intelligence was to present factual evidence and refrain from estimates or prediction—the jealously guarded prerogative of the Chief of War Plans—and both rules were rigidly enforced. When the Joint Army-Navy Intelligence Committee (JANIC) first met in October 1941 the Army wanted it to collate, analyze, and interpret information, and make judgments of enemy capabilities and intentions. But the Navy insisted on holding JANIC to facts, not interpretation. The Navy won.

Of course such limitations had fateful consequences. The broken Japanese diplomatic cipher gave us minute details of Japanese movements toward Singapore and the Dutch East Indies, in China and Indo-China, toward Thailand, and on the borders of the Soviet Union. Our analysis of radio traffic had the various bits of the Japanese fleet accurately pinpointed most of the time. The movements of ships and troops down the China coast and into Indo-China was clear to the Navy from ship call signs. Our embassy in Tokyo regularly filed perceptive economic and political analyses.

Unhappily, all the data thrown up by this vast information network never landed in one place at one time where the facilities existed to analyze the facts and project their implications. Donovan and his staff at the Coordinator of Information's office were not receiving this vital flow. On November 1 and December 1, Japan made changes in naval call signs so unusual as to hint strongly at preparations for some offensive. The changes were followed by the sudden "disappearance" of the Japanese aircraft carriers. U.S. inability to locate the ships by intercepting radio calls indicated the carriers were near Japan and could communicate on wave lengths we were unable to detect. At the same time diplomatic reports from Tokyo pointed to approaching political deadlines, first on November 25 and then on November 29, on which something would happen. Coded messages from Japanese agents in major ports, which we intercepted and read, told us what information Tokyo's warlords wanted to have about U.S. defense. Their sudden stepped-up interest in Manila and Honolulu should have been hard to miss.

But no one put together any coordinated analysis linking diplomatic reports, changes in call signals, and the disappearance of the carriers, all signs that a Japanese fleet might be steaming somewhere under radio silence, and that the "somewhere" might well be Hawaii or the Philippines. All the pieces of information were available in Washington, but no one put them together in a mosaic that might have cushioned, if not avoided, the blow against Pearl Harbor.

Though Pearl Harbor underlined Donovan's insistence that there be continuous screening and evaluation of all intelligence by a professional corps of experts, his ideas required a powerful push from the British to make them respectable. When Churchill came to Washington two weeks after Pearl Harbor for the conference codenamed Arcadia, he urged his new allies to make subversion an essential feature of Allied grand strategy. And he won his point. Donovan's concepts of guerrilla and psychological warfare, propaganda, economic pressure, and sabotage were meshed into Allied doctrine.

Yet in the months after Pearl Harbor a strange intelligence drama unfolded in Washington's centers of power. Churchill may have persuaded Roosevelt of the correctness of Donovan's position, but Donovan had not stilled the fears and anxieties of those who opposed him. Yes, he had access to the President and could preach to him about the importance of clandestine operations. And yes, Navy Secretary Frank Knox was his friend. But he had few other sympathetic ears. Moreover, Donovan was increasingly torn by his longing to get into the fighting on the front lines at a time when American forces were being driven from the Philippines and Japanese ships dominated the Pacific. On February 21, 1942, he even sent Roosevelt "an appeal from a soldier to his Commander-in-Chief" proposing the formation of a task force to go to the rescue of the beleaguered American boys in the Philippines and asking that he be "permitted to serve with this force in any combat capacity."

While Donovan wrestled with his urge to return to the battle front, everyone in Washington was trying to walk off with a slice of his franchise. J. Edgar Hoover resented a rival and fought for as much intelligence turf as he could get. He ended up in charge of secret intelligence operations in Latin America, an area from which the OSS was totally excluded. Nelson Rockefeller hacked out an exclusive franchise to report and analyze political and economic intelligence there, as well as conduct propaganda. Byron Price headed the Office of Censorship, Lowell Millet the Division of Information of the Office of Emergency Management. Playwright Robert Sherwood edgily divided his time between writing FDR's speeches and running the Foreign Information Service under Donovan, while he was bucking for an independent information franchise. Archibald MacLeish had the Office of Facts and Figures. It seemed as if anyone with access to Roosevelt could get a charter for himself.

Hoover had shown his total incompetence for sophisticated war-time intelligence activity early on. His handling of the "Popov Affair" might well have been a tip-off for his future legendary secretiveness and over-simplified way of thinking. Popov was a Yugoslav who had been recruited as an agent by the Germans, but who had decided to work for the British. He would prove one of the best and most effective double agents of the war. Six months before Pearl Harbor the Germans ordered Popov, operating out of England, to go to the U.S. to set up a Nazi spy network. The British promptly got in touch with Hoover, hoping the FBI would help Popov develop a fake network in the U.S. that could feed misleading information back to Berlin, much as the British counterpart to the FBI, MI-5, had done with Popov in England.

Hoover viewed the whole affair with hostility and suspicion and held Popov off as long as he could. Even when the Yugoslav gave Hoover a list of questions the Germans had asked him to answer, the FBI director did not react, although one of the questions asked for detailed information about installations and defenses at Pearl Harbor. Hoover failed to find this line of inquiry important enough to pass on to the Army and Navy. For a while the British watched in disbelief as Hoover frittered away the opportunity for building a controlled network of disinformation. Then they began to pressure the FBI director. MI-5 had a stake in Popov it did not want to lose. Hoover, the British said, had to leak some information back to Berlin through Popov, at least to preserve his British credibility. Grudgingly, Hoover agreed, but without letting anyone know what he would tell Berlin in Popov's name. Popov returned to England without knowing what he had sent and had to bluff his mission to his German controllers.

This fiasco, however, did nothing to diminish Hoover's influence on intelligence activities or upgrade Donovan's role. Still inexperienced in the bureaucratic infighting of wartime Washington and not really interested in it, Donovan gradually lost ground.

Donovan's first wartime charter from the Joint Chiefs of Staff was a severely limited one. He could operate the OSS under JCS direction only to obtain intelligence through espionage and to provide whatever area or other studies the military might request. Despite Pearl Harbor, despite Donovan's most eloquent pleading, and despite the precisely reasoned memos of his legal staff, the OSS did not have immediate access to the most vital single intelligence source, the communications intercepts, nor would other military intelligence flow regularly into OSS offices. Donovan's Research & Analysis staff, trained to integrate and assess the most diverse information, had to scratch for bits and pieces. Donovan had been effectively stripped of his intelligence coordinating function, the very idea he had sold Roosevelt on only a year earlier and which was the bedrock of OSS activities.

Donovan operated under the restrictions as best he could. At the same time, however, he kept fighting for a broader charter and wider responsibilities. Progress was measured more in inches than in yards, and the OSS was often thrown for a loss. Relations with the White House were a shambles. Increasingly, Donovan's access to Roosevelt was blocked by Admiral Leahy, who served FDR both as top military aide and as chairman of the Joint Chiefs. Harry Hopkins always kept a cold eye on Donovan, not being overly fond of anyone with Republican and Wall Street backgrounds and associations. Hopkins' distrust spilled over to Donovan's staff. At one point early in the war, Hopkins banned Captain Jim Rand from the White House, where he had been assigned to develop and keep up a war room. Hopkins had learned that Rand was the son of the head of Remington Rand who had been critical of FDR's war policies.

The Joint Chiefs of Staff did not issue their final definitive directive for the OSS until October 1943, twenty-eight months after Donovan's appointment as Coordinator of Information. The original vision had been shrunk and mauled, but what was left had been tempered and hardened in the bureaucratic jungles as well as in the field. At last the OSS had explicit authority to maintain liaison officers with Allied intelligence services, to get information from and give support to underground groups, to conduct propaganda, and to accumulate and analyze economic, political, and military information that would be used to prepare studies on how to "enforce our will upon the enemy by means other than military action."

When I left for London that October the battle of Washington was over. The OSS was an established organization, overqualified perhaps for the narrowed task given it, but ready to serve. It would remain an independent organization, but that independence would remain strictly circumscribed. In effect, the OSS would be the handmaiden of whatever theater commander wanted to use it. Already it was apparent that MacArthur in Australia cared little for the OSS. That left Europe as the OSS's major area of activity for the remaining years of the war.

How did the OSS work? How did the pieces fit and how did Donovan manage them? Donovan loved to move an idea into action, whether it involved a psychological thrust or a physical blow at the enemy. His watchword was "the perfect is the enemy of the good" and he used it as he moved about improvising and implementing on-the-spot operations which in any other part of the American war machine would have required months for study, debate, and clearance. It was a motto that lent itself more readily to effective action than it did to tidy organization. Then, too, the sweep of his interests was enormous. He traveled constantly and adapted to new circumstances quickly and flexibly. Action, he felt, should be made to fit the rapidly changing situations that war and battle threw up. And in such situations he never tired of driving home his motto about the perfect being the enemy of the good. His flexibility and adaptability would often confuse those who lacked the mental agility to keep up with him.

But for all his refusal to let organizational detail or procedure stand in the way of action, his building of the OSS over three years from a virtual one-man operation to a globe-trotting organization involving some 13,000 people (including agents, support forces, maintenance, etc.) was a considerable administrative achievement. Moreover, he kept the OSS running with reasonable effectiveness and few disasters, despite the work of its enemies at home and abroad. He kept his fingers on everything, but was still able to delegate authority, and when he did he expected his men to act on their own. Certainly he did, and his freewheeling ways would often send his branch chiefs up the wall. But they gave the OSS much of its thrust and energy while organizational cohesion was preserved by the vision he imparted to his chiefs.

To keep on top of all this, Donovan used a Secretariat of half a dozen young and bright lawyers—who tackled the mountains of important official mail and cables from all over the world that piled up on Donovan's desk every morning. They talked to Branch and Office Chiefs coming in with suggestions, requests for approval, and cries for help. This was delicate. The Branch Heads and Chiefs of Offices, there were 30 of them, were accustomed to giving orders. They had to be persuaded that the Secretariat was able to expedite matters instead of delaying them, that it would help in avoiding rather than multiplying errors, and that it could free Donovan himself from much of the detail and routine communication work, thus giving him more time for overall operations and policy.

Each day started with a staff meeting at 9 o'clock that would last about half an hour. Donovan would brief his staffers on general matters, overnight reports or sudden emergencies, and then ask for their comments or for reports that needed his approval. Shortly after 9:30 he was back at his desk where his mail had been sifted and sorted so that the most urgent documents and cables received overnight were ready for him with comments and recommendations. He worked through the overnight accumulation swiftly, correcting mistakes, demanding more information where it was needed, and overruled subordinates when he thought that necessary. By 10:30 he was ready to plunge into a full day's round of conferences and meetings that had usually begun with a working breakfast at his home. He saw everyone: theater commanders, American and Allied diplomats, agents, his own chieftains, cabinet officers, bureaucrats, and journalists. It was a rare lunch or dinner that was not devoted to the conduct of the war or to OSS operations. And after his day ended, often at eleven or midnight, he would read estimates of enemy capabilities, strengths, and weaknesses, economic or strategic reports, and at least scan virtually all the reports Dr. Langer and his academic colleagues at Research & Analysis had prepared.

His methods were certainly unorthodox and his personality cut across the military grain.

In a way, Donovan was an unlikely head for a major power's intelligence service. He resembled neither Admiral Canaris nor Reinhardt Heydrich, his German counterparts, nor the British secret service types featured in Alfred Hitchcock movies. Rather he was a roly-poly man, soft of voice and manner belying the sobriquet ''Wild Bill'' he had never been able to shake, he had soft blue eyes and a gourmet's demeanor. But most important was his curiosity. Donovan was curious about everything and everyone. And he backed up his curiosity with a sharply-honed lawyer's mind that realized earlier and better than most, that ''stranded'' information was not much good. It had to be analyzed, dissected, and fitted into the larger whole that modern warfare required.

He was one of those men who seems larger than life. He was in perpetual motion and engaged in constant activity and struggle. Yet for all his devotion to the big picture, he always made time for the small one, for lucid and concise analysis of his own views and the views of others.

To understand Donovan meant understanding his past and the events that had shaped him. He was a soldier and a scholar, a private man and a public man. He belonged to that pioneer generation of Americans who saw their country rise to global power before its people were ready to take on the duties that power required. Donovan was ready. In 1916, as a young lawyer, he had toured the battlefields of France and visited Germany and Poland for the Rockefeller-funded American War Relief Commission. Once the U.S. entered the war Donovan stood in the trenches, emerging with a reputation for integrity and bravery. Soon after the armistice, in 1919, Donovan was drawn into the maelstrom of the new age. Roland Morris, the U.S. ambassador to Japan, asked him to go on a mission to Siberia to evaluate the Kolchak White Russian government in Omsk. He kept a diary on the voyage from Vladiovostock to Omsk that documented his broad interests and acute political insights. President Wilson had committed 5,000 American troops to Russia. The State Department was eager to broaden U.S. involvement. But Donovan and Morris agreed that further U.S. aid was wasteful. The Kolchak government was too weak and too disorganized to wage effective war against communist-trained peasants mobilized by "whip and pistol." Donovan recommended covert action against the communists as the most promising approach to the Siberian mess. He maintained this faith in subversion through World War II and the cold war.

In 1920, Donovan was again in Europe to study how private capital could help rebuild Europe. Again his diaries revealed an all-absorbing curiosity about the social, economic, educational, cultural, and political workings of governments and societies. He had access to European leaders as well, men like Beneš and Masaryk in Czechoslovakia, and in a few days' stay would compile area reports that look like early drafts of those that the OSS Research and Analysis Branch produced twenty years later.

Back home, he returned to the legal profession. In 1921, he was named U.S. Attorney for Buffalo. When the Teapot Dome scandal broke, Attorney General Harlan Stone brought Donovan to Washington as chief of the Criminal Division. He needed a man of high repute and scholarship, and his former student—Stone had taught Donovan at Columbia Law—filled that bill. Ironically, perhaps, one of Donovan's first jobs at Justice was organizing the FBI and picking its first chief— J. Edgar Hoover, an appointment he would have cause to regret. Before leaving Justice, Donovan rose to chief of the Anti-Trust Division, then the second-ranking spot in the Department.

After quitting government, he opened his own law firm in New York and quickly carved out a reputation for handling cases that called for investigating, collecting, collating, and analyzing large amounts of information and drawing and presenting reliable and persuasive conclusions to judges, juries, legislative committees and other public bodies. The amount of information required in defending 135 coal companies and 24 oil firms in separate anti-trust actions was enormous. In the oil cases he gathered a staggering 18 tons of documents, and had them indexed and cross-referenced so that they were available virtually on a moment's notice. He marshalled squadrons of lawyers and special investigators to defend DuPont before Senator Nye's committee investigating "merchants of death." In these litigations he devised methods for people to do work computers now do. He even invented a filing system which later became a standard for the OSS.

Thus both in government and in private practice Donovan became adept at managing large organizations and at dealing in a comprehensible way with huge masses of data. These skills would stand him in good stead in developing the OSS, as would his abiding interest in national security matters.

Donovan recognized early the growing menace of Hitler and the Nazis. He spoke out against the Nazi and fascist dictatorships long before it was fashionable to do so in his political circles. In 1936, he wrangled permission from Mussolini to visit the Ethiopian front, and later talked to General Badoglio, then commanding Italian forces in Libya. A year later Donovan was in Spain to watch the 4th Spanish Army regain the heights above the Ebro river. In 1938, he attended the German army maneuvers near Nuremberg, and visited Czechoslovakia and the Balkans. At home, he said bluntly that appeasement at Munich meant war and that the U.S. would be in it.

When war broke out, Donovan was both a prophet and a hero in search of a role. FDR's decision to name Stimson Secretary of War was a bitter personal disappointment. And Stimson's hostility to intelligence filled him with foreboding. Navy Secretary Frank Knox was Donovan's strongest link to official Washington. In 1936, when Knox ran for vice-president on the GOP ticket, Donovan had acted as his unofficial campaign manager. In 1940, it is probable that Knox suggested to FDR that he send Donovan to London on a fact-finding mission.

Churchill was delighted with the mission and made sure Donovan saw everything—from coastal defenses, radar sites, and Spitfires, to the Royal Navy's Operational Intelligence Center. The two men got on well and the initial contact would prove important for the future. Back in Washington in early August 1940, Donovan was loaded with ideas, reports, manuals, and requests for weapons. He told Roosevelt and Knox that Britain would hold out if given ships, arms, and supplies. And Donovan arranged for the British to receive intelligence reports from U.S. consular officers on the continent.

On December 6, FDR again sent Donovan abroad, this time on a 22,000 mile voyage to assess the strategic situation in the Mediterranean, the Middle East, and the Balkans. He visited Gibraltar, Malta, Egypt, Greece, Bulgaria, Yugoslavia, Turkey, Cyprus, Palestine, Iraq, Spain, and Portugal. It was the kind of wide-ranging trip that would become an OSS standard. Donovan believed in taking first-hand looks and nothing was easier in the OSS than getting travel orders.

Donovan's trip has gone into the history books. In Bulgaria he persuaded Czar Boris to delay for eight days giving German troops permission to cross his country and attack the British in Greece. The delay gave the British breathing room to firm their foothold. He brought a message from FDR to the Yugoslav government in Belgrade, arriving just when Prince Paul, the regent, and his government were negotiating with Hitler in Berchtesgaden about joining the Axis. Roosevelt's exhortation to resist went instead to General Simovic, already planning an anti-German coup. Days later, Simovic and a group of Serbian officers overthrew the regent. Churchill credits Donovan's activities in Belgrade with delaying Hitler's attack on Russia a crucial five weeks, weeks that left the Wehrmacht at the gates of Moscow in winter instead of in the fall, and susceptible to the ravages of ice and cold.

On his return to Washington Donovan told the President that America needed an intelligence and covert operations capability. Preparations for irregular warfare were as important as building orthodox military strength. FDR, softened up by a year of Donovan's rhetoric and solid front-line reporting, did not need much more persuasion. By mid-year he agreed to set up the Coordinator of Information's office, thus beginning Donovan's Calvary through the Washington bureaucratic jungles.

That Donovan's prescience, vindicated at Pearl Harbor, made little impression on the U.S. military establishment is perhaps understandable, given the still raw state of American preparedness. But that the OSS operations in North Africa did not establish the organization more firmly as part of the Washington establishment must remain one of the minor mysteries of the war. Rarely had intelligence and diplomacy meshed as smoothly as they did in preparing operation "Torch" and helping it triumph.

That North Africa was the OSS's first testing ground was no accident. Donovan had pinpointed the area as a critical one in his report to Roosevelt 18 months before the American landings in November 1942. It became more so as Russian pressure on the Allies to mount a second front increased. Both London and Washington agreed that a successful assault on the European continent could not yet be launched. The Canadian attack on Dieppe earlier that year with the loss of 3,500 men out of 5,000 had testified to that. North Africa was the most logical site for attack and the decision to land there was made on July 22, 1942.

That most remarkable of American diplomats, Robert Murphy, had given the OSS a headstart in North Africa where he served as a kind of American proconsul. There wasn't much of a U.S. presence then, perhaps a dozen foreign service officers scattered among consulates in five cities from Tunisia to Morocco. So in late 1940 Murphy persuaded French authorities to let him bring in 12 observers, ostensibly to assure the British then blockading the African coast that food shipments allowed through did not get into German hands. These observers were also allowed to use secret codes and employ couriers who carried locked pouches.

Donovan inherited the observers when he was named Coordinator of Information in mid-1941. Able to send out uncensored reports, they became the nucleus for the first operating American intelligence network of the war. And Donovan wasted little time building on the base they provided. He named Marine Colonel William Eddy, English professor at the American University in Cairo and fluent in Arabic, as his chief in North Africa. Eddy moved fast. He set up clandestine radio stations in Tangier, Algiers, Casablanca, Oran, and Tunis. Links had been forged to British intelligence at Tangier and Gibraltar. By the summer of 1942, Washington and London received a steady stream of radio reports on all ships and cargoes leaving and arriving in North Africa, on the attitude of the French army and the civilian population, and on the details of all port and defense installations.

On June 11, 1942, the War Department ordered Eddy to Washington to make an oral report on the overall situation in North Africa. Opposition to the Germans ran deep, Eddy reported. If properly armed, 35,000 men could be raised in Algeria to help the Allies. General Juin, the French commander, would not interfere, nor would other French authorities who paid only lip-service to the German-Italian control commission that had its hands on everything military—airplanes, supplies, radio communications. Eddy predicted easy landings at Port Lyautey, Oran, and Algiers, but not at Casablanca, which was well fortified and where stiff resistance should be expected. This report had a powerful effect on the decision to land in North Africa even though fewer than half the troops the military planners wanted would be available and ready.

During the months before the North African landings, a German thrust through Spain or from Italy was always a possibility. Large elements of the French army in North Africa were anxious to resist this and, with many French civilians, were prepared for resistance to any German occupation. Eddy and his men helped organize and supply this resistance while at the same time soliciting the support of native Moorish, Algerian, and Tunisian leaders. Combat groups of Moors and Riffs were formed and plans were made to cut off power and seize key positions at the time of the landings. Guns and ammunition were stockpiled. People with expert knowledge that would be valuable to the invasion planners in London were shipped out by night schooner to Lisbon or Gibraltar. One big catch, brought to Washington, was the chief pilot of Port Lyautey harbor who guided the fleet in on D-Day.

OSS Research & Analysis scholars under Bill Langer and Sherman Kent delivered studies of the French North African railways, the capacity of the rolling stock, the condition of the roadbed and track, terrain maps, charts of reefs and channels, tidal tables—all assembled from manuals, engineering journals, and other sources available in the Library of Congress. In November 1942, the months of preparation paid off. As the ships approached their destinations along the coasts of Morocco and Algeria, Allied Army, Navy, and Air officers with the invasion fleet received detailed information on what to expect at every landing point. They had maps and diagrams of airport locations and measurements, and of port dimensions and facilities. They knew the disposition of the French fleet, the batteries actually being manned, and the number of planes on every airfield, with the amount of aviation gas available at each. They were aware of conditions of wind, weather, and tide and they had the expert advice of guides who knew the harbors. Before and after the landings, they were advised, by OSS representatives who accompanied them, on terrain, on locations of French headquarters and German Armistice Commission offices, and on the officials on whom they could rely for assistance in the administration of civil affairs.

Squads of friendly Frenchmen, Moors, and Riffs were instructed to cut telegraph and telephone lines and to obstruct public utilities generally. Still others were to go just before H-Hour to detonate mines on roads and beaches. Groups were assigned to beachheads and landing and parachute fields, with flares to signal troops in from ships and guide them inland.

Meanwhile, in Algiers, Bob Murphy had been authorized directly by President Roosevelt and General Eisenhower to initiate any arrangement with the military authorities that would assist the military operation. When the BBC, shortly before midnight on November 7, sent out the message "Allô, Robert, Franklin arrivé," American troops were due to enter

Algiers in two hours. Resistance forces in Algiers, on this signal, quickly took over the police and power stations, military headquarters, and communications and transport centers with little opposition. Murphy went to the home of General Juin, Commander-in-Chief of Ground Forces in Algiers, and had to wake him up to tell him that an American expeditionary force was about to land all along the coasts of French North Africa. Known to hate the Nazis, Juin was nevertheless shocked. He said: "If the matter were entirely in my hands, I would be with you. But, as you know, Darlan is in Algiers. He outranks me and no matter what decision I might make, Darlan could immediately overrule me." Murphy replied, "Let's talk to Darlan." A telephone call brought Darlan over within 20 minutes. He, too, exploded at Murphy's news, but eventually agreed not to resist the invasion. Only Darlan had the standing to persuade the French commander in Morocco, General Noguès, to stop fighting and make Morocco safe for Allied troops. According to Murphy who was present on the telephone with him, Darlan not only got Noguès to end resistance in Morocco but quickly persuaded Boisson, the Governor General of French West Africa, to deliver Dakar without firing a shot and urged Esteva, Governor General of Tunisia, to resist the invasion of German airborne troops.

Donovan's men had successfully prepared the way and almost entirely eliminated resistance to the landing of only 110,000 American and British troops along 1,200 miles of Atlantic and Mediterranean beaches. Military planners in Washington and London had estimated that they would need 500,000 men to take and hold French North Africa, and that 10,000 Allied casualties could be expected. The actual cost turned out to be under two hundred men.

The OSS had won its spurs in North Africa, but unhappily not yet in Washington. Military men would find it increasingly difficult to ignore the contributions that intelligence sources and irregular forces behind enemy lines could make. But ignore them they did. And much of the war of words that continued in Washington was aimed at making the brass understand how the OSS could be used.

As Allied military might grew and the invasion of the European continent became a clearly focused object of policy, London became the center of military planning. And it was in London that the OSS had to be sold all over again—to the British and to our own generals taking command of the invasion forces.

It was a task Colonel Bruce was fulfilling with brilliance and panache when it was my good fortune to join him in October 1943.

2. London

DONOVAN HAD sent David Bruce to London in February 1943 to take over a small OSS headquarters. Already, London teemed with American generals and officials. The great build-up for the D-Day invasion had not yet begun, but there was no longer any doubt that the real "second front" would be launched from England against France rather than from North Africa against Italy or the Balkans. The OSS needed an imposing presence in London. And more than most men of his times, Bruce was that: cultured, widely read, tough-minded, and with the manners and breeding of a Virginia gentleman and that perfect assurance that allowed him to treat everyone as natural equals—American brass, English peers, and leaders of governments-in-exile.

When Bruce arrived in London he had been involved in shaping U.S. intelligence policy for a year. Early in 1942 Donovan had taken him aside: He was to organize and direct a secret intelligence service for OSS, the core of its future operations. Bruce, known to be the most unflappable of men, was nonplussed. He had been with Donovan from the beginning. As much as any man, he understood Donovan's thinking and what he was trying to accomplish. But this went even beyond his far-ranging talents, for all his having been so many things in life—accomplished lawyer, legislator, newspaper publisher, farmer, and member of the Board of Trustees of the National Gallery of Art. He protested that he knew nothing about secret intelligence.

Donovan was unperturbed. "Nobody else does. And besides, I've already taken care of that."

The next day Bruce was in New York to settle final details of the arrangement Donovan had made with the British to help train OSS agents and indoctrinate them into the finer points of secret intelligence. Bill Stephenson, named by Churchill as head of British intelligence and propaganda activities in North America, made a camp he had set up in Canada available for training OSS officers. Dick Ellis, another experienced British pro, helped establish training centers, mostly around Washington. Progress was rapid because it had to be. The Americans learned the intelligence ropes quickly. They were sent to London and neutral capitals—mostly Berne, Ankara, Madrid, and Lisbon—to give the OSS a face and a presence.

Donovan did this by putting his staff in direct touch with as many of their counterparts in American, British, and European government-in-exile organizations as possible. The process was strenuous as I was to learn during my time in London. The heavy workload of the office had to be squeezed around long lunches and working dinners. We would pool and save our ration tickets to give two dinners a week in the flat five of us shared at 87 Harley House. On other evenings we counted on the menu of the U.S. officers' mess to entice foreign and military colleagues to tell us what they were up to and to hear about the OSS.

I had arrived in London toward the end of October 1943 and presented myself to Bruce. In this, my first visit to London, I surely contributed to the impression that moved Malcolm Muggeridge to comment: "Ah, those first OSS arrivals in London! How well I remember them, arriving like *jeunes filles en fleur* straight from a finishing school, all fresh and innocent, to start work in our frowsy old intelligence brothel.'' The British traitor Philby, then a high official in British intelligence, was no less unkind, characterizing us as ''a notably bewildered group'' whose arrival was ''a pain in the neck.'' Yet only a year later that ''bewildered group,'' working entirely on its own, was preparing, outfitting, documenting, and dispatching 150 agents into Germany itself. And ninety-five percent of them returned safely.

Bruce gave me an office in his command suite at 70 Grosvenor Street which housed the OSS European headquarters. The five-story brick office building was smack in the middle of the war-time American compound in London. It was halfway down the street from the U.S. embassy. On opposite sides of the Square, soon to be known as Eisenhower Platz, were U.S. military headquarters. Our headquarters was bland, grey, nondescript. It had elevators, for which we were thankful, and was heavily guarded inside the front door.

In offices adjoining mine were Walter Giblin, a lieutenant colonel fresh from Wall Street; Lester Armour, a Navy commander fresh from Chicago's La Salle Street; and Junius Morgan, a Navy captain from the House of Morgan at 23 Wall Street. Giblin, gruff and hardboiled at the crust, soft and gentle inside, was the Executive Officer. It was his job to wheedle the transport, housing, and equipment the OSS needed from skeptical Army service and supply types. He was superb at this task. Believing it important to impress on his sources that the OSS was really a military outfit, he acted the stern disciplinarian and was affectionately known as ''the Gauleiter.''

Junius Morgan had the much less difficult task of handling the Navy. This gave him time to accumulate and handle the European currencies and gold which agents would need when they got to the continent. Junius shared this responsibility with Bob Alcorn, one of Donovan's earliest recruits. Occasionally the two of them could be seen sitting on the floor counting out the contents of bags full of bills and coins they had managed to acquire, we never knew where or how.

Lester Armour had the title of ''Coordinator.'' His forte

was applying a skeptical eye and common sense to whatever was going on. Instructing me on how we should help our commanding officer, he exclaimed one day: "Our job is to sit here and screen the bullshit."

The atmosphere was informal. I recall an occasion when we gathered for a meeting in Junius Morgan's office. Raymond Guest, a lieutenant commander in the Navy, fresh from the polo fields of Long Island and Virginia, was in attendance. He was the chief of our maritime unit—three fast motor boats that the Royal Navy would not let out of their harbor. Guest barked at me: "Lt. Casey, get that chair." Having somehow skipped basic military training, I said: "Get it yourself." That moment of tension passed. Later that afternoon, Captain Morgan called me in. "Raymond has been here to say that I ought to call you before the mast. I don't know how to do that. But, do try to be nicer to Raymond." I must have succeeded because when Raymond Guest went back to Washington in October of 1944, he rented me his family's townhouse on Alford Street off Park Lane.

The London in which we lived and worked had the feeling of a city under siege. The beleaguered atmosphere enveloping the city came from the buildings drab and unpainted, the preponderance of uniforms of all sorts and varieties, the scarcity of motor vehicles, and the strangely mingled sense of shabbiness, devastation, and commitment. After long days at 70 Grosvenor Street, we would feel our way home in the blackout, hoping not to tumble down a flight of stairs into someone's air raid shelter in the basement. Later on, in those days of the little blitz, we would expect the air raid sirens to send us for a while down to the basement for shelter. But after we discovered how long the odds were on a bomb picking you out of the millions in London, we would go to the roof where we learned to tell whether the sound of the anti-aircraft came from Hyde Park or Regents Park or St. James's Park so we could put the chimney between us and any falling shrapnel. We admired the calm with which the English lived amidst the dangers of war and fortitude with which they gave up so many of their comforts.

As we settled into our new life, the mission of our tiny

headquarters group came into clearer focus. We had to sell ourselves and our organization to the various constituencies that made up the strata of wartime London. Our most indefatigable salesman proved to be Donovan himself, who came often to London.

Whenever he could find time between visits to British and American headquarters, and discussions with allied leaders, usually including Churchill himself, he would hold court in a large suite at Claridge's.

These sessions would always go well into the morning hours. His barber and the overnight cables would be on hand at 6 a.m. to clear the way for an early breakfast. The thing that sticks most powerfully in my mind is my amazement at how and when he found time in four or five hours of privacy to get enough sleep and still go through the half dozen or more books which I or Bob Alcorn or John Wilson would pick up for him. One of us would go to the Bumpus book shop on Oxford Street and get any new books about military, political, legal, or diplomatic events, whatever we thought he'd want to know about. Waiting in the General's suite, I would turn pages in these books and find them filled with underlinings and marginal comments.

The drive and vigor with which, on the next day, he would press headquarters generals and army commanders to make fuller use of OSS capabilities proved he got all the sleep he needed.

Those capabilities, however, proved as hard to sell in London as they had been in Washington. Grudgingly, the British conceded that American wealth and power required a U.S. intelligence capability, but they preferred to engage the OSS in new projects and to do so under British tutelage. Much to his later chagrin, Donovan agreed to British supervision. That meant we could not mount a single operation on our own without the approval of our hosts. Understanding the panoply of British clandestine operations—from intelligence and subversion to sabotage and resistance activities—became a necessity of survival.

Certainly the British set-up differed from ours. One fight Donovan had waged and won in Washington was to keep

espionage, counter-espionage, analysis, propaganda, support
for resistance groups, and the operation of small guerrilla
bands behind enemy lines all together in one organization.
The British had separate organizations for most of them—for
their intelligence, resistance, commando, and propaganda activities.

The oldest of the British secret organizations was known
as MI-6 or SIS for Secret (or Special) Intelligence Service.
MI-5 was responsible for internal security in Britain. (As
MI-6 resembled our own postwar CIA, MI-5 was a rough
equivalent of the FBI.)

One of MI-6's most important divisions was Section V,
which gathered information about foreign espionage in England. Eager to find out as much as possible about enemy
intentions and intelligence targets, MI-6's Section V was willing to give German agents plenty of rope and time in which
to hang themselves. Obtaining information required risks. It
was an attitude that MI-5, charged with internal security, did
not share. And it took some time for the two "fives" to stop
their internecine warfare and cooperate in capturing and turning around as many agents as possible. But by 1943 there was
not a single independent German agent left in Britain. They
were either in jail or sending fake reports back to their Nazi
contacts.

Section V maintained voluminous files on the two German
espionage agencies, the Abwehr run by the military and the
Sicherheitsdienst (SD) run by the Gestapo.

Perhaps the most important arrangement Donovan made
with the British was gaining access to these files for the counterespionage division of the OSS known as X-2. Norman
Pearson and Hubert Will, X-2 representatives in London, were
able to use the wireless traffic of the German intelligence
services intercepted and decoded by the British. These files
came from the biggest intelligence coup of the war. MI-6's
cryptographic organization, the Government Code & Cipher
School, had broken many German codes and read virtually
every radio message that passed between German command
centers. These messages were the bulk of all communications
because land-lines could not handle the heavy traffic Hitler

required from his staff and his generals. MI-6's code-breaking ability would prove invaluable throughout the war and was the basis of most of our intelligence activities. Next to breaking the German codes, success in neutralizing German agents in England and playing them back against the Nazis was the major achievement of British intelligence. Most of the credit belonged to MI-5, which soon took over the "playback" operation, and checked out the reliability of German agents who voluntarily offered to double back.

Although set up under the Ministry of Economic Warfare in 1940, Special Operations Executive was the most swashbuckling of the British organizations. It had a charter for sabotage, subversion, and supporting resistance groups in occupied Europe—and sought to enact Churchill's exhortation to "set Europe ablaze." European goverments-in-exile, however, were appalled when Special Operations pulled acts of sabotage that had little military significance and led only to brutal German reprisals. As a result, SOE proceeded more carefully on the path of sabotage, restricting its direct French operations, for example, to only 50 sabotage jobs, most of them minor, in the three years preceding 1944. Nevertheless, it was a potent and venturesome outfit. Headquartered in drab buildings at and around 64 Baker Street, Special Operations Executive had settled agents and established communications all over Europe, China, and southeast Asia, directing a global network of 10,000 people.

When I came to London, Special Operations Executive was run by General Colin Gubbins, a Scot from the Hebrides, who had succeeded Sir Charles Hambro, a friend of Donovan's. A regular army officer, Gubbins had served in Russia against the Bolsheviks after World War I and against insurgents in Ireland and India before specializing in unorthodox warfare at the War Office. When World War II broke out, he was chief of the British military mission in Warsaw. Later he led troops into Norway. After France fell, he was told to develop a British guerrilla force able to harass the Germans should they invade England.

At the end of the war, General Gubbins took stock of his

outfit, explaining the rationale behind SOE's formation and use:

> *"[T]he problem and the plan was to encourage and enable the peoples of the occupied countries to harass the German war effort at every possible point by sabotage, subversion, go-slow practices,* coup de main *raids, etc., and at the same time to build up secret forces therein, organized, armed and trained to take their part only when the final assault began. . . . In its simplest terms, this plan involved the ultimate delivery to occupied territory of large numbers of personnel and quantities of arms and explosives. But the first problem was to make contact with those countries, to get information on the possibilities, to find out the prospects of getting local help, and an even more immediate task was to find someone suitable and willing to undertake the first hazardous trip, then to train him and fit him for the job and ensure communications with him when he had landed. But all contacts with occupied territories closed when the last British forces returned to Great Britain in 1940, so the first man to go back to any country had to be parachuted 'blind' as we say, i.e., there was no one waiting to receive him on the dropping grounds, no household ready to give him shelter, conceal his kit, and arrange his onward passage. . . ."*

By the fall of 1943 Special Operations had three years experience under its belt working to sabotage the Nazi war machine, to build up underground forces in occupied countries, and to plan for their post-invasion support of regular Allied troops. Although SOE operated from Greece to Norway, the focus of its attention was France, where the invasion would take place.

Special Operations provided clothing, forged identity cards, and signal plans; scheduled air operations, ran small boats, and handled wireless traffic; and helped develop cover stories for agents, gave the pre-departure briefings, set up links with resistance groups, and arranged for reception committees to meet boats or parachute drops. In short, Special Operations

Executive provided the infrastructure for all successful clandestine operations abroad, including, later in the war, those of the OSS.

British propaganda was run by Political Warfare Executive (PWE), an organization that operated out of Bush House in London and at Woburn Abbey in the English countryside. The propaganda produced by PWE was some of the slickest of the war and often drew admiration from the old German master himself—Dr. Paul Joseph Goebbels. The BBC beamed a rich and varied news program into occupied Europe that was listened to with pathetic eagerness and irrespective of risk. Just how much the Nazis feared British "white" propaganda—news—was made clear by the stiff penalities they imposed on those who listened.

Britain's "black" propaganda—the real stuff—was a lot more devilish. In the ancestral halls of the Dukes of Bedford, Sefton Delmar, who had covered Hitler's Germany for the Beaverbrook papers with both panache and imagination ran PWE's "black" operations. His crew was a motley and fascinating bag. On the one hand there was a band of talented journalists and scholars who knew Germany and the Nazi leaders, their history and their psychology. On the other, as a kind of back-up, Delmar had gathered a group of refugees and prisoners of war of German, Italian, Slavic, and Balkan extraction. His writers used both the available "ethnic" talent, and the flow of intelligence from Germany that Delmar had organized—including current newspapers and magazines, radio broadcasts, and prisoner of war interrogations—to produce rumors known as "sibs." These were spread around Europe through radio broadcasts and news sheets that seemed to come from within Germany or the occupied areas. They were designed to create conflict and undermine morale.

A daily newspaper, "Nachrichten für die Truppe" or News for the Troops, was produced by Psychological Warfare and flown by Allied pilots on the "milk run" for distribution to German units. The pilots took big risks, flying lightly armed planes vulnerable to German attack. Later in the war, we Americans shared in this operation when John Elliott, today chairman of Ogilvy & Mather International, raided advertis-

ing agencies and newspaper, magazine, and broadcast offices
for talent and brought it to England to help out.

A radio station beamed directly at German soldiers proved
even more effective. Every night at 6 p.m., with a crack of
drums and a blare of trumpets, a jubilantly boisterous German march would burst from radio sets tuned to almost the
same band as "Radio Deutschland" in Munich. In crisp German the announcer would say: "Here is the Soldiers' Radio
Calais, broadcasting on wave bands 360 metres 410 and 492
metres together with the German shortwave Radio Atlantic,
on wave bands 30.7 and 48.3. We bring music and news for
comrades in the command areas West."

"Soldatensender Calais" and "Kurzwellensender Atlan-
tik" reached not only troops and submarine crews but civilians all over Germany. Dr. Paul Joseph Goebbles on
November 28, 1943, wrote in his diary: "In the evening the
so-called 'Soldatensender Calais,' which evidently originates
in England and uses the same wave lengths as Radio Deutschland—when the latter is out during their air raids—gave us
something to worry about. The station does a very clever job
of propaganda, and from what is put on the air one can gather
that the English know exactly what they have destroyed in
Berlin and what they have not." Effusive tribute, indeed, from
one pro to another.

Calais did all it could to suggest to the Germans that the
war in the west was no war at all, just a "Sitzkrieg" in which
all military effort was futile and ludicrous. Worse than that,
military efficiency was positively dangerous. "Units which
show themselves smart and efficient," said Calais, "are
drafted to the Eastern Front. Promotion in France is a sure
way to death in Russia."

News item after news item illustrated the general theme
that France was regarded as a theater of lesser importance;
and that in quality of manpower and armament, the troops in
France were far inferior to those on the Eastern Front where
Germany's fate was being decided. Hammering home the pri-
ority of the Eastern Front had a specific propaganda purpose:
After the allied landings in France, we would be able to tell
German units there that their High Command had written

them off, that they would be sent neither reinforcements nor supplies, that their front did not matter.

The London Controlling Section (LCS) was perhaps the most imaginative secret operation of the war. LCS was in charge of deceiving Hitler and his generals as to the target of the invasion. It did so by hoodwinking the Germans into believing that a huge phantom army on Britain's coast was real, ferocious, and ready to smash across the English Channel to the Pas de Calais and then invade Germany, rather than invade Normandy, the real target. What's more, it kept the Germans believing that myth—even after the Allies had landed—and thus tied up vital Nazi troops between Paris and Le Havre for several weeks after the landings.

LCS was run by John Bevan, a World War I friend of Winston Churchill. In peacetime, Bevan had pursued a quiet career as a London stockbroker. But he had an acute nose for danger. On a business trip to Rhodesia in 1937, he discovered the Nazi menace when two German saboteurs turned up intent on disrupting the output of copper Britain would need in time of war. He promptly returned to London and went on active duty with his old regiment.

In many ways the LCS crew was an odd bunch to operate so closely to the center of political power. Perhaps a dozen men in all, they worked at Churchill's underground headquarters at Storey's Gate. Bevan's executive officer, Sir Ronald Wingate, was a classicist who spoke obscure Arab and Indian dialects and had served as an agent for various small Crown colonies in India and the Middle East. Dennis Wheatley wrote horror stories in civilian life and had turned his fertile imagination from plotting unbelievable novels to thinking up credible military falsehoods. In the years that followed, LCS even floated a body ashore so the Germans would find it and be fooled by the false information planted on it, built phantom armies, planted false intelligence on neutral diplomats, misled, manipulated, and deceived. And Bevan used his clout with Churchill to have his "scenarios" acted out by generals and ambassadors. Even Churchill and Roosevelt reflected Bevan's "direction" in their speeches and in public and private appearances.

Our British allies, however, were just as adept in the "non-fiction" of intelligence work, and had accumulated a vast store of data on German power, tactics, and strategy. Over at Oxford Circus, on the top floor above Peter Robinson's department store, John Austin, an Oxford don, had, since Dunkirk, presided over a constantly expanding group of scholars: The Theatre Intelligence Organization. They collected and collated nuggets of information that came in from all over and from all sources—aerial photographs, radio intercepts, transcripts of prisoner of war interrogations, captured documents, reports on enemy censorship, press clippings, results of beach sand tests conducted by small landing parties, interviews with refugees and escapees, as well as agent reports. This four-year flow of information had been faithfully catalogued and indexed. It could be pulled out of filing cabinets and consulted as needed. Detailed maps and three-dimensional models of defense installations were available. The accumulation of information was truly staggering.

Out at Oxford, Fred Wells, a classicist, ran the Inter-Services Topographical Department. He had a staff of geologists, geographers, hydrographers, economists, draughtsmen, and photographers. They gathered every kind of detailed information about coastlines and terrain, tides and currents in and around Western Europe, and built models of the shorelines, beaches, and coastal strong points.

At the War Office in Whitehall, another group under Eric Birley, the reigning expert at Oxford on the armed forces of the Roman Empire, performed valuable work analyzing the enemy's Order of Battle. Birley kept the official tabulation of the location, composition, and experience of all units of the German army. His files and incoming reports were the key to understanding the enemy's capabilities and intentions.

Finally, all this data was stitched into overall policy by the Joint Intelligence Committee which functioned as part of the War Cabinet offices. The group was chaired by V.F.W. Cavendish-Bentinck of the Foreign Office and had on it a representative from the War Office, the Admiralty, the Air Ministry, and the Ministry of Economic Warfare. This five-man committee was served by a Joint Intelligence Staff of 10, typical of the British genius for having tight little groups handle functions that in the U.S. spawned huge bureaucracies. Coordination with the Joint War Planners—a group that included Combined Operations and the London Controlling Section—was close and friendly. As Cavendish-Bentinck puts it, "the donkey work was done in the departments. To get quality work and good security the important thing is to keep the 'bloody' numbers down."

The Joint Intelligence Committee was brisk and business-like. It reviewed, revised, and finalized intelligence appreciations and estimates. It met once a week with the Chiefs of Staff to discuss its judgments and assessments, and took questions for further analysis. The Committee's track record was very good. It predicted the German assault on Russia. It refused to panic when Hitler pounded at Moscow's gate, despite Washington's fear of imminent Soviet collapse. It wrote analyses stressing Russia's economic strength and fighting spirit as key factors, and predicted that the tide would turn when the Germans reached a place on the Volga River, known to history as Stalingrad.

By anyone's reckoning this was an imposing structure for intelligence and clandestine operations. The British had everything we still lacked: experience, seasoning, tradition, trained talent, contacts in Europe they had spent three years rebuilding. To some extent the haughtiness they displayed toward the OSS was justified, even from the long perspective of thirty years. British objections to our intrusion made sense, certainly more sense than the obstacles the OSS had encountered trying to get established in Washington. Nevertheless, British aloofness and often downright hostility brought its own host of problems that took all of Bruce's charm, tact, and intellectual ability to resolve.

There was one field where the British prized American expertise and where there was little if any of the friction bred by the teacher-pupil relationship we had in other areas with our English friends. This was economics, at first blush perhaps an esoteric intelligence area but on closer inspection an integral and vital part of any clandestine operation against an industrialized enemy. OSS economists showed their mettle first in picking bombing targets whose destruction would hurt the enemy's war-making potential the most. In fact, the American specialists in various British ministries and offices did much valuable original work applying economic analysis to strategic bombing. They developed criteria and doctrine for target selection and carried out cost-benefit analyses on the relative merits of bombing factories that made aircraft engines, assembled planes, and produced ball-bearings, or in attacks on marshalling yards, locomotives, roads, bridges, oil storage depots, and other critical targets.

Part of their effectiveness was luck and timing. Back in April 1942, John Wilson and Russell Dorr had arrived in London to put OSS economists together with economists in the British Ministry of Economic Warfare. Target analysis had top priority. A year and a half later American economists were everywhere in London. Charley Kindelberger came into the OSS from the Bank of International Settlements in Basle to direct our London economic team. He worked out of the Ministry of Economic Warfare but had specialists working with the U.S. Eighth Air Force, the British Air Ministry, the Home Office's damage assessment project, and anywhere else where targets were picked and bomb damage analyzed.

The American talent working in this area was prodigious, as the future careers of those who took part would testify. Kindelberger's stars included Walt Rostow, later to become Lyndon Johnson's National Security Advisor, Robert Roosa, a future Undersecretary of the Treasury for Monetary Affairs, Charles Hitch, who would become President of the University of California, and Carl Kaysen, who was to head the Institute for Advanced Studies at Princeton.

By the time the air war escalated in 1943, this group was a known quantity for both the British and the American generals streaming into London. And as Allied air armadas expanded their attacks against Germany and the continent into a round-the-clock venture, the advice of OSS economists was sought and valued more and more. Nothing brought their role home more sharply to me than a massive raid against the ball bearings factories at Schweinfurt, shortly after my arrival in London. On October 14, 1943, the 8th Air Force sent out 291

Flying Fortresses against Schweinfurt; 60 planes did not come back, a 19 percent loss ratio and four times our average loss on similar raids. The attack also cost us 600 casualties, a pace of attrition that shook U.S. flyers across England with many wondering about their chances of completing 25 missions and returning home alive. That the Germans lost an estimated 100 planes in the attack, a third of their defending force, did not make our losses easier to bear.

Clearly, some changes in strategy were needed. At the very least, Allied air forces had to have better data on the effectiveness of trade-offs between enemy targets destroyed and Allied planes shot down. The air war lacked an intellectual and strategic basis. The OSS provided one through the work done by the Research and Analysis branch's Enemy Objectives Unit developed by Ed Mason, an economics professor from Harvard, in Washington. Its theoretical work would be hotly debated, many of its suggestions rejected, but nevertheless EOU, as it was quickly known in our alphabet soup, became our first important contribution to the European war—and to the image others had of us. As we shall see, the Enemy Objectives Unit would play a key role in determining how Allied air superiority could best support the invading armies.

If 1942 had been the year of the OSS's organizing itself in Washington and of being tested in North Africa, 1943 was the turning point for OSS operations in Europe. We arrived in London as the new boys in school, untested, unknown, scorned and derided by some in the intelligence community, welcomed by others, ignored by few. However amateurish our efforts may have seemed—and in fact were—we represented the power and wealth of the United States on whose broad shoulders all hope of victory rested. As the year wore on, the OSS was slowly and sometimes grudgingly inducted into the mysteries of intelligence as the British and the governments-in-exile practiced them. In 1943, we sent our first agents into Europe, ran boats, supplies, and freedom fighters between Scotland and Norway, and planned air strategy for allied bombings of the Reich. By 1944, the year of Overlord, the OSS in London had girded itself to play a separate and equal role with the British and others in bringing Hitler to his knees. This would be the year when the American amateurs took on a professional sheen, and much of the seemingly random planning of the previous months took concrete shape.

3. Breaking into Intelligence

THE INITIAL British reaction to OSS and any American intelligence was summed up best by Lt. General Sir Frederick Morgan, who headed the planners at Chief of Staff to the Supreme Allied Commander (COSSAC):

"As regards Intelligence, there was at that time no doubt in anybody's mind that British developments were far ahead of American developments. The British had already been at war three and a half years and had, therefore, had time to perfect their Intelligence network throughout the world. They were well served everywhere by a variety of agencies and were already in possession of a stupendous quantity of information on every conceivable topic. The United States, on the other hand, had had little more than a year of war so far, and moreover, I understand that their neglect of military intelligence in peacetime had been even more glaring than our own which is to say a good deal. The Americans were therefore happy to concede the direction of the Intelligence setup of COSSAC to the British."

Well, I'm not sure how happy we were about it, but given the touchy OSS relationship with our own military there was not a great deal we could do—beyond go along and get along. Donovan soon regretted his commitment not to send American agents into Europe from Britain without British approval, but he could not change it. Moreover, even without such an explicit agreement, the British could easily have stopped any independent effort whenever they felt it risked their own operations. They controlled the air and the sea and all movements in and out of Britain.

Sir Claude Dansey, for one, viewed any other clandestine activity on the continent, whether foreign or British, as a mortal threat to the security of his own networks. Intelligence reports were more likely to cause confusion than elucidation unless each report was systematically evaluated, cross-checked, and worked into an overall appreciation of the military situation, he believed, and, accordingly, MI-6 held us at arm's length. Dansey made sure that Bill Maddox and his Secret Intelligence Branch were given only processed reports, little raw intelligence and no information about sources. We suspected that one reason for Dansey's reluctance was his embarrassment over the paucity of MI-6's direct information from Europe in general and Germany in particular. It was a suspicion Professor Hugh Trevor-Roper confirmed after the war: MI-6's coups were due mostly to code-breaking. Its spy networks on the continent had been destroyed by the sudden German sweep across Europe. For most of its on-the-scene information, MI-6 had to rely on the intelligence services of allied governments-in-exile. And that was another reason Dansey did not want OSS to do much on its own. He insisted that contacts with those governments run through MI-6. Still, our relations with MI-6 were tolerable. Kenneth Cohen and Bill Dunderdale, for example, were frequent visitors at 70 Grosvenor Street and, within the limits Dansey had set, could not have been more helpful. Cohen would prove especially valuable for his knowledge of the French underground. He had wide dealings with refugees from the continent. And more than most at MI-6 he had succeeded in building up new British intelligence networks in France, staffed mostly by Frenchmen. Dunderdale had broad experience in Russia and Eastern Europe that went back to World War I, and now he was responsible for liaison with the French and Polish intelligence services.

Still, Donovan and Bruce never stopped trying to change MI-6's mind. They argued that American troops and their commanders going into Europe needed direct intelligence from their own sources. The British agreed to American sources on the continent as an ultimate goal—after an American zone of operations had been established. Meanwhile, the only feasible method of preparing and conducting operations from Britain was jointly with the British and the governments-in-exile in London.

Nor was British opposition to independent American action limited to England. It extended to North Africa, the one reasonably independent OSS fiefdom, and one which was destined to play a key intelligence role in the invasion of southern France in August 1944. Earlier that year, after General Alexander Patch took command of the U.S. 7th Army, his G-2 (military intelligence) chief, Colonel Bill Quinn, visited the French desk of OSS headquarters in Algiers. Quinn realized quickly that Henry Hyde, chief of SI in Algiers, had valuable intelligence operations inside occupied France that could be an important resource for the forthcoming Allied invasion.

The British, however, viewed this budding relationship between American comrades-in-arms with alarm. They told Quinn never to go directly to producers of mere "raw" intelligence, but to rely entirely on the processed and evaluated intelligence that came from British headquarters. Quinn held his ground, and the conflict shot up the chain of command. Soon Field Marshal Alexander, the British commander, called Patch to complain that Quinn seemed to be young and inexperienced and needed to be taught the rules. Patch said, "We're all young and inexperienced," and backed Quinn. It started the most productive intelligence relationship between an Army G-2 and an OSS unit in the entire war.

Bruce had sent Henry Hyde to Algiers in February 1943 to set up an independent OSS intelligence operation inside occupied France. Hyde had the kind of background for the mission not found often among young pre-war Americans. He spoke French and had been educated at Harvard and Cambridge. He was bright, smart, discreet, persuasive, and instinctively tactful.

Within two months Hyde had settled into his Algiers milieu. He made contact with his French and British colleagues, learned their intelligence ropes, and convinced them of his own skills and abilities—the essential self-selling job the OSS had to perform wherever it went in the early days. He also began recruiting agents. He quickly found two jewels to be known as Jacques and Toto.

Hyde, Jacques, and Toto hoped to create a network of agents made up of members of Toto's hiking club in Clermont-Ferrand and Jacques' friends from a Jesuit finishing school in Lyon. Jacques had an aunt in Montpellier and an uncle in Lyon. Jacques had contacts all over the city right into Vichy police headquarters. In fact, he had a friend who ran the Lyon police and could provide fake papers. Toto knew radio hams and former French army radio operators he was sure he could recruit. An ardent hiker, he remembered possible "safe" houses in the mountains of the Massif Central.

All this fitted smoothly into Donovan's objectives of establishing OSS-operated intelligence chains in each of the three main areas through which an invading army would have to march—the Rhône valley in the southeast, the Garonne Valley in the southwest, and the Massif Central in the heart of France. Now the only problem was getting the two Frenchmen back home so they could start working. It proved a bigger problem than Hyde had anticipated. He couldn't find anyone to fly Toto and Jacques into France. The British Special Operations Executive had three Halifax planes in North Africa but they were fully scheduled. Hyde knew he had to move or his agents would go stale. Quickly, he began to play on the contacts he had built up over the last few months.

Dodds-Parker, the SOE station chief, offered to give him a set of travel orders and a letter of introduction to the SOE French desk in London. Hyde might be able to talk his way onto a plane to England. Colonel Eddy, the OSS commander in North Africa, saw no ready alternative and approved the mission to London. So one day in May 1943, Hyde, Toto, and Jacques arrived at Prestwick airport in Scotland in British battle dress. The MI-5 officer at the gate was alert enough to find the strange trio, only one of whom spoke English, suspicious. He asked what was up. Hyde showed his American passport and asked to call Colonel Bruce in London. What was Hyde doing in Britain, Bruce wanted to know, and why hadn't his visit been announced in advance? All right, Hyde could come to London to discuss it. Bruce would arrange for transportation on a DC-3 to London the next day. That gave Hyde a chance to shoot a round of golf at Prestwick with his mystified agents acting as caddies.

An amused Bruce listened to Hyde's story, then regretfully told him of Donovan's agreement with Sir Stewart Menzies of MI-6 that the OSS would not launch any independent intelligence missions from England. Not so, Hyde argued. His mission was actually a North African undertaking and he would report back to OSS North Africa, not to Bruce. England was merely a springboard that would not figure on the organizational chart. Bruce laughed and said he'd back Hyde if Hyde felt he could get away with it.

A day or two later, Bill Maddox, Bruce's intelligence chief, took Hyde to meet Sir Claude Dansey and General Marshall-Cornwall, respectively Number 2 and 3 behind Menzies. Dansey did not mince words. He lashed out at the young Americans with that special fury he reserved for anyone who threatened MI-6 turf. Why have you come here? Don't you know about Donovan's agreement not to mount any intelligence missions from the British Isles? What makes you think you can add one iota to what we are already doing? We have centuries of experience and have been working in occupied France since 1940. You are a bunch of amateurs. Don't you know that one bad apple can contaminate the whole barrel?

Sir Claude dripping fire and ice could be intimidating. But Hyde belonged to a breed as unflappable as the British. He came right back. He had responsibility in North Africa. It was an American theater. American troops might be required to land in the south of France. They were entitled to their own agents. England would only be a jumping-off place. His agents were unusually promising, chances for their organizing a real intelligence network in central and southern France were very good. It was an area not exactly studded with allied operatives. Dansey was impressed. He agreed to consider Hyde's request. Two days later, Bruce called an impatient Hyde and told him that Toto and Jacques' mission had been approved.

In July 1943, they were dropped blind within a two-mile walk of one of Toto's girlfriends near Clermont-Ferrand. Within a year they had 2500 agents and sub-agents and 37 radios sending in reports to Algiers.

Eventually, even our relations with MI-6 improved. About the time Hyde mounted his lone American assault on the continent, Bruce opened negotiations with Sir Claude Dansey on a joint undertaking that grew into the Sussex Plan. The project called for dispatching 120 agents in teams of two, one observer and one radio operator, into France just ahead of the invading armies. The Sussex teams were to report from key points in France on German troop movements. It was to be a tripartite operation with French, British, and American agents in civilian clothes. They were to be organized into 30 teams for the British combat zone in France and another 30 for the American battle area. Sussex took months to ripen—official approval was not given until November 1943 and the first teams were only dropped into France six weeks before the invasion—but it did ease some of the strain between Grosvenor Street and "Broadway"—the codename for MI-6.

Basic to the strain, of course, was the continuing dependency that bound us to the British, and which for all our understanding of their reasons, we were anxious to break. We had gotten a taste of independent action in North Africa, and were getting more of it in the neutral capitals. There, free of our British tutors, we could develop our own contacts and sources. In turn, the flow of American information from the neutral cities enhanced the OSS's position in London's intelligence community.

Because the neutral capitals—Lisbon, Madrid, Stockholm, Berne and Istanbul—had regularly scheduled passenger flights for both Berlin and London, they served as windows on occupied Europe and as meeting places for "our" and "their" people. Our people expected to be overheard and watched, and routinely assumed that any contact or source they cultivated might be working for the other side.

Each city held its special intelligence attractions. Everything crossed at Istanbul: East and West; Africa, Asia, and Europe; Slavs, Teutons, and Anglo-Saxons. Lisbon was the escape hatch west for refugees, downed Allied airmen, and others trying to evade the Nazi net. Traffic moved the other way through Madrid, where sympathies lay with the Nazis. Berne and Stockholm were windows on Germany. Trade was conducted through both. Businessmen traveled back and forth everyday. From Berne we could look into Italy, Austria, Yugoslavia, and the Balkans. Stockholm was a center for Danes, Norwegians, and Finns coming in and out of their occupied countries.

In all these capitals, the atmosphere favored independent development. OSS officers grew up faster than in London or Washington. They moved around openly under their own names and conducted independent operations. Take Gregory Thomas, who ran the Iberian peninsula for us out of Madrid. He was a tall, suave businessman, an executive of Coty perfume, which he had sold all over Europe. It was a background that gave a light, personal touch to his dealings with refugees, businessmen, and double agents who thronged Madrid and Lisbon on a thousand different errands and missions. At the same time, he built up extensive intelligence networks from Barcelona and San Sebastian into southwestern France. They paid off big when the Allies invaded southern France.

Bruce Hopper, a Harvard professor of government, ran OSS operations in Stockholm under the most difficult conditions: The British hobbled any American effort to mount independent missions into Denmark and Norway and the U.S. ambassador did not want to rock any boats. About all Hopper could do was poke his intelligence finger into northern Norway. He did manage to stir some dust in Stockholm, though, and to score a major coup inside Germany.

The name of the game in Sweden was ball bearings. As

allied air attacks cut into German output, increased shipments of Swedish ball bearings took up the slack. Efforts to dam the flow got nowhere, despite very liberal preemptive buying arrangements with SKF, Sweden's leading ball bearing manufacturer. SKF's Göteborg plant alone supplied 5 percent to 7 percent of German needs, and the percentage was much higher for specialized types of bearings.

To shame or pressure the Swedes into cutting back we needed more information. Hopper recruited a shipping clerk in the SKF Göteborg office who provided a flood of details: on shipments, on serial numbers and quantities, on exports of ball bearing tools and machinery, on lathes made at an SKF plant in Lidköping and shipped to Schweinfurt, and so forth. He lasted from December 1943 to May 1944, when the Swedish secret police arrested him. By then, however, we had what we needed. Exports were much larger than the Swedes admitted. In May, a U.S. Economic Warfare Mission arrived in Stockholm. Armed with our intelligence, it won Swedish agreement to stop the shipments.

Swedish businessman Eric Erikson proved our most valuable Stockholm find. Early in the war he had been blacklisted by the Allies for trading with the Germans, but his sympathies did not lie with the Nazis. After we had pulled him to our side he pretended to plan a synthetic oil plant in Sweden. Erikson contacted August Rosterg, a fellow Swede, who owned the controlling interest in a German synthetic oil firm, Wintershall. Rosterg freely gave Erikson much valuable information on German oil manufacturing and supply. In October 1944, he even helped Erikson arrange a tour of Germany's synthetic oil industry. When German oil plants became a major bombing target, Erikson's reports provided a vital blueprint.

Some of the best OSS sources in Stockholm, however, were other foreign services. The Poles, for one, sent us their intelligence reports in return for our helping them with supplies and transportation. A similar arrangement was reached with the Hungarian Minister in December 1943. Estonian, Latvian, Lithuanian, Dutch, and Belgian refugee groups and diplomatic representatives were equally helpful.

Berne was our showcase. There Allen Dulles built a center to rival London. He spun threads all over Europe, often to the chagrin and discomfort of Sir Claude Dansey who held Switzerland to be his personal fiefdom. But Dulles operated on his own. He fostered the impression that he had direct ties to FDR and was empowered to act and make decisions alone. His contacts within the German Reich widened over the months.

In the summer of 1943, Fritz Kolbe, an official of the German Foreign Office charged with handling cable traffic with diplomatic posts all over the world, had made his way to Berne carrying 16 telegrams taken out of the files of the Foreign Office in Berlin. Kolbe traveled first to the British embassy where, he told Dulles, he had been thrown out as a suspected plant or *agent provocateur*. Dulles quizzed Kolbe and scanned the cables he had brought signed by von Papen in Ankara, von Neurath in Prague, Abetz in Paris. Dulles was convinced that Kolbe sincerely wanted to work for the Allies, and, under the code name George Wood, Kolbe made the trip from Berlin to Berne 5 times, bringing with him copies or photographs of over 1,500 official cables.

This stirred up a fierce storm in London. Sir Claude Dansey had been in charge of British intelligence operations in Switzerland since before the war, and was hostile towards American activity there. He charged that the OSS was falling for an obvious plant with Kolbe, and was jeopardizing established sources who had been developed over long periods of time. In both London and Washington, the case was handled as a counterintelligence matter, both because Kolbe might be acting under German intelligence control and because some of this information could be put to counterintelligence use. When our Wood cables stood up as valid—cables intercepted between the German Foreign Office and German embassies abroad—Dulles's Wood reports gained acceptance as perhaps the greatest espionage coup of the war.

Back in London, we were becoming familiar with the various governments-in-exile. Because exiled governments had little tangible to offer—their homeland, after all, was in enemy hands, their resources were meager, their troops had to be equipped by us—intelligence and control over indigenous resistance forces were their most prized possessions. They got information from their homeland no one else could, instigated sabotage, and directed resistants.

None were more important than the French. France was our invasion target. Though the regime in exile and the resistance at home were riven with factions, both were active, strong, and eager. De Gaulle even had territory in black Africa that acknowledged his authority, and while for a long time Algeria did not, it represented a considerable power base. London was full of French staff. And de Gaulle had wasted little time building a Free French intelligence service. It was called the Bureau Centrale de Renseignements et d'Action and in acronym-crazed London was quickly known as BCRA. Colonel Passy, the nom de guerre for André Dewavrin, and a veteran of the French Deuxième Bureau, served as de Gaulle's loyal and often intractable intelligence chief. He had started with very little and gradually built up the service. By the time I arrived in London, Passy was ensconced in a 27-room suite at 10 Duke Street behind Selfridge's. From there he directed an impressive bureaucracy in London and a far-flung network of espionage, sabotage, and resistance activities in France itself. One of Passy's deputies ran a staff of 80 to 100 people who sifted through huge sacks of mail containing reports, maps, drawings, and photos received from France. His staff was organized into readers, classifiers, cross-checkers, and compilers. By 1944, BCRA was distributing reports to the entire London intelligence community twice a day. The monthly output of this information factory averaged 200,000 mimeographed sheets, 60,000 copies of maps and sketches, and 10,000 photographic reproductions.

Passy had put one of his veteran operatives in charge of the "Mail Room." Colonel Rémy had organized the first espionage networks inside France after the collapse and built them up across a third of the nation before settling in London. His network "Confrerie de Notre Dame" sent in detailed plans for Hitler's Atlantic Wall before its construction began and the 300 members of the Alliance network produced a huge detailed map of the Atlantic Wall as it stood a few months before D-Day.

Gilbert Renault-Roulier, his real name, was a deeply religious Breton. Before the war he had handled investments and financing for the Eagle Star Insurance Company in Paris. When France fell, Renault-Roulier had been overseeing the making of a film about Christopher Columbus in Spain, and traveled constantly between Madrid and Paris. He managed to escape to London, contacted Passy, and in August 1940 was on his way first to Lisbon and then to France to spin the fragile webs of an intelligence network.

Both Passy and Rémy were thoughtful, bright, quick, intelligent men with a firm grasp of their new craft. They were prickly and bent on maintaining both *honneur* and *gloire*. Friction with the British and Americans was constant. The French were often kept out of top strategy planning and had to suffer other security restrictions, which they often broke. Discovery would lead to mutual discomfort and recrimination. There was, for example, the matter of certain information the British did not want the French to send home, but which the French sent anyway. Because the British had long broken the French code, they read the messages and were furious. The French pointed out that reading one's allies' mail was not cricket. The result was a suspicious stand-off. On another occasion MI-6 smelled a security breach when Colonel Passy pinpointed the invasion site between Calais and Cherbourg. Because the French were not privy to invasion planning, somebody must have leaked. In fact, no one had. Passy's Czech planner, Colonel Miksche, had simply deduced the area by a process of logical elimination, and Passy had accepted the deduction.

It was a moment of bitter satisfaction for the Frenchman. He often raged at being kept in ignorance. He did understand the Anglo-American fears of French leaks, though grudgingly, and his anger in no way diminished his effort and support on behalf of the Allied cause. But his anger flared often. The British got first crack at Frenchmen coming into England, for one, and signed up the best material at the Royal Patriotic school. He thought the OSS played too close with

de Gaulle's major rival, General Henri Giraud, who ruled in
Algiers. And he did everything he could to stop links developing between resistance units in France he did not control
and Allen Dulles's OSS operation in Berne. On that one he
had little trouble lining up British support because MI-6 was
equally opposed to the OSS establishing independent ties to
France. What griped Passy and the French the most, however, was the Anglo-American refusal to understand the intricacies of French politics that dominated so much of de
Gaulle's thinking. The Free French wanted to come out on
top in the muddle of French politics, a muddle, they knew,
that would reappear as soon as the Germans had been defeated. The British were somewhat more sympathetic to that
view than we were. For Roosevelt, whose dislike of de Gaulle
was well known, winning the war came first, last, and always. Consummate domestic politician that he was, FDR
tended to shove foreign politics—as distinct from foreign policy—into the background of his thought and concern. Besides, he was afraid that de Gaulle would emerge as the man
on the white horse and plunge France into military dictatorship.

The Poles in London ran one of the most efficient and
ambitious of the exile intelligence services. Colonel Gano
developed large networks both in Poland and in France where
hundreds of thousands of Poles had found refuge. Most were
clustered around Toulouse, the jumping off place for those
escaping to England through Spain. After France fell, the
Polish army set up a tourist bureau in Toulouse for ex-soldiers
who wanted to fight again. The Vichy authorities were not
yet well enough organized to do much about it, nor about
the many Poles who decided to stay in France and fight the
Germans from underground. Blessed with a long tradition
of resistance, the Poles quickly became prominent in the
movement. They set up intelligence chains and recruited
Frenchmen for them. Soon the Poles were running many espionage outfits in France.

Two radio operators from the Polish Foreign Office,
stranded in Toulouse, found an out-of-the-way villa, built a
transmitter, and, having remembered wave lengths and

schedules to Madrid, established radio contact with the Polish embassy there. Their "fist"—the touch of their fingers on the transmitter, a common way for radio operators to recognize one another—was recognized in Madrid, and they were given a direct link to London. It was the beginning of the Polish F-2 network that eventually spread all over France and into North Africa. By 1944, F-2 had 700 full-time and 2000 part-time workers, with 90 percent of its membership French. Polish agents also roamed Germany and, of course, Poland.

In the months before D-Day the Poles were particularly good on locating buzz bomb installations along the Pas de Calais and reporting rocket tests inside Poland. Equally important were Polish reports on German troop movements to the Russian front, on activity in Belgium and northern France, and on bomb damage in cities all over Germany. In London, Thadeus Lisicki, an electronics engineer of considerable skill and innovation, had set up a Polish radio station that stayed in constant communication with agents and proved to be one of the most valuable information gathering points of the war.

As with the Free French, politics did not make the Poles easier to deal with. No one was more fiercely anti-German. But the Poles could not forget that Stalin had stabbed them in the back and carved up their country with Hitler. The situation became impossible after evidence mounted in 1943 that the Russians, not the Germans, had shot and buried 4,500 Polish officers in the Katyn Forest. On April 25, 1943, the Russians broke off diplomatic relations with the London Polish government. The Poles, Moscow said, had insulted Russia by suggesting the International Red Cross investigate the Katyn Forest mass murder. The breach threatened our collaboration with both Poles and Russians, but the Poles never relented in their efforts to help crush the Nazis.

Belgian intelligence also played a major role, especially as the invasion neared. Judge Fernand Lepage, head of the Belgian Sûreté de l'Etat working out of London, had eight to ten effective intelligence networks operating in Belgium and in that part of northern France the Germans administered from Brussels.

One of the largest Belgian "chains" was the work of vet-

eran Walthère Dewé, who had run the famous La Dame
Blanche network in World War I. Worried about German intentions, he asked to be put in charge of the Belgian Army's
Telephone and Telegraph Service well before the Nazi invasion. He proceeded to build up an intelligence service inside
that system and staffed it with present and former employees
of the Belgian Postal Communications Service. Dewé's network survived his capture, and at its peak had 1,500 operatives. Other Belgian networks, also heavy on engineering and
industrial talent, were used not only in Belgium but in Germany as well. Their information on German radar and secret
weapons sites was accurate, the guidance on bombing targets
valuable, and their assessments of bombing damage and of
rail traffic between Germany and France shrewd and telling.
Other Belgian agents penetrated military sites, German railroad offices, factories, and laboratories. One Belgian came
up with plans for coastal defenses, another put troop deploy-
ment details on a map and sent it to England.

One Belgian network was headquartered inside the communications center of the Belgian national railroad and used
its system to keep in touch with agents and get advance
teleprinter information on German troop and supply movements. Because the railroad communication system was independent of other Belgian telephone and telegraph lines,
workers could install automatic telephones, a teletype machine, and a radio-telegraph connection to London. The system was so sophisticated that agents could tap into it from
their own phones. Nor was Belgian intelligence limited to
networks providing sophisticated technical information. Much
of it came from day-to-day observation by ordinary citizens
with contacts in the underground. It does not take much training for a man to note divisional insignia on a troop train or
to spot tank cars on a freight train and note the direction in
which the train was traveling. Such fragments were collected
by a huge corps of "amateurs." According to some estimates, as many as 75,000 Belgians were connected with intelligence work at one time or another, with 5,000 more or
less full-time agents. They worked under tough conditions.
Belgium is small and flat. The Germans had little trouble

tracking down transmitters. Operators dared not stay on the air longer than a few minutes. Couriers carried most reports out through France, Spain, Portugal, and Gibraltar to England.

The Germans had been ruthlessly efficient and effective in eliminating all Dutch intelligence networks that operated after Holland's fall. And for years the Dutch government in London failed in its often haphazard efforts to re-establish them. The reasons were more personal than tactical. Queen Wilhelmina's exile government lacked trained personnel. The Dutch Intelligence Chief, "General" François Van't Sant, was needed as aide and confidante of the Queen. There was no one else with the contacts and the experience to replace him until 1943 when Major J. M. Somer showed up in London. An old intelligence hand trapped in Holland, he only managed to escape in 1942. And then it took him the better part of a year to reach England. The story is crazy outside the context of World War II, perfectly logical within it. Somer first got to Switzerland, traveled to the Dutch West Indies, and from there to England. By then, all contact with Holland had been lost. Not a single Dutch agent had been in touch with London from September 1942 to March 1943. Yet a year later, Somer had parachuted enough men into Holland to organize 20 new networks and set up a dozen transmitting stations. Radios, however, were as little use in flat Holland as in flat Belgium. The Germans could locate them in minutes. So most Dutch intelligence took circuitous routes to Britain. For a while, coastal ships took the information to Sweden. When the Nazis caught on, the traffic shifted overland to Switzerland. Couriers carried microfilmed reports to Geneva. The reports were hidden in book covers and shipped via Lufthansa to Lisbon and then to London. Messages took about four weeks, but by the end of 1943, we knew everything about every German headquarters and division in Holland.

The Danes were in a class by themselves. Their commitment to opposing Nazism was total, their skill and dedication unmatched. They organized early and the whole country was seeded with the spirit of resistance, which brought rich dividends of military and political intelligence. We were one of the beneficiaries, and ties between the OSS and the Danes were close from the beginning. Many of the Danish resistance remain close friends to this day.

The Danes had one advantage most others did not, a functioning government of their own even under the occupation. Thus military and naval intelligence could regularly supply London with information and do so with relative ease. A Danish journalist in Stockholm, Ebbe Munck, worked closely with MI-6 in processing raw reports sent by Lt. Col. Nordentoft of Danish Military Intelligence. The reports were then radioed to London or flown out of the country.

The system worked smoothly until the Germans cracked down in the summer of 1943. In August, the Gestapo arrested several of Nordentoft's top aides, forcing him and other regular line officers to flee to Sweden. The Danes had to start over from scratch, and they did, much to the Germans' chagrin. Svend Truelsen, a lawyer and former reserve officer, buckled down to organizing an entirely new intelligence apparatus. No member of the old network could be used, lest the arrested Danes break under German torture and reveal their sources. Brazenly, Truelsen moved into the office of the Danish Agriculture Council and established his new intelligence service in the Ministry's postal department.

He found two Copenhagen postmasters with intelligence experience whose jobs put them above suspicion. They put together a new staff of couriers, mostly country postmen and hotel porters who did not know enough to implicate anyone else. More sophisticated information was gathered by those with a reason to move around and talk to people—doctors, vets, teachers, clergy, engineers. Many were told to work on their own and form separate intelligence networks.

What really undermined German efforts to crush the Danish underground was the Germans' own brutality weeks after they put Nordentoft's operation out of business. Nazi plans to round up all Danish Jews on one day and deport them aroused Danish fury as nothing else did. And in that crunch the Danes defied the Germans and hid the Jews. Here's what happened:

On Friday morning, September 30, 1943, the day before

Rosh Hashanah, Rabbi Melchior told about 150 members of the congregation in the Copenhagen Synagogue that "last night I received word that tomorrow the Germans plan to raid Jewish homes throughout Copenhagen to arrest all Danish Jews for shipment to concentration camps. They know that tomorrow is Rosh Hashanah and our families will be home. By nightfall tonight, we must all be in hiding."

That night they were, 7,000 Jews sheltered in Christian homes, most of them near the water. Over the weekend, the underground organized 100 small boats that carried most of the threatened Jews to Sweden and safety. The Danish people formed a protective wall for their country's Jewish population throughout the war, and doing so, behaved courageously.

4. The German Atom Bomb

WHEN WORLD War II broke out, there was only one company producing heavy water in Europe on a commercial scale. That was Norsk-Hydro at their power plant at Vemork, next to Rjukan, between Oslo and Bergen in south central Norway. It had begun operating at the end of 1934 and in 1939 was producing only 10 kilograms per month.

In 1940, Norsk-Hydro's limited output of heavy water was sold to laboratories throughout the world. The Germans had bought only small quantities. Joliot-Curie, working on atomic research in his laboratory at the Collège de France, theorized that heavy water could work as a moderator in achieving a controlled nuclear explosion. He warned the French Minister of Armaments of the potential significance of the Norwegian heavy water plant. The French minister sent to Norway Jacques Allier, a businessman brought into the French Deux-ième Bureau, to buy the entire Norwegian heavy water inventory. If he was unable to buy it, he was to contaminate it with either cadmium or boron, which would make it useless for nuclear purposes. The Germans had already tried to buy the whole Norwegian heavy water stock through I. G. Farben, but Norsk-Hydro's general manager declined the order. Instead, he sold all 185 kilograms on hand to Allier along with priority rights to all future production. He also told Allier that Norsk-Hydro didn't want "one centime" until France had won the war.

When the Germans marched into Rjukan, the last town in Norway to surrender, they found that the entire stock of heavy water had been shipped out some weeks earlier. They lost no time in launching plans to expand the capacity of the Vemork plant.

When the British government learned that the Germans, on occupying Norway and Belgium, were increasing Norwegian heavy water production and had seized 3500 tons of uranium from Union Minière in Belgium, the Ministry of Supply was directed to study what would happen if an atom bomb was detonated in the center of a large British city.

With their occupation of Europe, the Germans had an impressive array of nuclear assets—Europe's only heavy water plant; the uranium of Czechoslovakia; a half-built cyclotron; a group of physicists, chemists, and engineers at work on nuclear research; the best chemical engineering industry in the world; and the results of American nuclear research freely published in U.S. scientific periodicals.

By 1942, alarming reports were coming out of the Scandinavian window on Germany. A wireless message from Danish intelligence reported that Werner Heisenberg, now in charge of nuclear research at the Kaiser Wilhelm Institute in Berlin, had come to Copenhagen to consult Niels Bohr on the morality of a physicist engaging in the construction of a nuclear bomb. Bohr had concluded from the conversation that Germany was well on its way to building a war-winning weapon. A Swedish theoretical physicist wrote from Uppsala that Heisenberg was conducting extensive nuclear experiments in other German laboratories. British intelligence had determined primarily from study of German scientific literature, that of 16 top German scientists, 15 were involved in nuclear research and the 16th was excluded on racial grounds.

Lief Tronstad, who had designed the Vemork heavy water plant and been consulted by the Germans about expanding it, came out of Norway to London with the clear conviction that heavy water output was of the highest importance to the German military.

In mid-March, SOE got a Rjukan man, Einar Skinnarland, out of Norway. He was briefed and then parachuted back to Rjukan, where he established contact with Jomar Brun, chief engineer at the heavy water plant. Discussions with German scientists had convinced Brun and his colleagues that the Germans had a military purpose in expanding heavy water production. Brun provided drawings of the plant that were microfilmed and concealed in toothpaste tubes, smuggled into Sweden, and flown to Britain. On June 19, 1942, Winston Churchill arrived in Hyde Park, New York, for a meeting with President Roosevelt that had, as Churchill later reported, the atom bomb as "the most complex and, as it proved, overwhelmingly most important" subject on the agenda. Roosevelt came with a report from Vanevar Bush that there were six basic methods of exploiting nuclear energy—four involving the separation of uranium-235 and two involving the extraction of plutonium from a uranium pile moderated by either graphite or heavy water. As Churchill wrote in his memoirs:

> *"We both felt painfully the dangers of doing nothing. We knew what efforts the Germans were making to procure supplies of 'heavy water'—a sinister term, eerie, unnatural, which began to creep into our secret papers. What if the enemy should get an atomic bomb before we did! However sceptical one might feel about the assertions of scientists, much disputed among themselves and expressed in jargon incomprehensible to laymen, we could not run the mortal risk of being outstripped in this awful sphere."*

On Churchill's return, the War Cabinet decided that the Norwegian heavy water had to be taken away from the Germans. It had increased its production from 3,000 pounds a year to 10,000 pounds and there were no industrial uses.

Three options were looked at. Bombing was strongly opposed by Major Lief Tronstad in London for Norwegian intelligence, because of the danger to the civilian population. Even though SOE had a four-man team waiting for weather good enough to allow them to parachute in and set up a base camp on the Hardanger plateau, 30 miles northwest of Vemork, a sabotage operation was viewed as too uncertain. The third option, a Combined Operations plan, was selected. Thirty-four commandos would be carried in on two gliders, each towed by a Halifax bomber. The two lines would be let go over the Hardanger plateau and the gliders, with troops, demolition equipment, guns, and folding bicycles, would glide silently to the edge of the lake that fed the turbines at the Vemork plant. The men would bicycle to the plant, kill the guards, enter the plant, and destroy first the machinery and then the existing stock of heavy water. The attacking force would then split into small groups of two and three and head for the Swedish border.

When the Norwegian section of SOE studied the plan, they came back with a long list of objections—both the glider tow and the escape into Sweden, each about 400 miles, were too long under Norwegian winter conditions; cloud cover could make it difficult to find the landing site; air currents and the rough terrain made a glider landing on the Hardanger plateau too risky; the ice would not be strong enough to bear the weight of a glider with its men and equipment; and the bicycles would be useless in snow or on ice-coated roads. But the pressure from Washington and London to put the heavy water plant out of action was so great that the Combined Operations plan was on.

Two gliders, towed by Halifax planes, carrying 34 commandos took off for Norway on October 19, 1942. Only one of the Halifaxes returned. On October 20, a wireless message from Norway reported that the other Halifax and both gliders crashed. Fifteen of the men were killed on landing. Four survivors were so badly injured that when they were found and brought to Stavanger Hospital, a German medical officer poisoned them. Fourteen of the surviving commandos were shot by a German firing squad pursuant to Hitler's decree that sabotage teams were to be shot at once.

This disastrous mission told the Germans how concerned the Allies were about their nuclear research and gave them time to strengthen the protection around the plant. It in no way lessened the urgent demand in London and Washington to take the only heavy water plant in Europe away from the Germans.

Colin Gubbins decided that an SOE sabotage party could do what Combined Operations and its commandos had failed to do. The SOE saboteurs parachuted into Norway in February 1943 and succeeded in blowing up all the plant's electrolysis tubes and destroying half a ton of heavy water. The saboteurs escaped, though the Germans sent some 3,000 men out to look for them.

Nevertheless, only five months later, reports surfaced that the plant at Vemork was expected to reach full production again by August 15, 1943. Shipments of heavy water were going from Vemork to Germany under very heavy guard.

Back in America, General Leslie Groves suspected that the Germans were close to making a bomb. Groves convinced General Marshall to propose to the Combined Chiefs of Staff that Vemork be made a first priority bombing objective. The Combined Chiefs, without consulting the Norwegian government-in-exile, decided that the Germans had strengthened their security to the point that bombing was the only remaining alternative.

Only two of the seven hundred bombs dropped by 154 Flying Fortresses in the valley in November 16, 1943, hit the electrolytic plant. Although no bombs fell in the town itself, twenty-two Norwegians were killed. The Norwegian government protested formally that a saturation air attack was carried out without advance notice and that it was "out of all proportion to the objective sought."

The only accomplishment of the air raid was to convince the Germans that Allied determination to stop heavy water production and undercover agents and commandos in central Norway were so strong that they could not rely on getting heavy water from Vemork.

We learned after the war that three days following the raid German authorities approved the erection of a heavy water plant in Germany. A Montecatini electrolytic plant in Italy, using a different process and having only half the capacity of the Vemork plant, was turned to heavy water production.

In late January of 1944, London was informed that all heavy water equipment, 14 tons of fluid, and 613 kilograms of heavy water, was ready to be brought to a Norwegian port from the plant at Vemork and shipped across the Baltic to Germany. The War Cabinet reacted with great alarm. Orders were wirelessed to SOE contacts in Norway, Einar Skinnarland and Knut Haukelid, to destroy the heavy water shipment. Haukelid had received a supply drop from the RAF in November 1943 that included some explosives, and he radioed for authority to sabotage the shipment in transit. Col. Wilson, head of SOE's Norwegian section, got the approval of the Norwegian Defense Minister and wirelessed it to Haukelid.

Haukelid went down into Rjukan to meet with Skinnarland's brother-in-law, Gunnar Syverstad, who tested the heavy water concentrations in the plant's lab; Alf Larsen, who had succeeded Brun as chief engineer at Vemork; and Kjell Nielsen, Norsk-Hydro's transport engineer, who had the shipment plan. They went over four possibilities for attacking the cargo. They could blow up dynamite stocks next to the railway line running from the Vemork plant to Rjukan as the cargo was passing. They could blow up the ferry that would carry the railway cars, with the cargo, across Lake Tinnsjö. They could attack the railway cars as they proceeded by rail to Heröja. Or they could sink the ship carrying the water across the Baltic to Germany.

Exploding the dynamite pile was rejected because it would jeopardize workers; there was no time to organize a direct assault on the railway cars; and an attack on the ship in the Baltic seemed too uncertain. On the other hand, if the Tinnsjö ferry could be sunk, the lake was deep enough that the cargo could never be salvaged.

Haukelid went to work studying the schedules and the route of the three ferry boats that plied the lake. He figured out that it would be the Hydro that would make the early run south on that Sunday, that it would take half an hour to reach the deepest part of the lake, that it would traverse water deeper than 1000 feet for about 20 minutes. If an explosive was set for 45 minutes after scheduled departure, a ten-minute delay in casting off or a faster than usual trip would still find the Hydro in deep water.

Now the explosive would have to be designed and put together. Haukelid wanted the ferry to go down suddenly enough to exclude the possibility that it could be maneuvered into shallower water after the explosive went off, yet slowly enough that the passengers would have a chance to swim for the shore. To accommodate these objectives, he figured that the hole should be blown in the bow so that the screws and the rudder would lift clear of the water and the rail cars roll forward into the lake. In case this did not happen, the hole should be big enough that it would bring the ship down inside the five minutes he figured it would take as a minimum to reach shallow water.

Everything was ready to go except a plan for escape and a contingency plan should the Hydro somehow manage to get its cargo to the railhead. Syverstad and Rolf Sörlie would leave Vemork and join the underground. Hansen would return to his surveyor's job as if nothing had happened. Larsen, as chief engineer, would be suspect. To protect him and to give the Germans a scapegoat, he would head for Sweden with Haukelid. Nielsen, in charge of transport, would be most suspect, but Skinnarland asked if he could find a way to stay so that London could retain a contact at the plant. This dilemma was resolved by having Nielsen's sister arrange for him to go into a hospital in Oslo for an appendectomy on Saturday, February 19. Thin as this seems, it worked.

In London, back-up arrangements were mounted. The Norwegian underground was asked to send enough men to Skien, near Heröja, the scheduled port of embarkment on the Baltic, to attack the German convoy and destroy the heavy water. The RAF and the Admiralty were requested to sink the cargo in the Baltic, if it got that far.

A little before midnight, Lier-Hansen drove Haukelid and Sorlie to the station-dock at Mel. Some 20 German soldiers were playing cards inside the station. On the ferry, most of the crew were below deck playing cards. Haukelid and Sorlie walked on board, kept on going to a hatchway leading from the passenger saloon to the bilge. Telling a Norwegian member of the crew that they had something to hide, Sorlie and Haukelid, with twelve feet of plastic, detonators, and timers, and each with a Sten gun bulging under his coat, went down the hatch and worked furiously to fix the plastic in a circle against the ship's hull, tape the detonator fuses, and set the timers to go off at 10:45. After connecting the electric detonators to the fuses, Haukelid and Sorlie walked off the boat and Lier-Hansen, after picking up Larsen, drove them to Kongsberg, where they boarded the morning train for Oslo.

A little after 10:00 a.m., the Hydro with 53 passengers and two flatcars loaded with 39 drums of heavy water lashed to its deck, started down the lake. The explosive went off on schedule. It took four minutes for the flatcars to roll off and the ferry to sink. In that time, 27 people on the deck were able to jump into the water. All of them were saved. The remaining 26 went down with the ship.

In April 1945, the dismantled high concentration plant was found in Bavaria, together with uranium and heavy water on the brink of going critical, lacking about 700 liters of additional heavy water. The Germans were never able to get out of Norway much more than half the heavy water they needed. Nobel prize-winner Wagner, one of the physicists driven out of Germany, had in 1942 told the American government that the Germans would produce a nuclear weapon in two years. If Vemork had been allowed to maintain its rate of heavy water output through 1943 and 1944, he might have been right. Haukelid, who, with his companions, implemented the decisions taken at the top by Churchill and Roosevelt and the Combined Chiefs of Staff, and approved by his own government, is entitled to the last word. In his book *Skis Against the Atom,* he concludes:

> *"Of all the 'buts' and 'ifs' which follow all historical discussions, none are so unstable and encumbered with variable values as those which come as an aftermath of war.*

*** *If Adolf Hitler's failure in producing the decisive weapon of the Second World War was due to lack of foresight, lack of proficiency, lack of willingness by his scientists, lack of freedom of research, or lack of heavy water, it is in this connection a matter of little consequence. The final result was that it failed. * * * When a war is going on there is no free exchange of ideas across the front lines, and the political leadership has a tremendous responsibility. Everyone can imagine what an atomic weapon in Adolf Hitler's hands would have led to. It was under this threat that the allied governments gave their soldiers and scientists their means and their orders.''*

5. Missiles and Rockets

YEARS BEFORE the atom was split in Berlin, the Germans had been working for almost ten years on building that other component of the modern strategic arsenal, the long range missile. The German army had been stimulated to take an early interest in rocketry by the Versailles Treaty, which prohibited the development of artillery over 3 inches in caliber, but which was silent about rockets. In 1930, Captain Walter Dornberger was assigned to develop rocket weapons for the German army. In 1932, he hired as his technical assistant 20-year-old Werner von Braun. In 1936, a joint Army-Air Force rocket establishment was created at Peenemünde, on the northern peninsula of the island of Usedom. When World War II was launched, Dornberger and von Braun had at their disposal a 300-mile water range along the southern shores of the Baltic and numerous small islands on which tracking stations could be placed, as well as a supersonic wind tunnel, a liquid oxygen factory, a pilot factory for developing mass production techniques for rockets, and a string of supporting workshops and laboratories.

During 1943, reports prepared by Admiral Eugenio Minisini, head of the Italian torpedo works, and Professor Carlo Calossi, a world renowned electronics expert, had been spirited out of Italy by an OSS mission headed by Lt. John Shaheen. Minisini and Calossi had provided a detailed description of all the weapons in production and all those under development at the Italian torpedo works. There was a detailed account of both and German research on what they called "guided missiles," "winged bombs," and "winged torpedoes," comparing various methods of propulsion and guidance, and projecting the range and explosive power they could deliver.

Donovan, Shaheen, and Major Jim Rand had been at the Salerno landings when guided missiles launched from German planes had hit the cruisers Savannah and Philadelphia. Rear Admiral H. K. Hewitt, in command of the invasion fleet, called in Donovan, who had come to be looked upon as an all-purpose problem solver. Donovan turned to Shaheen and Jim Rand. Rand was advised that the only immediately available defense was to go after the planes.

In London, the British had early on known about secret weapons Hitler had under development. The British naval attaché at Oslo had received a batch of papers accompanied by a note signed "a well-wishing German scientist." The papers, which came to be known as the Oslo Report, described German progress on two radar systems, a system of blind bombing, a form of proximity fuse, and a rocket program. They also disclosed that glider bombs and other new weapons were being investigated at an experimental station at Peenemünde on the Baltic coast. The Oslo Report had been filed away, discounted on the basis that it was unlikely that any one scientist would be reliable on so many technical subjects as rocketry, radar, guidance systems, and acoustical bomb detonation. The predictions of the Oslo Report on radar systems and navigational guidance devices had already materialized. Now the emergence at Salerno of guided missiles strengthened the report's final warning that the Germans had a rocket under development.

In London, intelligence pointing to a German long range

rocket program had begun to accumulate. During 1942, Danish intelligence started to send in reports that unidentified flying objects were appearing over the Baltic heading north and either crashing into the sea or exploding in the air. Early in 1943, a Danish agent, who had already established his credibility by sending in detailed photographs of newly installed radar aerials on German night fighter planes, sent in 3 detailed reports about trials on the Baltic coast of a rocket that could carry 5 tons of explosive over a distance of 130 miles. Other reports took the warhead up to 10 tons and the range to 180 miles.

In the early months of 1943, a conversation between two German generals who had been captured in North Africa after El Alamein was recorded at the London Cage where high-level prisoners of war were gathered for interrogation and allowed to talk with each other in rooms wired for sound. General von Thoma expressed surprise to General Cruewell that London was not already under rocket bombardment. He went on to describe a visit to a firing range in Germany where self-propelled unmanned bombs were being tested over long distances. He said that the officer in charge had expressed great confidence that these weapons would be operational and reach London the following year.

Dr. R. V. Jones, a physicist attached to MI-6, had established his reputation during the Battle of Britain by identifying beams that the Germans were transmitting to pinpoint targets over England. He learned to read the beams and could frequently forecast the target, time, route, and height of the German attack. Jones was also able to defeat German air defenses by confusing their radar with radio waves and physical reflection, using balloons and metal strips.

Now turning his attention to the German rocket threat, Jones wanted to pursue his usual method of accumulating fragments of information and piecing them together slowly and quietly until he knew what they meant. But the circulation of new agents' reports and a transcript of General von Thoma's conversation did stir up alarm over in the War Ministry. Military Intelligence at the War Office decided that the Prime Minister and the Secretary of State for the Home Department, Herbert Morrison, should be warned of a possible rocket attack. On April 11, 1943, the Chiefs of Staff had a paper compiling agent and interrogation reports together with staff speculation on German long range rocket development. Within a few days, General Ismay, Chief of Staff to the Minister of Defence, had spoken to Churchill suggesting that a single investigator be designated to report on the German long range rocket threat and available countermeasures. He suggested the name of Duncan Sandys, Churchill's son-in-law who had been responsible for weapons research and development in the Ministry of Supply and had also commanded an anti-aircraft rocket squadron. On April 20, Sandys was named and authorized to call on all the intelligence and scientific resources of the British government.

Sandys arranged for intensified aerial reconnaissance of the Baltic coast and areas of France within the estimated rocket range of London. Agents all over the continent were briefed to look for information about a German rocket, where it might be made, how it might be fueled, how and where it might be launched.

The accumulating evidence made it clear that something important was going on at Peenemünde. Jones, who had been left out of Sandys' inquiry, still had responsibility at MI-6 for receiving and interpreting agents' reports dealing with new weapons.

Starting in June, reports started to come from inside the rocket establishment itself. First, the Polish Home Army's underground intelligence service compiled a comprehensive report including a sketch map of Peenemünde, a description of the flying weapons seen there and how they were launched and steered, and an analysis of the security and facilities at Peenemünde. Then, a report locating the positions of anti-aircraft guns, compiled by workers from Luxembourg, was brought out and passed to MI-6 through a French network. At about the same time, a Belgian network sent details of a German flying bomb. Given all this information, different conclusions were reached. Jones was pretty sure the Germans had a flying torpedo or bomb in a fairly advanced stage of development. Sandys was searching for German rockets and

Professor Lindemann suspected the whole thing was a German hoax.

In the bureaucratic contest that developed, Sandys had enough clout to get first crack at air photos of Peenemünde. Jones had more experience in working with the photo interpreters and got to the agents' reports first. He was also far more resourceful in obtaining his own intelligence sources. A seemingly insignificant piece of evidence satisfied him on the importance of Peenemünde. He spotted a captured German document that showed Peenemünde was given priority for the distribution of gasoline. This, in his mind, ruled out any possibility that the weapons development at Peenemünde was a hoax.

Of much greater importance was Jones's analysis that if a long range flying weapon was being developed, the Germans would probably use their best radar units to plot its trial flights. In his early work on the German bomb guidance systems, he had learned of the German Air Signals Experimental Regiment. He now asked that the location of its units be closely watched. In the early summer he got a report that this regiment had a detachment at work on Rugen Island, just north of Peenemünde, and on the Danish island of Bornholm, 75 miles away. Jones immediately asked his friends at Bletchley to make a special effort to read the transmissions of these signals detachments strung out along the Baltic.

At about the same time, photographs taken over Peenemünde came in showing what were described as long cylindrical objects with pointed ends. One of them, painted a dazzling white, was standing erect on its fin tails.

Agents in France and Belgium began reporting large concrete installations near Watten and other towns on the Pas de Calais. Air photos of these installations were brought in. A report from Switzerland said that the Germans were "announcing that a novel and decisive air attack would soon be made using liquid air bombs and other 'hitherto unexploited' " methods of unprecedented destructive power.

All this was enough for Sandys to propose that the Ministries of Health and War Transport review their evacuation plans and for Churchill to call a meeting of the Cabinet Defence Committee on July 29, 1943.

Sandys presented the photographs of the rockets. Lindemann argued that the whole thing bore the earmarks of an elaborate deception plan. Real rockets would hardly be painted white and left lying about so that aerial reconnaissance could hardly fail to pick them up. He didn't believe that the Germans had built a rocket. It would have taken the British more than five years to do that. Churchill had been impressed by Jones' role in the battle of the beams and had specially invited him to the meeting. Called upon to speak, Jones took apart Lindemann's arguments against the existence of long range rockets. It had already been demonstrated that the enemy had rockets of long range and great destructive power. All that was in question was how long it would take for them to be used. Still, he pointed out that pilotless jet-propelled aircraft might be more advanced. He reviewed the evidence that Peenemünde was an important research station and pointed out that it was not in the German interest to mount a deception that would encourage the Allies to attack it. The decision of the meeting was to order Bomber Command to make the heaviest attack possible on Peenemünde as soon as conditions were suitable, to attack rocket-related installations in France as soon as they were located, and to direct Sandys to work with Jones to examine and report on the pilotless jet-propelled aircraft.

Peenemünde was a long way off, and Bomber Command was not willing to risk an attack there until the nights got longer. On August 17, 65 Pathfinder aircraft and 433 heavy bombers raided Peenemünde. That night, in one of the most successful spoof attacks of the war, 8 British Mosquitos succeeded in drawing more than 200 German fighters away from Peenemünde to defend Berlin. Nevertheless, the attack cost 41 British planes. The attack killed some of Peenemünde's top scientists and damaged dozens of buildings at the German army's rocket research establishment known as Peenemünde-East, but did not touch Peenemünde-West, where the Air Force was developing the robot aircraft, which London would come to know as the V-1 or buzz bomb.

A major result of the Peenemünde raid was that the Germans decided to move the rocket testing grounds to Poland. A new rocket testing ground was established at a former Polish army firing range at Blizna, between Cracow and Lvov.

Only a few days before the Peenemünde raid, an intelligence report had come in from Berlin that dispelled some of the fog that had developed in London from the profusion of reports about the German long distance weapon program. From a source in the German army, it stated categorically that the army had test fired over 100 rockets and that a pilotless aircraft had also been tested at Peenemünde. Priority over artillery and anti-aircraft production had been given to both weapons. Late in August, one of the pilotless airplanes had overshot its mark and crashed on Bornholm. Intrepid Danish intelligence agents had taken photographs of the main parts of this buzz bomb and made a sketch of the whole weapon. Several copies of this find were made and sent by separate routes to London by the end of the month. We began to hear that German prisoners-of-war were stating that they had seen rockets shoot straight up into the air at Peenemünde.

The existence of two weapons was now accepted. The debate turned to when and how they would be used, how much damage they could inflict, and what should be done.

Kenneth Cohen's Alliance network produced a report, replete with convincing detail, that an anti-aircraft regiment had been formed to operate more than 400 catapults sited between Brittany and Holland. It would be headquartered near Amiens. The first hundred catapults able to fire a bomb every 20 minutes would be operated from around Amiens, Abbeville, and Dunkirk in November. It claimed that fifty to a hundred bombs would suffice to destroy London.

The watch that Jones had put on the German Air Signals Experimental Regiment six months earlier now paid off. Detachments of this regiment turned up on the air transmitting ranges and bearings on a moving object which took off from Peenemünde and flew at a speed of about 400 miles an hour. Jones sitting at Broadway in London would be looking at each trial of the flying bomb.

In October, a report produced by a French intelligence

agent, Michel Hollard, came in from Switzerland. Hearing about unusual construction at Auffay between Rouen and Dieppe, he went there posing as a workman. Fifty-yard strips of concrete, clearly the emplacement of some kind of ramp, were being installed. Using a compass, he established that the strip was pointed directly toward London. Learning that the laborers, mostly Germans, were working in three shifts around the clock, he radioed this to London. A return message instructed him to follow up on this information and a new aerial survey of western France was ordered. He had one of his agents, an engineer, get a job at the site and draw a plan of every building under construction. And Hollard had four of his agents join him in a bicycle tour of northern France that turned up, by early November, more than 60 of these mysterious sites. The agents reported that the one building they had been able to examine closely had no metal parts. Wooden rollers and rails led from the building to the ramp pointed at London. This told the British scientists that a magnetic steering device would be used. Sir Stafford Cripps, who had been asked by Churchill to turn his legal talents to sorting out the evidence on the robots and rockets, reported on November 17 that the threat from pilotless aircraft was serious, but that much of the evidence about rocket production was "being manufactured by inquiries we ourselves have launched," and that its destructive effects had been overestimated.

At the beginning of November, Jones had asked for air reconnaissance over Peenemünde and Zemplin to look for something that looked like a launching installation for a winged missile. Weather had prevented the flight until November 28. Then, the photos brought back to England clearly showed 3 long ramps rising and pointing toward the sea. These ramps were identical with those found at every ski site in France. It was established that there were more than 100 such sites in France that were to be used for firing the winged missile being tested over the Baltic. The Joint Intelligence Committee estimated that the Germans could launch 500 bombs a day on London. Morrison's staff at the Home Office topped this with estimates that 100 sites firing 20 robots a day, each carrying a ton of explosives, could deliver the same quantity of fire and blast as that which had inflicted the devastating fire storm on Hamburg earlier in 1943.

Jones restored calm and reality with a report on Christmas Eve of 1943. From Bletchley's reading of the Peenemünde test shots, he was getting not only the speeds and points of impact of the flying bombs but also the intended target. Thus, he could show from the Germans' own trials during December that if the flying bombs had been launched from the ski sites in France, only one in six would have hit London. The dimensions of the bomb could be estimated from photographs. The number of bombs to be stored in the ski-shaped buildings could also be estimated. The warhead was estimated at between half a ton and a ton and a half. Jones' report hit range, speed, rate of fire, and height almost on the nose. All the information needed to assess the buzz bomb and develop countermeasures was on hand six months before the first bomb was fired at London.

6.   Dealing with the Enemy

IN THE early months of 1944, I heard for the first time of Rankin C. This was a contingency plan for the occupation of the continent in the face of a conditional surrender by the Germans. When work on Rankin C was begun it might have seemed a routine precaution any staff planner would take, had it not been for a series of messages Dulles sent from Berne suggesting that the rumbling opposition to Hitler inside Germany might be the real thing, and that the Nazi regime might collapse without the dreaded invasion of France.

The first of what would total some 150 messages that passed between Berne, London, Stockholm, and Washington, clattered over the airwaves at the turn of 1944. It told us about a mushrooming conspiracy inside the Reich which Dulles called "Breakers." The conspirators wanted to get rid of Hitler, form a new government, and bring the war to an end. The originators of what would go into the history books as the July 20 plot were a formidable group headed by General Beck, Chief of the German Army General Staff until 1938, and by

Carl Goerdeler, former Mayor of Leipzig. Both had opposed Nazism since the mid-thirties. The underground they built eventually had military, political, trade union, and intellectual components. It operated with facilities and protection provided by officers of the Abwehr led by Admiral Canaris and his deputy, General Oster.

Dulles's principal source was a young Abwehr officer named Hans Gisevius, posted in Zurich as a Vice-Consul. Gisevius established his credibility by telling Dulles that the Germans had broken one of his own codes and intercepted a message about the anti-German group in the Italian government. It included Count Ciano, who was Mussolini's son-in-law and his foreign minister, and Marshal Badoglio. When Hitler saw the intercept, he sent it to Mussolini with his compliments. Days later, Ciano was no longer foreign minister and had taken refuge in the Vatican.

Dulles had reason to take the conspiracy seriously, even though neither he nor anyone else I knew ever contemplated cutting a deal with the Germans whereby they would surrender in the West and hold off the Russians in the East. But the existence of so widespread and powerful an opposition within the Reich offered the Allies an opportunity to save millions of lives. Those ready to act against Hitler, Dulles reported, included key men in the Wehrmacht and the Abwehr. They had opposed Hitler for at least five years. General Oster, number two in the Abwehr, had first risked his life in 1939 when he tipped the Dutch that Hitler planned to attack Holland and Belgium on his way to France. He had also warned the Norwegians on the eve of the Nazi attack on Norway.

By 1944, the conspiracy was still deliberately small in numbers, to lower the risk of discovery, but the conspirators were spread throughout Nazi society and many were in key positions. Already they had almost been successful in killing Hitler. In March 1943, Fabian von Schlabrendorff, one of the conspirators who survived to write about his experiences, placed a British-made plastic explosive bomb (the Abwehr had seized the device from a resistance group) on a plane taking Hitler to his headquarters in Rastenburg on the Eastern Front. The bomb was timed to go off shortly before the plane was to pass over Minsk. It malfunctioned and did not explode. Hitler landed safely. When von Schlabrendorff learned of his failure, he calmly took a courier plane, flew to Rastenburg, strolled into the Führer's craft and took out the parcel with the bomb in it. A careless British worker had saved Hitler's life.

Unconditional surrender entered the vocabulary of World War II in January 1943 after the Casablanca conference between President Roosevelt and Prime Minister Churchill. It was a term casually tossed off, yet it changed forever the character of the war and the world that emerged afterwards. Certainly, it robbed the Allies of repeated opportunities to exploit internal dissent. Before Casablanca, dealing with the enemy had paid big dividends. Bob Murphy, for example, practiced his wiles on French authorities in North Africa, and his brilliant diplomatic poker saved Allied lives. He convinced Admiral Darlan to order French generals not to resist Allied landings in exchange for a pledge to re-equip French forces. Washington applauded the move.

But only nine months later, the unconditional surrender formula immensely complicated negotiations with the collapsing Italians. They started off briskly and hopefully enough. The OSS dispatched a mission under Lieutenant John Shaheen to talk to Italian flag officers in the hope of putting the Italian fleet under Allied control. Shaheen carried an ace— a letter from a new York Italian-American, Marcello Girosi, to his brother, Admiral Massimo Girosi, a member of the Italian chiefs of staff. Shaheen's group steered a rubber dinghy to Calabria province on the tip of the Italian boot and got the letter, approved by Donovan himself, to the Admiral. It got to the Italian high command just after King Victor Emmanuel had fired Mussolini as his prime minister. Marshal Badoglio, Mussolini's successor, was looking for ways to open surrender talks with Eisenhower. The letter looked like the perfect key.

Badoglio wanted an agreement that would allow Italian forces to fight with the Allies in driving the Germans from Italy. On July 27, he dissolved the Fascist party and rescinded a law giving supreme power to the Fascist Grand Council.

Clearly he figured that ending fascism in Italy was a precondition to peace. But Badoglio had not counted on unconditional surrender and FDR's stubborn determination to cling to the full meaning of the term. Roosevelt chose that moment to announce that ''our terms to Italy are still the same as our terms to Germany and Japan—Unconditional Surrender.''

The following day, Ike, worried about the risks of the coming invasion of Italy, made a conciliatory speech. He praised Italy for dumping Mussolini and promised peace with honor. Badoglio agreed to a secret mid-August meeting in Lisbon between his envoy, General Castellano, and General Bedell Smith. The talks moved like molasses. Both men constantly had to check back with Rome and Algiers. Finally, two agreements were ready. Smith and General Kenneth Strong, Ike's G-2, had drafted a ''Short Form Agreement'' that the Italians seemed ready to accept. Back in London, however, the British Foreign Office had laid out a Long Form Agreement. As Italian emissaries read the 42 clauses they grew more and more alarmed. The humiliation the text heaped on Italy was complete. Naturally they stalled.

Eisenhower, meanwhile, read intelligence reports of a steady stream of German divisions pouring into Italy. Arguments over surrender terms should not delay the invasion, he insisted. Finally, Churchill intervened and, as General Strong reported later, ''swept aside all quibbles and objections by declaring that the important thing was to ensure the success of the invasion and thus save precious lives. Eisenhower was given authority to use the Short Terms. After the Italians had signed these he was to give them the Long Terms for transmission to their government.''

On September 3, the Italians signed a short but tough armistice agreement that nowhere mentioned ''unconditional surrender.'' Two weeks later, an appalled Badoglio received a document entitled ''The Unconditional Surrender of Italy.'' On September 29, Badoglio met Eisenhower and asked him to scrap the phrase to which no Italian negotiator had agreed. Ike refused. He had to obey his civilian superiors. Still, he offered this concession: a personal follow-up letter explaining that Italy was now cooperating with the United Nations. Haggling over details lasted six weeks, weeks in which Italy was ready to help the Allies land and block the Germans from moving in heavy reinforcements. Instead, Hitler rushed in fresh troops that Field Marshal Kesselring stationed on the hills above Salerno where they nearly blasted the Allies back into the sea. Thousands died in the long and bloody march up the peninsula—a march that might have started in Rome or Florence, instead of so far south.

As the rendezvous with Overlord neared and we learned more of the nature of the July 20 conspiracy—and of Russian activities aimed at undermining the German regime—the view grew that something had to be done about the albatross of unconditional surrender, a redefinition if nothing else. The Soviets had no problem with the term and had set up a Free Germany Committee and a League of German Officers as a nucleus of a postwar regime, or, better, one that could take over once the Nazis collapsed or were ready to be pushed out. Headed by General von Seydlitz, the committee was geared to Soviet war aims, which meant a communist German beholden to the Soviet Union. Moscow wanted the July 20 plot to fail, and, as Dulles reported, warned its own underground cadres inside Germany to do nothing in support of the plotters.

In early April, Dulles was informed that the German resistance was ready to move against Hitler. On April 7, Dulles reported that:

> *"The opposition group led by Tucky (General Beck) and Lester (Carl Goerdeler) say that at this critical point they are now willing and prepared to try to start action to oust the Nazis and eliminate the Fuehrer. Theirs is the only group able to profit by a personal approach to Hitler and other Nazi chiefs, and with enough arms at hand to accomplish their ends. Their group is also the only one in Germany having enough power in the army and with certain active army chiefs to make the coup feasible."*

Dulles added that General von Rundstedt and General von Falkenhausen, German commanders in the West, were ready to help the Allies land once the Nazis had been ousted. Such readiness, however, was conditioned on "assurances that, once the Nazis have been overthrown, the group may negotiate directly with the Western powers about practical action necessary. The group is especially concerned that they should not have to negotiate with Moscow, but that the dealings be carried on through London and Washington. The group cites as precedent the procedure followed, though in reverse, in the instance of the recent negotiations for peace with Finland." This condition was clearly unacceptable and Dulles consistently told his German contacts that we would never deal with the Germans without Soviet participation. Nevertheless, Dulles urged that some encouragement be given the conspirators. As he explained later: "I was convinced that whatever the result of 'Breakers' might be, the fact that an attempt was made to overthrow Hitler, whether or not successfully, would help to shorten the war."

Eisenhower, Churchill, and Marshall all shared Dulles's point of view for reasons of their own. Ike would just as soon not have taken the risk of Overlord if other means for winning the war were available. Churchill was still haunted by the World War I slaughter in France he had witnessed. Marshall shared both men's concern, but as he told Sir John Dill, the Washington representative of the British Chiefs, "they were up against an obstinate Dutchman who had brought the phrase out and didn't like to go back on it."

Early in April 1944, Roosevelt again displayed his obstinacy by rejecting the Joint Chiefs new draft on unconditional surrender. It would take two generations to change German attitudes, he said, and he was not "willing at this time to say that we do not intend to destroy the German nation." FDR had bought the State Department line that Hitler had to be beaten without help from any internal German opposition. Otherwise, the "stab in the back" legend that had haunted post-war Germany would never be laid to rest. The die had been cast against supporting the German resistance.

Still, Ike did not give up. At the end of April he and Bedell Smith gave Under-Secretary of State Edward Stettinius, a memo once again redefining unconditional surrender. In it,

Ike suggested that Allied heads of state announce a "clarified" policy the German generals could accept and that would
allow them to quit fighting. Specifically, he wanted to spell
out methods of demilitarization, purging Nazis from the German government, seizure and trial of war criminals, orderly
transfer of population, and restoration of religious and trade
union freedoms. Announcement of the redefinition was to
come four weeks before the invasion to allow the message to
get through to the German people and to the German army.
Once a bridgehead had been established, Eisenhower would
call on the Germans to surrender.

Nothing came of the idea, however. Stettinius sent the proposal to Secretary of State Cordell Hull in Washington, along
with Bedell Smith's conclusion that without such a declaration the Allies could not exploit the crisis in the German army
sure to arise in the wake of a successful landing. But Hull
and FDR turned thumbs down on the idea. Nor did Ike have
any more luck with Churchill, though a host of British advi-
sors urged the Prime Minister to press for clarification of
unconditional surrender. In a minute dictated on April 19,
1944, Churchill said: "The matter is on the President. He
announced it at Casablanca without any consultation. I am
not going to address the President on the subject. For good
or ill, the Americans took the lead and it is for them to make
the first move."

Early in May, the conspirators inside the Reich came up
with a new scheme, a specific military proposal, which Dulles radioed to London. Dulles said: "The opposition group
which includes Beck, Rundstedt and Falkenhausen . . . were
ready to help our armed units get into Germany under the
condition, that we agreed to allow them to hold the Eastern
front." The military proposals were imaginative and daring.
German commanders promised help to Allied parachute divisions dropped over Berlin, and to amphibious troops going
ashore near Bremen or Hamburg. Hitler would be trapped in
his bunker home on the Obersalzberg in Bavaria. Finally,
although Rommel had not been lined up yet, the hope was
that he would give aid to Allied troops landing in France.

Late in May, Ike was still looking for a way of rephrasing

unconditional surrender to make it more palatable to the German generals and their concept of honor and obligation. He even got playwright Bob Sherwood to draft a speech—with the assistance of SHAEF's political adviser, William Phillips, and General McClure, head of SHAEF's Psychological Warfare Branch—that took another crack at redefining unconditional surrender. Eisenhower planned to deliver it after the landing. Washington, however, remained silent. Finally, Churchill wrote Ike that "this is a matter that really must be dealt with by governments, and cannot be the subject of friends' talks. I never read anything less suitable for the troops."

Still, the conspiracy moved forward. Over in France, as we were to learn later, von Rundstedt and Rommel were being approached to join the plot even as they were preparing to destroy Eisenhower's expected invasion of France. They did not join, but listened with interest and did not turn the plotters over to the Gestapo. The German military governors of both France and Belgium were fully committed to the conspiracy. And Rommel's chief of staff, General Hans Speidel, was in it up to his ears and was wooing Rommel as hard as he dared.

7. Battleground Behind the Lines

BRITISH AND American commanders planning the invasion of
Europe from London never fully trusted either the Free
French or the various resistance movements mushrooming
across France itself. For one thing, the French always seemed
to put their own fractured, intractable, and enormously complicated domestic politics ahead of winning the war. For another, the resistance movement was widely regarded as
unreliable and was difficult to control from London. The
prevalent view was that any assistance given the invasion of
France by the resistance was a bonus, not an essential or
integral part of military strategy.

For the generals at SHAEF the French resistance movement might be as good and as important as the OSS and
Special Operations Executive said it was. On the other hand,
the resistance might be a chimera and not materialize in the
crunch. Sure, there were thousands of Frenchmen eager to
fight the occupier, as many as 150,000 by some estimates.
But they had to be organized, armed, and directed. Could

the still nascent and loosely knit resistance movement quickly become a cohesive striking force sufficiently under our command and control to make a military contribution to the invasion? That belief required an act of faith. The OSS officers in Grosvenor Street, who had worked closely with Colonels Passy and Rémy and the others who made up the French intelligence service of BCRA, were willing to make that commitment. But selling the idea to our generals and their planners wasn't easy. The wall of distrust had yet to be breached. In the meantime, the distrust showed up dramatically in the paucity of arms and equipment the allies dropped to the maquis and other French resistance groups. Arms deliveries to those areas of France where the invasions were planned was a lower priority than the air lift to Yugoslav and Italian partisans.

The history of the French resistance movement was one of the more ambiguous, contradictory, and confusing episodes of the war. A short review, therefore, of how it got to the stage it did in the months before D-Day is essential to understanding the nature of the discussions that permeated London about the pros and cons of the resistance.

There was, first of all, the fact that so few Frenchmen heeded de Gaulle's call of June 18, 1940, to rally to the Cross of Lorraine and the cause of Free France. For all the humiliation of defeat and German victory, the Nazis proved shrewd conquerors. They allowed the Vichy government to function over a large area of unoccupied France. Vichy had the trappings of power, including a 94,000 man army—the Armistice Army. And despite imposition of a military government, French civilian authorities remained at their posts and functioned largely as before. Marshal Pétain, the hero of France, had the stature to keep the officer corps and a large proportion of the French people loyal to the new regime. A carefully staged propaganda campaign blamed the British for the French defeat, and was widely believed.   •

Yet men and women all over France—individually, separately—walked against the tide and made the decision to resist. The results were many strands of resistance that would prove difficult to fuse later on. There were, first of all, the indigenous resistance movements like Liberté and Verité, later merged under Henri Frenay, and Libération led by Léon Jouhaux. There was the resistance de Gaulle and his followers organized first in London, then in sub-Saharan Africa and in Algiers. Special Operations Executive's F Section organized a second wave by sending agents into France from London. A small but important resistance effort was fostered by intelligence officers of the embittered French general staff.

Finally, the German invasion of Russia on June 22, 1941, brought yet another resistance group in to the open—the communists. There was some irony in this. Only a month before, the communist newspaper, Humanité, called for the formation of a "Front Nationale" of all political parties and the assertion of a neutral position between Germany and England. After the German invasion of the Soviet Union, however, the communists quickly turned the "Front Nationale," into a strong and effective resistance movement. The front's military arm, the Franc-Tireurs et Partisans or FTP, was soon established as a painful thorn in the German side, especially in the north.

Thus, before the end of 1941, all five resistance groups—indigenous, Gaullist, communist, and those inspired by the French Armistice Army and by Special Operations Executive—were operational. Over the next two and a half years they waxed and waned, fought each other and the Germans, were brave and foolish, cowardly and astute. But over and over again the resistance's bottom line was written in black ink.

It did not seem to matter how hard the Gestapo cracked down or how successfully the Abwehr infiltrated the resistance. Every time the Germans cut down one network, others bloomed and took their place—and the longer the war lasted the more robust the resistance became.

One reason for the underground's continued growth was the German labor draft. Increasingly young Frenchmen were rounded up and shipped as slave laborers to German factories. Thousands of young men refused to go and fled into the mountains instead. By the end of 1943, some 50,000 were in the mountains and woods. They had been organized into small camps of 30 to 60 men each, sheltered in broken-down farm buildings or hastily built huts put up with freshly felled logs or whatever else was available. Soon a whole network of camps existed, with guards to watch for surprise attacks. If German troops or Vichy Milice forces were spotted, a camp commander would send a runner to warn the neighboring camps. Gradually, these men were being drilled, armed, and molded into small fighting forces.

The young men in the mountains, the "maquis," were a relatively late development in the French resistance movement. But with the invasion only six months off, their numbers became too large to ignore, and they became one more argument in the London debate on the relative merits and drawbacks of the resistance. These bands needed funds, food, and clothing. The older French underground groups helped them as much as their meager resources allowed. They also began to look upon them as the core of their "secret army" and to press London for help.

Among those arguing against the kind of massive support the French wanted were Sir Claude Dansey, the Air Marshals, and "F" Section of Special Operations Executive. Dansey worried about threats to the security of his MI-6 intelligence networks. The Air Marshals didn't want any of their precious planes to be used to drop supplies to the resistance rather than to drop bombs on German cities, and therefore tended to minimize both the size and potential value of the resistance forces. At SOE, Colonel Buckmaster was painstakingly organizing small, secret, self-contained cells directed by radio from London. These cells would move into action for specific assignments as their territory became significant for invading armies. Wholesale supply drops to large resistance forces did not fit into so meticulous a concept.

The French wanted to act on a massive scale. Resistance leaders clamored for arms and explosive drops. They proposed an elaborate program of sabotage and direct attacks on German headquarters and forces in France. Again they pointed out that sabotage could be more effective than aerial bombardment and could cause greater destruction at a lower cost of life. It was an argument that carried the day very often. Anglo-American suspicion surfaced all the time. If weapons were dropped, one argument went, how did we know the French would use them to fight the Germans and not each other? How did we know they wouldn't squirrel the arms for use in a postwar struggle for power? Distrust remained so high that the French were never fully apprised of the invasion plans and had to work with us ignorant about exact details and timing. With the situation growing more serious day by day, Michel Brault, a leader of the French resistance, flew to London in January 1944. An accomplished Parisian lawyer with the quick wit and flair that marked practitioners of French jurisprudence, Brault was taken to see Churchill and plead for his cause. The Prime Minister was impressed, as he always was by courage and daring. Representatives from the RAF, SOE, and de Gaulle's headquarters joined the meeting. The discussion was terse though often heated. SOE and the RAF reiterated their well-worn arguments against committing massive supplies to the resistance: Such commitments would hurt the air war against Germany and disturb the delicate clandestine operations of Special Operations Executive. This time Churchill would not listen to them. Supporting the resistance, he said, would have priority. All planes that could be spared from the air war would fly supply missions, even at the expense of bombing secret weapons sites. Unfortunately for the French resistance, even Churchill's promise did not then pry loose the needed planes.

Weeks later, SOE broke ranks. On February 1, 1944, Yeo-Thomas of the RF Section of SOE in charge of liaison with BCRA, returned to London from a survey trip of France. He too was given an appointment with Churchill, and apparently made a more effective and dramatic case than Brault had been able to. His account of the maquis, their organization, their will to fight, and their need for arms and clothing, moved Churchill. He promptly dictated a memo ordering the Air Ministry to make available to the RF section 100 serviceable aircraft able to fly 250 sorties during a "moon period." Within 48 hours, Yeo-Thomas had at his disposal 22 Halifaxes, 12 American Liberator bombers, 36 British Stirlings, 6 Albemarles, and some smaller aircraft.

But Churchill's second decision to step up aid to the French resistance did not resolve the dispute in France's favor. Though British squadrons did increase supply drops into France in February, few American planes took part because of the refusal of the U.S. Army Air Force to cooperate with the plan. The Combined Chief of Staff of Special Forces Headquarters—the combined SOE-OSS operation—were told that they would not get American planes on a regular basis. They would have to make do with the charity of local U.S. airbase commanders. USAAF's position, of course, frustrated OSS efforts. We felt foolish urging the French resistance to tool up for paramilitary activities in support of the invasion without being able to provide planes to drop guns and ammunition. French officers in London, not unreasonably, felt that Washington's hostility to de Gaulle explained why the United States refused to arm the underground. Donovan and Bruce strove as hard as they could to dispel that notion. Sometimes they had the support of Secretary of State Cordell Hull in urging that more American supply drops were necessary to keep up French morale, maintain their fighting capability, and dispel their suspicions of our political intentions. Gradually, Donovan's persistence began to pay off. In mid-March, OSS got 11 U.S. planes for one daylight drop in the upper Isère Valley southeast of Annecy. In late March, we succeeded in having two squadrons assigned us, and in April we could count on a small fleet of 32 planes to fly regular supply missions. Most of the actual war material dropped into France during 1944 did come from the U.S. But by then America supplied the bulk of Allied hardware everywhere.

The debate on how best to use French resistance forces grew much hotter and more intense in the months before the invasion, fueled by the growth and impatience of the French resistance forces themselves. The French generals in London kept pushing Plan Vidal. It called for the resistance to seize large areas in the heart of France. Once seized, these outposts would give the Allies ''ports of entry'' for airborne troops and supplies. French and Allied soldiers could then strike at the enemy's rear. SHAEF thought the plan too bold and too

risky and would have none of it. Yet despite the formal
SHAEF rejection of Plan Vidal in February, the notion lin-
gered on. The French never really gave up on it. As supplies
to the resistance began to increase and French forces grew in
size and strength, local commanders began to implement the
Plan Vidal in more or less open defiance of London directives. In March, we could identify 18 "controlled areas"
where airborne forces could land with some safety. In April,
the count reached 29. Intensified Nazi efforts to round up
more slave labor prompted more Frenchmen to take to the
mountains, especially in the Massif Central, the Ain, and the
Haute-Savoie.

We learned quickly, however, that "controlled areas" was
a relative term. For the most part, they were controlled as
long as the Germans did not challenge that control in force.
In March, for example, the Wehrmacht wiped out a band of
500 maquis bivouacked on the isolated Glières plateau near
Lake Annecy. The group had been supplied on March 10
when we sent out a fleet of 30 planes that dropped 580 containers filled with everything from sten guns to aspirin. A
week later, German planes twice carpeted the plateau with
bombs and German artillery was brought up through the difficult terrain. The big guns quickly found the range and plastered the plateau with shells. Infantry moved up behind the
cannon and in a week's combat German and Vichy forces
numbering 10,000 men wiped out most of the maquis; 83
captured survivors were executed. Although the attackers suffered nearly 1,000 casualties, it was a more expensive loss for
the French than for the Germans. The maquis had ignored a
cardinal rule of guerrilla warfare: "Don't fight pitched bat-
tles, retreat and disperse to fight another day." Needless to
say, this engagement did not raise the resistance's stock with
the skeptics in London.

Communications and command arrangements with the resistance moved to the front and center of our concern. Our
ability to use these forces depended on both. Resistance leaders operating behind the lines and officers commanding invading troops would have to be able to communicate quickly
and effectively if their operations were to mesh. Radio contact

alone could not accomplish this. We needed men in Allied uniforms to advise the resistance on Allied needs, and specialists attached to the invading armies who understood the resistance to advise Allied commanders on what French forces could deliver.

The concept of putting men in uniform behind the battle lines was a novel one, and one of the most effective of the war. They were to go in teams of three—an American, British, and French officer or non-com—and were known as "Jedburghs." One would be appointed the leader, another his deputy, and the third served as radio operator. Sending them in uniform had a double purpose. First, it would show the flag and boost the hopes and morale of the resistance forces they would advise. And second, the uniform offered some protection against reprisals if captured. Indeed, the Führer had issued orders to shoot anyone caught behind the lines, in uniform or not. But the Wehrmacht adopted an attitude of enlightened self-interest. As long as they adhered to the rudiments of the Geneva convention, chances were the Allies would too. Thus the uniform did offer some protection to volunteers inexperienced in clandestine work and speaking at best a barely passable French that would give them away as quickly as their uniforms. All in all we trained 300 volunteers and organized them into 93 teams. They were all dispatched into France after D-Day. Other uniformed commanders were the OSS Operational Groups (OGs) and the British Special Air Services (SAS) detachments. Armed with automatic rifles, machine guns, bazookas, and explosive charges, they went in to strengthen maquis units fighting the Germans and to block or divert enemy forces. Our OGs were made up of 15 French-speaking men. We had 14 of them ready by D-Day. The British had 2,000 soldiers in their SAS and they operated in larger units than OSS Operational Groups, though their aim and purpose were similar.

Right up to the end of May, the Americans, British, and French accepted as dogma that resistance forces should lie low until specifically ordered into action. But like so much dogma in the hectic weeks that were the countdown to D-Day it would be subject to sudden, unexpected change.

8. Air Targeting, Sabotage, and Interdiction

EISENHOWER AND his invasion planners had two preconditions to making the invasion succeed. We had to have air superiority over the Channel, the landing area, and its approaches, and the movement of German reinforcements to the beachhead had to be disrupted and delayed. Among the many debates that crackled through various military and intelligence commands in London, none was fiercer than on the relative merits of bombing from the air and of sabotage on the ground and how these two methods of operation could be meshed most effectively. The British had used both since the day after Dunkirk, but with indifferent success. Sabotage operations mounted by Special Operations Executive agents had led to savage German reprisals and pleas from government-in-exile and local resistance groups to stop. Bombing missions flown against targets in occupied Europe had led to heavy loss of civilian life and resulted in similiar pleas. Few agents could yet act in Germany itself, while bombing attacks had only marginal impact on industrial production and failed to shatter German morale. The British had abandoned daylight air raids as too costly. Instead, they flew against the Reich at night and followed a strategy of "area" bombardment rather than precision bombing. Their planes lacked the needed accuracy. Indeed, the RAF was lucky if it found a town the size of Schweinfurt, where most of Germany's ball-bearing industry was concentrated, let alone hit targets in it. After the war the United States Strategic Bombing Survey explained the purpose of "area" bombing this way:

> *"It was believed that city attacks offered a means of destroying German civilian morale. It was believed that if the morale of industrial workers could be affected, or if laborers could be diverted from the factories to other purposes, such as caring for their families, repairing damage to their homes, German war production would suffer. . . ."*

It was at best a dubious premise, and one, moreover, based on technological deficiency. Its moral underpinnings, given the savage destructions wreaked by firestorms from Cologne to Dresden, are still the subject of violent controversy. Among the early doubters of "area" bombing's military potential were the Americans, especially the American economists from the OSS who arrived in London in the spring of 1942. They were full of new ideas on applying economic analysis to industrial target selection and found the British woefully behind U.S. thinking in this area. Donovan had plunged into economic analysis as a major area of OSS concern from the beginning of the organization. He had picked a distinguished Harvard economist, Edward Mason (known in the immediate postwar years as "Mr. Marshall Plan" for his contributions in formulating the foreign aid program), to head up the economic unit of the OSS Research & Analysis Branch in Washington. Mason recruited a group of talented economists including Walt Rostow and Carl Kaysen (who soon showed up in London) and set them to work on economic analysis as a base for industrial target selection, choosing those industries for attack that were most vulnerable to bombardment, that could not easily be dispersed, and that were the most vital to the German war effort. The degree of sophistication these studies achieved in the early years of the war was far superior to what anyone else was even contemplating.

British economic analysis, while broad and detailed, was wedded to the big picture rather than the structural economic models that showed relationships among the various functioning parts of an economy and how these could best be disrupted. The British focused on evaluating the overall German supply and production positions, not on how the pieces fitted together. The Ministry of Information, for example, had compiled a "Bombers' Baedeker" that listed every industrial target in Germany and occupied Europe without making any distinction among them. The Air Ministry had assembled a collage of the Luftwaffe and its operations that was totally bereft of judgments. In fairness to the British, they had little need then for information on relative value and vulnerability of specific targets. Their bombing was too inaccurate. Targets were selected on an ad hoc basis from a list of important but largely unrelated industries.

The U.S. air force began to arrive in England in the fall of 1942 and as American air strength grew so did debates over strategy. Once the 8th Air Force's Flying Fortresses squatted on British fields, Air Marshal Harris wanted them to join his night raids on Germany and pulverize the Nazis into submission. The Americans demurred. The Flying Fortresses were larger, heavier, faster, and better armed than the British craft. They also carried more accurate bomb sights. Precision bombings, the Americans figured, would help end the war more quickly by crippling German industry directly, not through its workers. After all, U.S. planes were able to drop ten percent of their bombs dead on a rectangle with a border of 100 yards around targets, and the rest fell within a radius of one mile. The best the RAF could do was come to a mile of the target and that only ten percent of the time. Still, Harris argued daylight raids would extract a fearful cost. Even the heavily armed Flying Fortresses could not keep the fast Me-109s and Me-110s at bay. British pressure on the Americans to join night raids continued on and off through most of 1943. The U.S., however, insisted on daylight raids, with, admittedly, indifferent success at first.

The problem was that greater accuracy in locating and hitting targets would not by itself justify the added risks of daylight attack. Greater sophistication in selecting targets whose destruction would significantly reduce enemy strength was needed. Neither British nor American brass had yet tackled that task. The result was one of those conceptual loopholes Donovan filled so well. OSS specialists realized quickly that available information would have to be analyzed much more extensively and presented in new forms. Forging the link between intelligence and operations became the task of the OSS Enemy Objectives Unit or EOU which was staffed by the OSS and the Board of Economic Warfare. It laid down guidelines for interrogations, air reconnaissance, and secret agents producing the raw intelligence. The EOU would then analyze and organize the information in a way to help operations pick targets that offered the greatest payoff.

The man who recognized the Economic Objectives Unit's potential for strategic planning was Colonel Richard Hughes, an English-born American who served as planning officer for the Eighth Air Force. Hughes arrived in England early in 1943, just after the big three Casablanca conference in January. That meeting had laid down a new directive for the air war named Pointblank. It set five primary targets in this order of priority: submarine construction yards, aircraft industry, transportation, oil, other war industry targets. The lack of discernment in this directive was equalled only by the lack of precision in the means available to carry it out. Hughes and others realized quickly that Pointblank was badly in need of intellectual embroidery. Fortunately, in February 1943, Donovan had brought Charley Kindelberger over from the Bank of International Settlement at Basle, where Kindelberger had served as a monetary economist, to head up the Economic Objectives Unit. Over the next four months Kindelberger and his staff worked up a series of papers that amounted to a general theory of strategic bombardment.

The EOU's first approach to greater refinement in target selection was to look for industries upon which the German economy depended. Electric power, oil, ball bearings, and steel were obvious selections. But their relationship to overall war production was less clear. The EOU, accordingly, studied major German plants to identify their vulnerability and their relationship to other industries and German fighting strength. These studies turned into "Aiming Point Reports" on a broad range of plants—aircraft, submarines, tank and truck assembly, synthetic oil, rubber, components of all kinds with emphasis on ball bearings, tires, and engines. British and American experts helped prepare the reports whose theoretical conclusions were buttressed by visits to similar plants in the U.S. and Britain. Each study specified the importance of a specific German plant within its industry, the function of individual buildings, the vulnerability of each part of the plant, and the areas that should be attacked, and also estimated the probable rate of recovery after a successful strike.

The Aiming Points were followed up by a series of "Target Potentiality Reports" that analyzed major German industries to compare their value as target systems. What impact would cutting production have? When would results of the cutback show up at the battle front? How long would the decrease last? The Target Potentiality Report on the German ball bearing industry was a good example of the process in action. It examined the effect a bombing attack would have that reduced ball bearing output at Schweinfurt by 60 percent. It also looked at how the Germans could insulate military production from such a loss: by cutting non-military use of ball bearings, stepping up foreign imports, drawing down stocks, converting equipment, and speeding repairs. The major disruption following such a raid, the report reasoned, would be felt during the second and third months. German production would begin to recover after that. A second raid, therefore, would be launched three or four months after the initial attack. Such a follow-up strike should yield a richer harvest of destruction because the Germans would not have had enough time to recover fully from the first raid. This was the report that provided the rationale for the first massive American raid on Schweinfurt on August 17, 1943, and for the follow-up attack on October 14, 1943. For all the heavy losses the U.S.

suffered in these raids, they were part of a rational bombing strategy.

Both Aiming Point and Target Potentiality reports were typical of the new style of military thinking. They focused attention on the complexities of determining relative vulnerability and importance of targets. A list of criteria was developed to put that relationship in sharper focus: What was the importance of a particular industry's output to overall war production? What was the degree of specialization in the manufacture of products critical to war production? What indirect effect would knocking out production have on other industries? How large is the plant to be attacked? What about the supply picture? Could other factories take up the slack? How easily and quickly could repairs be performed? What are the possibilities for substituting production from other sources? How vulnerable is the plant, how big, how easily can it be located? How strong are the defenses over the target and on route?

Next, Economic Objectives Unit experts drew a distinction between quick and slow moving items. Fighters, for example, were rushed into action as they tumbled off the assembly line. A month's production of fighter planes accounted for 25 percent of German frontline strength. Monthly submarine output, on the other hand, made up only 6 to 8 percent of the German submarine fleet. The conclusion to be drawn became clear: Attack the points of fighter production rather than the existing fighter force because lack of replacements will cripple the Luftwaffe faster than knocking down planes that are quickly replaced. On the other hand, attack submarines at sea rather than submarine yards. Replacement is slow; decimation of ships at sea will do the most damage.

Bombing priority given submarine yards was therefore, reduced drastically. Attacks on the aircraft industry were narrowed to single engine fighters because they alone could threaten U.S. daylight air supremacy and provide close support for German ground forces. Assaulting Germany's oil production was postponed because our bombers could not yet reach a large enough share of German synthetic oil production to make the raids worthwhile. Instead, ball bearings were moved into centerpiece position—an alternative method of diminishing German war production as a whole.

Later in 1943, Kindelberger and his colleagues went in for even more sophisticated economic analyses of German production strengths and weaknesses and how aerial bombardment could exploit them. They put together studies on the relationship between three key elements: current rates of fighter output, rates of combat fighter losses, and the impact of Allied attacks on plane assembly plants, and on factories making components such as engines, fuselages, etc. They concluded that intensive precision bombing of aircraft assembly plants would force the Luftwaffe to concentrate its fighter strength around such plants. This would allow the U.S air force to squeeze new production and destroy substantial numbers of fighters already in the air. The theory was put into practice in February 1944 when the U.S. Eighth and Fifteenth Air Forces pounded German aircraft factories for six days running, then launched carefully selected follow-up strikes. As a result, German production of single-engine fighters dropped from 1,200 a month to 400 in March. Moreover, German fighter losses in defending against these raids were heavy, so heavy that the Luftwaffe fighter force, at peak strength, was defeated over its own bases. The Allies would own the air for the rest of the war.

At the same time as the EOU was carrying out its theoretical studies, it also had to defend the U.S. air force against continued British pressure to quit daylight raids and join night assaults on Germany. The British argument had some weight. In 1943, the U.S. had not yet developed long range fighters, like the P-51, to protect Flying Fortresses on forays deep into the Reich. U.S. losses were heavy. The raid on Schweinfurt, in October, for example, had a much higher loss ratio than normal and led to growing nervousness within the U.S. command. British demands for joint action became insistent that fall, after the RAF had carried out a series of devastating raids against Berlin. The British argued that massive USAAF-RAF area bombing could bring the war to a quick end. An American, Major Walt Rostow, then stationed with the British Air Ministry, wrote a memo that caused a great stir in this debate by taking the theory apart with sublime assurance. It said:

> *I gather that you conclude that it is within the capabilities of our air forces, in the full settling of the German military position during the next six weeks, to cause by an intensification of area raids a total collapse of the German political structure and the acceptance of defeat.*

> *On the basis of the evidence available, and of our knowledge of the structure of the German government, and its capabilities with respect to the maintenance of order at home and in Occupied Territories, I regard that conclusion as unjustified.*

> *[I]f the German leaders choose to continue the war, there is no reason to believe that they will be incapable of mustering sufficient agencies of relief and repression to avoid a general loss of control over the population.*

> *I believe that collapse will come this time also from the top, and as a result of the military and military supply situation, literally defined. I see no evidence or reason to believe that area bombing, whatever its great virtues as a generalized drain on the structure of Germany and its military potential, is capable of precipitating a decisive crisis.*

Such strong expressions of American opinion added to the Economic Objectives Unit stature in the London intelligence community and boosted OSS prestige in the strategic debates. Unlike many other OSS branches, the EOU had won full access to both military and economic intelligence. It began to be looked to for operational conclusions and recommendations. Gradually, it influenced policy directly and did so at important centers of decision. Kindelberger and his top aide Harold Barnett enjoyed direct access to the staffs of Generals Eaker and Doolittle at the Eighth Air Force and of General Spaatz at the U.S. Strategic Air Forces. Walt Rostow began to have a greater say at the Air Ministry's target section, and he sat on the "Jockey Committee" where week-to-week target selections were made. Bill Salant and Phil Coombs logged some London time before moving to the target section of the Mediterranean Allied Air Force that pounded Germany from the south. Under Mason and Kindelberger's skillful direction, a network of talent and experience began to spread its influence throughout the Allied air forces.

This network became deeply involved in a sometimes acrimonious debate in late 1943 and early 1944 when invasion plans were firming up and the role of air power in supporting the landings was in debate. Clearly, the air forces could best disrupt German supply lines to the beaches. And they had to be disrupted, otherwise the success of the invasion was very much in doubt. The Wehrmacht had excellent networks of roads and rails in France. It could move troops and equipment to Normandy much more quickly than the Allies could by sea. G-2 estimates, updated constantly during the winter and spring of 1944, showed that the Germans could bring up 7 or 8 divisions just a day after the landing, 18 divisions after a week, and as many as 25 to 30 divisions after two weeks to face only 20 Allied divisions. Indeed, the prospect was so grim that the landings were postponed a month to beef up Allied attacking forces and improve reinforcement techniques.

Although few doubted the importance of air power in meeting this "transportation" threat, the air marshals were less than happy about prospects for taking part. Some pointed to the resistance and argued that underground forces could cut rail lines, blow up tunnels and canal locks, block highways, destroy railroad turntables, etc. And surely the maquis could draw off some German divisions to fight in the interior. But those who advanced such theories rarely presented them as an alternative to air strikes. Clearly, they were a supplement to, not a substitute for, precision bombing. But Harris, especially, was appalled at the prospect of bombing railroad yards. He and U.S. air chief General Spaatz were committed to pounding German cities day and night and wanted nothing to interfere with that goal.

This dispute found OSS economists and their British colleagues on the same side. And however reluctantly, the air marshals gave way, agreeing to make the strikes invasion planners thought necessary. But when it came to specific targets, the British and the OSS split company. The British kingpin was a man named Solly Zuckerman, a doctor who taught medical students anatomy at Oxford and Birmingham. He had been pulled out of academe first to investigate why people were wounded by exploding weapons, and then was told to carry out a nationwide survey of bombing casualties. He next made one of those giant conceptual leaps that seem to take place only in wartime. He became an adviser on bombing policy. Zuckerman had earned his spurs in that field as scientific adviser to Air Chief Marshal Sir Arthur Tedder during the Sicilian and early Italian campaigns. He had helped plan and analyze the air operations that broke enemy communications in Sicily and southern Italy.

When Tedder was transferred to England as Eisenhower's deputy, Zuckerman returned with him and became one of Ike's scientific advisers. In that position he developed what became known as the SHAEF Transportation Plan. It proposed bombing railroad marshalling yards as the best means to hamper German mobility and destroy German equipment. After all, Zuckerman argued, that approach had worked splendidly in Sicily and southern Italy. For the most part the British agreed with him, and so, it turned out, did the bulk of the Americans.

But not all of them. In January, Colonel Dick Hughes, the 8th Air Force Planner, still intent on improving strategic bombing for the air war, asked Kindelberger and his colleagues for ideas on how U.S. strategic air forces might be used best to support the invasion. On February 28, 1944, the OSS Economic Objectives Unit submitted a comprehensive paper, which dismissed bombing railroads in this short paragraph:

"Railroad Transport. *Axis railroad motive power is not a useful target system. Strategic attack on railroads is judged to present too great a cushion of civilian and long-term industrial use, and stand too deep in time to offer a chance of achieving military effects.''*

Instead, the memo suggested an oil strategy; the systematic attack and destruction of 23 synthetic oil plants and 31 refineries. Together these installations accounted for 90 percent of Axis oil output. Their destruction would all but immobilize German armies and thus assure their defeat in the field. Nor was total destruction a prerequisite of success. The memo argued that a reduction of better than 50 percent of Axis oil supply would crimp strategic mobility on the ground and in the air. It recommended strikes against oil ''which alone among the remaining target systems offers the opportunity, if completed, of bringing the German war effort to a close.''

The Allied High Command was thus faced with two separate and distinct proposals on how to conduct the air war. The battle of theories was formally joined on March 5, 1944, when General Spaatz, the commander of U.S. Strategic Air Forces, after a long evening meeting, accepted the OSS proposal for attacking oil installations. He ordered drafting to be completed and the plan presented to General Eisenhower. Zuckerman, however, had not remained idle. In the same weeks he had embroidered his original proposals and produced a paper entitled ''Delay and Disorganization of Enemy Movement by Rail.'' It was another version of the plan he felt was so successful in Sicily and Italy. Hughes promptly asked Kindelberger for a critique. Kindelberger radioed Bill Salant, one of his London economists now serving with the Allied air forces in Italy, asking how successful the Allies had been in disrupting enemy transportation from bringing reinforcements to the front. Salant replied that pinpoint bombing of bridges had been most effective in slowing troop movement, and that attacks on marshalling yards were of questionable value. He also pointed to one unique aspect of the Sicily-southern Italy campaign: traffic across the Straits of Messina. Allied ability to cripple ferry service had all but stopped German reinforcement of troops on Sicily. Equally important, Salant reported, was the unenthusiastic effort of the Italian railroads in repairing damaged and rolling stock.

Finally, he pointed out that the Italian rail system lent itself more to aerial bombardment than did the French system. Italy is long and narrow with parallel railroad lines running up both coasts. The French rail network is hexagonal in shape and therefore much harder to cripple with massive bombings. Besides, even in Italy, planners had moved away from the concept of attacking the whole rail system. Instead, they wanted to focus on key bridges and rail segments. Such systematic attacks would deny the enemy rail transport to the front.

In a series of sharp, pungent memos, Kindelberger summed up the shortcomings of the Sicilian strategy and the problems with applying it to France. He contended "that the principal factor contributing to the 300,000 ton reduction in Sicilian imports during the first half of 1943 was the gradual reduction in ferrying capacity across the Messina Straits, which was only slightly influenced by marshalling yard attacks.

It was also pointed out that an ordinary bomb crater on a running railroad track could be repaired in a matter of hours. Meanwhile civilian rail traffic would serve as a cushion and allow the Germans to keep military trains running, even if heavy damage to marshalling yards cut rail capacity by 50 percent and more. It was an argument Spaatz used in his espousal of the "oil" over the "marshalling yard" strategy. The enemy had brought 50,000 reliable German workers to France for the purpose of repairing damaged rail lines quickly. Destruction of synthetic oil plants and refineries would cripple German mobility for a much longer time and much more severely.

But there was a long range element in the OSS "oil" plan that bothered Eisenhower. He wasn't interested in long run impairment of German mobility. It had to be done quickly so that the enemy would have difficulty reinforcing the troops trying to dislodge the Allies from the Normandy beachhead. In other words, bombing had to be effective before D-Day and stay effective through the landing and beyond. The fact that bombing plants and refineries would not ensure the crippling of Germany transportation between D-Day and D plus 30 scrapped the oil plan.

The resourceful Americans would not, however, be deterred. Kindelberger and Rostow had already worked out a strategic alternative to oil and rail yards: bridges and rail lines. Spaatz had first opted for oil. Now he was ready to consider the bridge option. Pulling Bob Roosa aboard, Rostow and Kindelberger buckled down to working out the details of a comprehensive strategic bombing program. It was destined to destroy rail and road bridges in a large perimeter around the Normandy landing area. The perimeter would be long enough, the attacks would be sufficiently widespread and a sufficient number of bridges outside that perimeter would be destroyed to keep the Germans in the dark about the actual landing area. Targets included a string of bridges from the mouth of the Seine near Honfleur to Paris, and along the Loire from Nantes to near Orléans, plus selected viaducts and bridges on the few other lines that ran from the rail belt around Paris to Normandy. The OSS argument was simple. This option was cheap, effective, and would free enough heavy bombers to start strategic attacks on oil at the same time.

The Zuckerman forces at SHAEF took strong issue with this American proposal. Bombing, they argued, was not accurate enough to topple bridges. The attacks would be costly and a waste of time. Forces could be better applied elsewhere, namely against railroad marshalling yards. The argument boiled down to one of effectiveness and accuracy. Could bombers knock out bridges in the needed quantity?

Kindelberger said bombers could do the job. He pointed to the bridges being destroyed from the air in Italy. A bridge more than 120 feet long, he said, would take three weeks to repair. A bomb crater on a running railroad track could be fixed in a maximum of four hours. The bridge option required a limited number of aircraft. Kindelberger's views were given strong support by other planners. The Operational Research Units attached to both the British and American air forces agreed, so did the bomb-damage assessment group working out of the Ministry of Home Security. But their support was not strong enough, not in the early spring of 1944 anyway. Eisenhower stuck with Zuckerman. Still, the OSS plan was far from dead and would make a critical contribution to the Allied war effort just before D-Day and again during the Normandy campaign. The Americans, moreover, continued to believe in their strategy. Roosa spent long weeks collecting data on bridges leading into Normandy and on fuel and ammunition dumps in the Normandy area. He pored over atlases, talked to Colonel Passy's men, and pumped engineers and other specialists about bridge construction and design. Old road maps were consulted, weaknesses probed. When he was finished, the information was distilled into a bridge interdiction manual.

Zuckerman and his plan were not home free yet. Ike ran into trouble getting approval. Churchill worried that diverting air power from German targets to French transportation would allow the Germans to stiffen their air defenses and rebuild their fighter strength. The argument became so sticky that Eisenhower threatened to quit and go back to the U.S. for authority to carry out the Transportation Plan. Moreover, he insisted on assuming temporary command over both Harris and his British Bomber Command and Spaatz and the U.S. Strategic Air Forces. By mid-April Ike had more or less forced Churchill to back down, when a new issue surfaced that delayed implementation of Zuckerman's ideas another three weeks. Estimates of French and Belgian civilian casualties under the Transportation Plan were enormous and alarmed both Churchill and the War Cabinet. They refused to sanction attacks on rail targets in major cities or near other built-up areas such as the industrial belt in northern France and southern Belgium. Churchill and Eisenhower got into another hassle and Ike agreed to hold off attacking 27 of some 80 rail targets that had already been selected. Not content with that, Churchill fired off a worried telegram to FDR about the high casualty cost of the planned assault. Roosevelt closed off further discussion by siding with Eisenhower. No matter how regrettable the attendant loss of life, he wrote, he would not "from this distance" impose restriction on military action that might endanger Overlord or add to Allied casualties. But the invasion was now only little more than a month away, not enough time, really, to test the plan's effectiveness. Still, in

April and May, 80 rail targets were bombed. The G-2 evaluation at the end of May was bleak. The rail bombing operation had failed "to impair the enemy's ability to move up reinforcements and maintain his forces in the West." Clearly, the OSS plan would get another crack.

The debate over civilian casualties was not new, of course, and had shadowed many arguments over the ways and means of crippling enemy transportation and industrial output without punishing the civilian population. Earlier in the war, resistance leaders in occupied Europe were wary of sabotage by foreign agents, fearing German reprisals. Gradually, however, underground thinking began to shift. Resistance forces grew stronger and bolder. Reprisals lost some of their terror (if none of their horror) as they became part and parcel of everyday life. Reprisals could be kept in check or at least dealt with. Bombing raids could not. Death from the sky was too unpredictable for comfort and too inaccurate to make such sense. Yet both resistance groups and the governments-in-exile who directed them realized that the Germans were expanding their war-making potential within the occupied countries and that something would have to be done to curb that expansion. During 1942 and early 1943, opinion on the continent and in London swung back to sabotage, but it was preferable that acts of sabotage be committed by native agents rather than foreigners parachuted into the country. Resistance leaders argued with force and conviction that one Frenchman, Dane, Norwegian, or Belgian who knew where to place a pound of plastic explosive could do a better job than a squadron of bombers.

But like aerial bombardment, sabotage could no longer be a hit and miss affair. The same kind of creative thinking that went into formulating strategic planning for the air war had to be developed for meaningful sabotage. Targets that would create the most painful production bottlenecks had to be identified and pinpointed before they could be attacked. And it would require the same type of innovative strategic mind to do the target selection. Fortunately, we were elbow-deep in talent. Ed Dickinson, a top economic planner at the U.S. War Production Board who had talked himself into the Marine

Corps, was brought to London to head up a sabotage target-pinpointing operation. Dickinson began to give concrete shape to our well-worn arguments that sabotage on the ground was much more precise than attack from the air. Plastic explosives could be attached to the most critical part of a plant and its machinery. Sabotage allowed a precision the most sophisticated bomb sight could not achieve. Damage from plastic explosives often exceeded that of bombs, took longer to repair, and civilian casualties were lower, even if the Nazis did take hostages and punish civilians.

In July 1943, the RAF sent its lumbering Lancasters against the Peugeot motorcar works at Sochaux that was making tank turrets and aircraft engine parts for the Germans. The attackers missed the factory by the proverbial—and literal—mile, and killed hundreds of townspeople in the process. However deplorable the failure was in strategic and human terms, Henri Rée, the Special Operations Executive (SOE) organizer for the Jura, spotted wings of opportunity. Rée contracted Rudolphe Peugeot. If he would help sabotage his own factory Rée would keep the RAF away from the plant and avoid more serious destruction. Peugeot asked Rée to prove that he spoke for the Allies. By that time nothing was easier. The BBC had become a smoothly functioning answering service. Rée radioed London to request BBC broadcast of an agreed-upon message. The BBC complied and Peugeot promptly gave Rée plans of the factory, helped select points where explosives should be placed and had two trusted employees do the job. Frantic German efforts to crank up production again led nowhere. The Peugeot plant was never fully operational for the rest of the war. And when the Michelin tire family refused to adopt the Peugeot formula, the British called in the RAF. The Michelins watched unbelievingly as British bombers blasted their tire factory at Clermont Ferrand.

Schneider-Creusot was the French arms merchant and cannon maker who had traded shell for shell with the House of Krupp during World War I. Now its plants around Lyon were churning out arms for German use. In 1942, the RAF had sent 75 Lancasters against the Creusot works. The bombers did little damage to the plant but killed 1,000 French civilians. Rather than risk another raid with its uncertain prospect, British planners devised a plan to knock out sources of electric power that fed the complex. In August 1943, two French agents were parachuted into Burgundy. They were Raymond Basset, known as Mary, and André Jarrot, a postwar French minister, then known as Goujon. They organized sabotage teams and attacked four power stations, destroyed transformers, circuit breakers, and pylons; knocked down cables and high tension wires; and set fire to oil and coal dumps. In short, they crippled Schneider-Creusot's entire infrastructure system.

In the first six months of 1944, Special Forces Headquarters carried out 50 sabotage operations, three times as many as SOE had tackled in the previous three years, and all of them major actions. Plants were shut down anywhere from two days to six months; some were knocked out for the duration of the war. Moreover, it took over a ton and a half of plastic explosives to wreak all this havoc—less than the bomb load of a single Mosquito.

Nor were explosives the only tool at the disposal of saboteurs. Henri Frenay's resistance units had specialists in factories and installations through the south of France. His man in Toulouse was an immensely talented engineer who would put changes into prints, or write in a reversal of tolerance indications, or make deviations of a fraction of a millimeter in a mold. The result would be an undetectable malfunction in a component, just enough to wreck a gun or an engine after relatively short usage. Such technologically sophisticated sabotage could be much more devastating than bombs or explosives, because repairing blast damage is relatively easy. Malfunctions in the production process are much harder to detect and infinitely more difficult to reverse.

Paradoxically, perhaps, similar effects could be achieved by ordinary workers with little training in technical innovation. Throwing sand or pebbles into delicate machinery could have a devastating impact, so could a hundred small "mistakes" like misdirecting shipments, or slowing down production or "losing" parts, or screwing them on loosely; SOE and the OSS helped that kind of sabotage along by supplying the resistance with an abrasive grease that would wear out the parts it was supposed to lubricate.

Advice on how to commit factory sabotage was available on the air-waves, as part of Political Warfare Executive's black propaganda. PWE manufactured a "workers" radio station supposedly run by anti-Nazi electronic engineers who were building radio transmitters for a large German firm. The station would use the song "Lili Marlene" as its call signal, then switch to a German worker detailing grievances in various German factories. Sabotage instructions would follow. Sabotage instructions were also available, in greater detail, in an SOE pamphlet printed in all major European languages and profusely illustrated. Hundreds of thousands of copies were circulated throughout the continent. It became something of a sabotage bible.

The sabotage payoff, however, was to coincide with Overlord. Different patterns of sabotage were developed for each of three possible invasion points: across the channel, on the Atlantic coast, and in the Mediterranean. The centerpiece of the Allied sabotage plan was a series of simultaneous rail cuts designed to prevent designated German units from moving toward the frontlines. These rail disruptions were to be maintained while Allied forces plowed into Normandy. In addition to making the designated rail cuts, resistance forces were to knock out telephone circuits, thus impair German ability to move convoys; sabotage rail signals to cause collisions, derailments, and transportation bottlenecks; and attack sheds in which hoisting cranes and spare train engines were stored, thus preventing speedy repairs.

Information poured into London about every conceivable aspect of railroad operations and German troop train movement. Everybody from administrators to equipment men working on the tracks contributed to the flow of vital data. From this flow London was able to monitor troop and supply movement and to pinpoint possible sabotage targets. Maps and sketches provided detailed knowledge of bridge areas, stations, and depots. Technical data on French railroad equipment, from locomotives and rolling stock to switches and signal systems, abounded. It enable Allied experts to devise the most effective explosive charges for blowing up engines and cutting rails. We learned to neutralize signals, set rails ajar, remove essential pieces from rolling stock, increase the heat on axles to cause derailments, and set random fires. In Paris, the resistance set up a school to train saboteurs in the art of rail destruction. French rail experts were flown to London to brief French and other Allied officers. German documents that passed through SNCF offices were copied and sent to London, so were reports on soldier morale, trips made by high German officials, and trade of goods for the German account. All were relevant to Allied planning. Knowing the movement of a single secret troop or supply train could identify or confirm a change of enemy plans or strategic maneuver.

The French Post and Telegraph Service, the PTT, provided London with a study of underground telephone and telegraph lines the Germans used. Plans were included for making cuts that would interrupt enemy communications between the front lines and headquarters to the rear. Such cuts would force the Germans to abandon land lines and take to the air where we could pick up and read their messages. Finally, electric power lines continued to be attacked and blown up across France.

Thus in the spring of 1944, plans for disrupting enemy transportation were taking concrete shape. Nevertheless, the disputes on how best to use Allied air strength and the growing power of the French resistance continued right up to D-Day and beyond.

9. Countdown to D-Day

As SPRING tiptoed into London in 1944 few of us at 70 Grosvenor did not know or sense that the invasion was near. An atmosphere of feverish activity and excitement engulfed us that had, for all its deadly seriousness, some of the thrill of a big college football weekend. Several "Sussex" teams— teams of two agents, one French and one British or American dropped behind the lines to work closely with the resistance— were being dispatched into France in April. The "Jedburgh" teams, their training completed, visited London. American officers assigned to the OSS detachments that would go into France, attended briefings and indoctrination sessions, and stretched our social lives far into the night. The OSS itself was growing and changing. We had become a more experienced and professional organization, and we were gaining respect.

We had parachuted the first Sussex team into France in April, and more went out in May. Early reports on their activities were encouraging. They managed to blend into the landscape and into the resistance movement. The pace of parachute drops stepped up in May, when 9 agents were dropped on three nights, May 5, 7, and 10 respectively. Three of the two-man teams were American, what we called Ossex, one British or Brissex. A 9th man was part of the Pathfinder mission, yet another clandestine group directed from London. The Americans were assigned to cover Melun, Romilly, and Etampes. Three more two-man teams went later in May. The Americans in this group were posted to cover the crucial airport of Le Bourget outside Paris. By the end of the month, with the invasion only a week away, 13 Sussex teams had been dispatched into France, seven American Ossex and six British Brissex. Of the 13 teams, six had established radio contact with London and were firmly installed at their planned destination. Each team's observer—the roving contact man— had added a more convincing local cover story to supplement the more general version we had worked out for him in London. We had also begun to line up a chain of local informants in order to increase both the range and thoroughness of his coverage.

Our own OSS Operational Groups or OGs—the force once so ardently attacked in the Pentagon as Donovan's "private army"—were completing training. We had five in England, another six in North Africa. They usually were commanded by four officers and had a complement of 30 men who spoke at least adequate French. Their mission was similar to that of the Jedburghs—working in uniform, behind the lines—except on a larger scale and closer to the actual fighting. The British Special Air Service or SAS was fitted for similar duties. Organized into two British regiments, two French paratroop battalions, and a Belgian company, these were specially trained and hardened troops.

We knew there would be little point in sending special troops immediately behind the major invasion shorelines. The Germans had cleaned all civilians out of a thirty-mile deep strip behind the beaches from Normandy to the Channel coast. Normandy resistance groups, therefore, could take little effective action against reserves already in the bridgehead area. Population to the north and east was too dense and policing too thorough for the resistance to risk any kind of pitched battle. Sabotage and hit and run operations were about all that could be done there.

That left Brittany, the area northwest of the Loire, and the rail and road lines spreading east from Paris and down the Rhône Valley. Resistance units, moving in military force size, could expect to tie up and delay German forces in the Loire and Rhône areas. But the clandestine "directorate" in London (of which the OSS had at last become a tolerated member) felt that the Loire and the Rhône were too far away from the landing sites to risk attacking immediately after the invasion. The resistance should not swing into action until Allied forces were approaching their territory. Here too, sabotage would be the principal weapon against the enemy.

But Brittany was another matter. The three German divisions stationed there could be shifted quickly into Normandy. The terrain was congenial to guerrilla operations. True, the Gestapo had cleaned out most of the local resistance networks, but Bretons were tough and resilient. Many were ready to fight if armed. Most important, the Overlord plan called for an American army to attack Brittany and capture its ports, thus making Brittany a natural target for special troops that would go in just ahead of the invasion to coordinate action with the local resistance. Accordingly, one of the first Jedburgh teams was tapped for a mission to Brittany. The Jedburgh teams were to report on the strength and leadership of each resistance group in their assigned area, how they could be expanded, and what they needed in the way of training, organization, and weapons. They also carried a tag that was to become a common one for all special troops. It was a kind of passport. On one side, over General Eisenhower's signature in English, and on the other, over General Koenig's in French, it said:

"The bearer of this document is a regular member of the Allied Forces under the command of General Eisenhower whose object is the liberation of your territory from the enemy.

"It is required that you should give such members of the Allied Forces any assistance which they may require and which may lie within your power, including freedom of movement, provisions of information, provisions of transport where possible and provisions of food and shelter.

"The Supreme Allied Command counts upon your assistance in carrying out his wishes as expressed above, which are hereby endorsed by the French High Command."

Preparations were also made for OSS Operational Groups and Special Air Service (SAS) troops to move into Brittany ahead of the invading armies. Plans called for the SAS's French parachute battalion to go in first. They would wear red berets and the Cross of Lorraine badge sewed to their uniforms and would be the first Allied soldiers to touch down on French soil. The time for the drop was fixed at 11 p.m. on the night of June 5, 1944.

Auvergne was another area of concern. Colonel Emile Coulaudon, using the nom de guerre of Gaspard, had built up a resistance force of 3,000 to 5,000 men, and ran it pretty much as an independent fiefdom. On May 20, 1944, Gaspard had his men plaster the walls of town halls in his area with posters that, in effect, ordered a general mobilization against the German. By the end of May, his force had swelled by several thousand men as steelworkers, farmers, policemen, shopkeepers, school teachers, miners, and students heeded his call. On June 2, 800 SS troops attacked Gaspard's force and were beaten back. It was the first pitched battle of the invasion period. The SS defeat made it clear to the German high command that such a threat to the Wehrmacht's rear was unacceptable. Greater force would have to be applied to contain the maquis. In London, we worried about a second round of fight so we sent in three Jedburgh teams with orders to bring Gaspard to heel and stop him from taking foolish risks in the future. We committed men of considerable and diverse talent to the project: John Alsop, who would later run for Governor of Connecticut; Reeve Schley, who would become a Wall Street broker; and René Dusacq, a Hollywood stunt man.

While we at Grosvenor Street worried about Brittany, the Auvergne, and a thousand other details, our intellectual warriors on Berkeley Square continued to debate Solly Zuckerman on bombing strategy. In the final weeks it got hot and heavy. Charley Kindelberger, Bob Roosa, and Carl Kaysen continued their skeptical assessment of railroad marshalling yard bombardment. As they analyzed bombing results their conviction hardened that any traffic delays resulting from the bombing would hit civilian, not military, transport. German troops and supplies would get through. In late May, a SHAEF assessment concurred. Bombing, it noted, had failed to "reduce the railways' operating facilities so as to impair the enemy's ability to move up reinforcements and maintain his forces in the West." The Germans still had three times the capacity needed to support their military traffic.

The SHAEF assessment, coming less than three weeks before D-Day, fired up the OSS economists. They saw one last chance for putting the bridge-bombing strategy into action. Other signs, too, had been favorable. On May 6, authorization came to expand Zuckerman's plan for bombing marshalling yards to include bridges. Zuckerman disparaged the importance of bridges (and still did so in his 1978 autobiography *From Apes to Warlords*) but could not fully prevent the vindication of Kindelberger's thesis when, early in May, a handful of Thunderbird fighter-bombers knocked out the bridge across the Seine at Vernon, and did so at a fraction of the anticipated cost.

To overcome such resistance the OSS Enemy Objectives Unit went all out. Harold Barnett, Bob Roosa, and Carl Kaysen gathered all the intelligence they could that would help refocus Allied bombing on bridges, open stretches of tracks, fuel and ammunition dumps, and tank and truck depots. As they did, their work came to the attention of top American and British generals looking to improve their own intelligence performance. Wherever they turned, Barnett and company were heaped with job offers. Barnett went to SHAEF, Kindelberger to Montgomery's headquarters at 21st Army Group and later with Roosa to Bradley's headquarters, Kaysen for a while to the Allied Expeditionary Air Force (AEAF). With Rostow still at the Air Ministry, the Enemy Objectives Unit was well positioned to propagate its research recommendations in the places where big decisions were being made.

Barnett's desk at SHAEF became the linchpin of OSS efforts to change Allied bombing strategy in the weeks before D-Day. It was his job to see that ground intelligence was fully evaluated with a view to picking the fattest targets out of the most tangled evidence. He was in the thick of the dispute over the effectiveness of bombing railroad marshalling yards. With the help of Kindelberger and other analysts from both the OSS and the Ministry of Economic Warfare, Barnett was able to show that the Germans had plenty of rail capacity left, despite massive bombings of their transportation system. In fact, as late as May 20, using only official damage assessments, Barnett demonstrated that the Germans had three times the rail capacity, four times the wagons, and eight times the number of locomotives they would need to reinforce the beachhead, ship military supplies, and keep enough other goods moving to maintain the lifeblood of the Nazi economy. The French railroad system would still be able to handle 350 trains a day on top of the trains needed to keep the military supplied and the economy churning.

SHAEF planners bowed before the force of evidence and swung the major thrust of the Allied bombing programs toward targets favored by the OSS Enemy Objectives Unit: cutting bridges and open lines of tracks in remote places rather than hitting marshalling yards where cargo could be shifted quickly from damaged trains on ripped up tracks to other trains waiting on still intact rail lines. Kindelberger had argued for months that rail traffic could be made to break down 150 miles from the beachhead this way, and that it could be done without the massive destruction of French property and wholesale slaughter of French citizens that was actually taking place while the debate was going on. There was still time before D-Day, Kindelberger argued, to destroy the bridges spanning the Seine from Paris to Conflans, those across the Oise from its mouth below Pontoise northwest to the height of St. Quentin, and those on the Meuse and the Albert Canal from Dinant to the sea at Antwerp. Starting on D-Day, Allied bombers were to smash at the Loire bridges and four junction points on the grand ceinture around Paris. Raids were to be flown in cycles of 48 hours. Railroad marshalling yards were to be hit only after the invasion, and only when German traffic was stacked up in a yard, thus making the "content" —German trains—a worthwhile target whose temporary elimination would have direct bearing on German front-line strength. Attacking train concentrations weeks before Overlord was at best a futile effort. There was plenty of time to repair the damage. But post-invasion air assaults against the same targets would establish a double line of interdiction against German traffic. The first would run along the Seine and Loire, the second along the Albert Canal to Maastricht, then wheel south along the Meuse to Verdun, then west to Besançon, and finally to the Loire.

The OSS strategy was laid down in a paper produced jointly by the Enemy Objectives Unit and the Ministry of Economic Warfare just 16 days before D-Day. It was entitled "The Use of Allied Forces After the Establishment of the Bridgehead." Attacks on bridges and open tracks, the paper urged, should be supplemented by attacks on local supply concentrations. For starters the EOU pinpointed 21 ammunition dumps, 30 fuel concentrations, and depots where as many as 25,000 vehicles might be destroyed through aerial bombardment. The paper identified some 50 bridges and tunnels along the interdiction lines running as far north as Maastricht, a town lodged inside the Dutch appendix poking into Belgium, and as far west as Besançon near the Burgundian frontier with Switzerland. By May 20, after the U.S. Thunderbolt fighter-bombers had delivered the practical proof of their theoretical argument, the Americans had produced the basic guide to tactical air support of ground forces. It did not settle the argument once and for all—few arguments were ever taken care of that neatly in the rarified atmosphere of tactical and strategic thought—but the EOU's argument had gained at least equal weight with Zuckerman's.

The logic Kindelberger's team had pushed for four months became overwhelming. It could take up to three weeks to repair a bridge, but would take only hours to fix a track inside or near a marshalling yard or railroad center. The Allied air

chief marshals—Tedder, Leigh-Mallory, Spaatz, Arnold—
authorized the attacks on bridges spanning the Seine, the Oise,
and the Meuse. Success was spectacular. Stone and masonry
tumbled into the dusty river and powdered its banks from
Rouen to Montes-Gassicourt. Instead of the sour expectations
that 6000 tons of bombs might be needed to dump five bridges
into the river, the actual cost averaged only 200 tons of explosives per bridge. Compared to the expense of knocking
out a marshalling yard, the difference was even greater. And
by May 25, all routes over the Seine north of Paris were
closed to rail traffic and were kept closed during the critical
weeks after the landings. Henceforth Kindelberger's ideas
about bombing hard-to-repair bridges and hard-to-reach open
stretches of track would remain a major strategic option.

But the conflict about when and how to use the French
resistance could not be kept in balance as easily or as well.
We had all agreed in London in April that the underground
had to be leashed as long as possible. Maquis troops were to
be used in careful dosages and only in places where they
could directly benefit Allied troops by harassing the German
rear. The agreement, however, was hard to implement and
turned out to be even harder to keep. As D-Day neared, our
relations with the Free French, always frayed, grew markedly
worse. It is hard, really, not to have great sympathy for their
frustration. They were allies. De Gaulle had at last won and
cemented his position as the one resistance leader recognized
by all Frenchmen. He insisted on France being treated as a
major power. Yet the British and Americans did not trust him
enough to share the invasion plans with him and his men.
That friction surfaced explosively and dangerously just weeks
before the invasion.

Colonel Passy wanted to make sure that resistance leaders
in France understood de Gaulle's policy, which was also our
own: The resistance was to keep a low profile and not take
action until ordered to do so. So far so good. But what Passy
did to get that message to his front-line commanders was not
so good. He sent Lazare Racheline, a veteran organizer of
escape "lines" for downed Allied airmen and others escaping from France, to Brittany in a small boat. Racheline was

to deliver the lie-low message in person. He was to remind resistance leaders that French soil could only be freed piece-meal. Operations could only be launched district by district and as ordered from London. Dutifully, Racheline went to Paris where he gave his message to Alexandre Parodi, the newly appointed delegate general. He met Chaban-Delmas, the national military delegate, and Maurice Bourgès-Maunoury and Col. Ely who commanded FFI forces in the south and the north.

Meanwhile, back in London, the SHAEF staff was fit to be tied. Once again Passy had ignored orders. Racheline had blithely disobeyed a specific ban on his leaving the country. In effect, the French had smuggled Racheline out of England. If the Gestapo had picked him up, who knows what he would have told the Germans about the invasion plans? He knew little about them, but the Germans might have squeezed out of him enough pieces of information to blow the vast program of deception along the southern coast of England. The Germans believed that the major Allied blow would be struck against the Pas de Calais and not against Normandy. Protecting the ''grand deception'' was a major cause of ulcers among responsible officers. We never did know how long John Bevan and his scenario writers could keep it up, or how long the Luftwaffe would be fooled by the decoys that crammed air-fields and ports. For many British and French officers, Racheline's trip—and it had taken the better part of the month of May—was the last straw.

French officers, for their part, boiled with anger and frustration at being kept out of the last-minute planning. This close to the invasion, they figured, they had a right to be kept informed. Touchiness and resentment mounted. One scene that spring remains imprinted on my memory. We were standing in the Sussex operations room at 70 Grosvenor Street plotting yet another mission. As usual, Colonel Rémy stood in front of a large map, a pointer in one hand. He had always recommended where each Sussex team could be sent safely, and his recommendations had always been accepted. Now he pointed to a spot right behind the landing area and explained how his men had found a safe house there. We turned him down. Rémy was no fool. He promptly asked if the impending invasion was the reason for our refusal. And if so, couldn't we tell him enough about what was up so he could do his job properly? Everyone was embarrassed. We couldn't tell him, Francis Miller explained. It was forbidden. Rémy accepted our refusal with as much good grace as he could muster, but it made for an awkward moment. Eisenhower himself had suffered similar embarrassment with General Koenig. In fact, Ike had gone so far as to ask Washington for permission to tell Koenig. This was at first flatly rejected, but when Eisenhower persisted, Washington relented to the point of allowing him to tell Koenig the month but not the day set for the invasion.

On May 31, word reached Grosvenor Street that SHAEF had turned the policy for using the FFI and other French resistance forces upside down. We were told that instead of signalling the resistance to rise unit by unit and join the fighting on a gradual and as needed basis, all action signals to groups in every corner of France would be sent out simultaneously. A year's worth of careful planning and analysis were to be thrown out the window, conclusions reached about not exposing the FFI to Nazi retaliation until Allied forces were close enough to help were abandoned.

Our first reaction to the new order was one of gloom and foreboding. If issued as now planned it could touch off a national uprising. The Germans would have little trouble crushing the revolt, which would have grave long-term political consequences for us. Finally, and perhaps most importantly, our troops moving across France would be deprived of military support from the FFI. Bruce and Mockler Ferryman made our pitch to General Walter Bedell Smith, Ike's chief of staff, to no avail. The decision was firm. Eisenhower wanted all the help he could get when he needed it most—at the time of the landing. Others who argued our case did not get any further, but the debate was intense and did not split along nationalist lines.

Some suggested that the French really favored a general call-out, primarily for political reasons. Others thought—rightly as it turned out—that so many Frenchmen were so eager to smash the hated Boche that we could not stop them. Resistance would flare spontaneously almost everywhere. A policy of closely coordinated control was futile. Still others, including some within the OSS community, argued that the greatest contribution the resistance could make was to stretch German forces in France to the utmost. A sudden surge of resistance nationwide, they said, was the best way to achieve that goal. A final argument, and one that seems to have carried the most weight, contended that only a general uprising could keep the Germans confused about the site of our actual landing, and thus safeguard the Pas de Calais deception plan. It cannot be stressed enough how much depended on that deception plan. It permeated all Overlord thinking.

In the first days of June the signs of imminent invasion multiplied. The surest signal for us was the sudden appearance of General Donovan in London. He had materialized, out of thin air as it were, before the landings at Sicily, Salerno, New Hollandia, and Anzio. He was not about to miss the greatest adventure of the war. This time Eisenhower and Bedell Smith were determined that he would miss it, and stay back where a proper Major General should. He went to Admiral Stark with his plea for a seat on a landing craft. The Admiral was under orders too, but he relented to the extent of smuggling Donovan aboard the cruiser *Augusta*. Jack Small, my old boss in the Navy, now elevated from Captain to the recently restored rank of Commodore, turned up in London. Having successfully completed his assignment of getting enough landing craft built for the invasion, he felt entitled to see how they worked and wanted to ride one on to a Normandy beach. He, too, was turned down, but got a perch on the *Augusta* as a consolation prize.

On the evening of June 5th, as the invasion—with its 5,000 ships, 9,000 planes, 23,000 parachutists, 176,000 assault troops, and 20,000 vehicles—passed out of the hands of those left behind in London, apprehension, though not openly expressed, ran high. The last time the Atlantic Wall was stormed at Dieppe, 60 percent of the invading force was killed, wounded, or missing. General Brooke confided to his diary that "it may well be the most ghastly disaster of the whole war.'' Churchill told his wife that by the time she woke up in the morning 20,000 men might have been killed.

There was much to worry about and lots to hope for. We knew there were rocket sites ready to launch robot bombs at London, and we knew that broadcasting sabotage instructions all over France—as we had—could bring on mass reprisals and lasting recriminations.

We had received a wireless message from one of our new OSS agents at Chartres that the powerful Panzer Lehr division had returned from Hungary and moved in just behind the Normandy bridgehead. We did not know, although Montgomery's intelligence chief Brigadier Williams had indications and passed them along to General Bradley as the convoys sailed for France, that the German 352nd Division had just moved up from St. Lô to conduct exercises right behind Omaha Beach.

Despite the detail and precision of Dulles's messages from Berne about the plot to kill Hitler, few, if any, in London at that time would have imagined that there were German generals commanding troops behind the Atlantic Wall who were more interested in taking Paris from the Gestapo than in throwing back the Allied landings.

There was other good news, too. Of 59 German divisions in France, we knew that only 6 were in Normandy. Another six were in recently reinforced Brittany and 18 were across the Seine in the Pas de Calais, where the infantry divisions were two deep. There had been no sign that any of them were about to shifted to Normandy. We had blinded the Germans by knocking out their radar screens, except along the Pas de Calais—and those screens would be recording false impressions of approaching ships and planes created by R. V. Jones and his fellow wizards with tiny strips of tin foil.

On May 30, an American intercept of a report of a conversation that Baron Oshima, the Japanese Ambassador at Berlin, had at Berchtesgaden revealed that Hitler believed there were 80 or 90 divisions in Britain and that while there might be an initial thrust in Norway or Normandy, the main thrust would come on the Pas de Calais. Eisenhower and the SHAEF deception staff had as their original objective keeping the German 15th Army in the Pas de Calais and away from Normandy for 48 hours after the landings. Now, with Hitler believing that there was an army twice the size of the Normandy invasion force remaining in England, still greater opportunities were at hand.

10. Normandy

A FEW DAYS before D-Day, the German 352nd Division had positioned itself for military exercises right behind Omaha Beach, where the U.S. First Division was to land. At 3 A.M. on the morning of June 6, the 916th infantry regiment of the German 352nd Division was ordered to Isigny at the south-eastern corner of the Cherbourg peninsula to deal with an airborne threat that consisted of three British paratroopers, hundreds of exploding dummies, a chemical preparation ex-uding smoke, and a battery of victrolas amplifying recordings of gunfire, soldier talk, and troop movements. By the time the 916th returned from its wild goose chase at Isigny and joined in a counterattack on the Omaha beachhead, the U.S. First Division was sufficiently established that it could not quite be dislodged, though it came under withering fire.

At the other landing beaches, we were lucky in achieving initial surprise. Not only had deception planted firmly in the enemy's mind that the main thrust would come north of the Seine on the Pas de Calais, but when paratroopers and landing barges touched ground in Normandy, the Germans refused to believe it. Rommel had calculated that the invasion would be made at high tide so that the invaders would not have to make a long run across sandy beaches through concentrated crossfire. The landings were actually made between low and high water. German meterologists proclaimed on June 4 that bad weather ruled out invasion for a fortnight. These two considerations were enough to send Rommel home to Stuttgart for his wife's birthday, with plans to go from there to meet with Hitler at Berchtesgaden. Other generals exercising command over the German Seventh Army in Normandy were engaged in Paris, in Rennes, or some other place away from their command posts. When at 9:30 in the evening of June 5, a German wireless section in Paris heard the second half of the Verlaine poem signaling that invasion was imminent, word was sent at once to the German high command in the west. The message was recognized at the headquarters of the 15th Army on the Pas de Calais and its corps were warned that invasion could be expected within 48 hours. The 7th Army in Normandy, on receiving the message, ignored it, until at twenty minutes after one on the morning of June 6, the arrival of Allied paratroopers woke up its headquarters in Normandy. When this was reported to Rommel's headquarters, Speidel, his chief of staff, replied that this was not considered to be a major operation. By 6:00 A.M., von Rundstedt had decided that the invasion was for real. He had his chief of staff, General Blumentritt, request that Panzers be released to Normandy. General Jodl, however, decided not to disturb Hitler's sleep and told von Rundstedt's headquarters to handle the situation with its own forces until the situation was clarified. Not until four o'clock in the afternoon was von Rundstedt authorized to use two Panzer divisions already under his command.

On D plus 1, when Montgomery, Bradley, and Dempsey had their first meeting on French soil to take stock, there were 155,000 Allied soldiers in France. Twenty-five hundred men had been killed, another 9 to 10 thousand were wounded or missing, against the 75,000 casualties that COSSAC had estimated would be taken if surprise was not achieved.

Still, none of the D-Day objectives had been obtained. None of the four bridgeheads had been joined to form a consolidated front. The Americans had suffered heavy casualties at Omaha Beach and had only a tenuous hold on a slender strip of shorefront. The British had failed to reach Caen, the supply situation was bad, and the weather seemed likely to prevent substantial improvement very soon.

There was every prospect that the Germans would pour the full force of their Panzers into France and the crack divisions of the 15th Army into the bridgeheads. Three days before D-Day, General Strong, Eisenhower's G-2, had predicted that within a week of the landing, 3 Panzer divisions and 3 infantry divisions of the 15th Army would have crossed the Seine to fight in Normandy. Could the 155,000-man force on the Normandy beaches be built up rapidly enough to hold on?

The air force redoubled its efforts to block German reinforcements from reaching the beachhead. Leaflets were dropped to warn civilians to evacuate Caen, St. Lô, Coutances, Lisieux, Falaise, Argentan, and Vire. Rail centers were bombed from the air and rails were cut so that troops were compelled to detrain and walk as much as 50 miles to the front. As military police with walkie-talkies tried desperately to untangle the traffic, trucks moved so slowly that they were sitting ducks for new air attacks.

In the week after D-Day, resistance teams made 1,000 rail cuts. Three weeks after D-Day they had made 2,000. After June 7, not a single train crossed the area of Burgundy between Dijon, Besançon, Chalons, and Lons-le-Saunier, through which ran all the main and secondary rail lines between the Rhône Valley and the Rhine. Virtually every train arriving at Lyons from Marseilles would have to survive at least one derailment. Rail lines in the north around Lille were cut and kept cut from the day after D-Day until the end of June. Road movement became virtually impossible as fallen trees and blown bridges backed up convoys and resistance raiders attacked stranded trucks. One convoy coming from around Bordeaux got stuck in the sands of the Loire and had to be abandoned.

The German 11th Panzer Division took a week to get from

Russia to the Rhine and three weeks to get across France to Caen. One of the oldest and probably the best of the Panzer divisions, Das Reich, ordered to Normandy from Toulouse, normally a three-day trip, arrived 15 days late.

On D plus 6, American troops linked their two beachheads, Utah and Omaha, by taking Carentan. It seemed as though the Allies were winning the build-up race. American and British divisions were landing faster than German divisions were appearing in Normandy. The German High Command could still not make up its mind whether Normandy was a feint or the real thing, despite a great stroke of luck on D plus 1 when the Germans captured the operational orders of both the American 7th Corps at Utah and the American 5th Corps at Omaha. Analyzed at German 7th Army headquarters, they indicated such an expansion of the American bridgehead all the way to Cherbourg and the bay of St. Malo, as to indicate that this was no feint. Although the captured orders could have been intentionally lost to achieve deception, von Rundstedt and Rommel had enough evidence as early as D plus 2 to conclude that this was the invasion.

But Hitler held fast, defending his rocket sites behind Calais and Boulogne, believing that the Allies had twice as many divisions in England as they had. To keep German troops on the Pas de Calais as long as possible, all channels were to be used to propagate this post-invasion story:

1. *Because of the enemy's successful efforts to contain Allied forces in Normandy, General Eisenhower has been forced to divert forces from the Pas de Calais forces to the beachhead.*
2. *These forces are being replaced by fresh troops from the U.S.*
3. *The Pas de Calais forces, still directed by the same Army Group Headquarters, are ready to invade the Pas de Calais area. They wait only for enemy reinforcements to be drawn away by the diversion at Normandy. The date of the Pas de Calais invasion is a command decision to be made by General Eisenhower, who will act when he thinks best.*

To hold the 15th Army on the north side of the Seine, BBC and wireless messages went out to the resistance in Northern France and Belgium. Submarines and torpedo boats appeared off the Pas de Calais coast. There was intense activity in the English harbors and rivers and on the coast opposite the Pas de Calais. Wireless traffic between SHAEF and FUSAG (First U.S. Army Group) headquarters intensified while the divisional headquarters went silent to indicate armies on the move. Mine sweepers started to operate off Calais. Landing beaches around Calais were bombarded. Our highest hope was to keep units of the German 15th Army away from Normandy for just another few days.

MI-5's double agents struck the decisive blow in the days following D-Day. Back in London, it had been recognized that the first prerequisite for any continuing intelligence contribution to the invasion effort would be that the credibility of individual agents be maintained as long as possible. Col. Roger Fleetwood Hesketh, the chief scenario writer at SHAEF, had started several weeks before D-Day to lay the groundwork to enhance the credibility of one agent in particular—a Spaniard codenamed Garbo who was an Abwehr agent working for the British. On the eve of D-Day, not far enough ahead to do the Germans any good but enough to impress them, Garbo reported to Madrid that the invasion was on the way. SHAEF authorized Garbo to radio General Kuhlenthal—the Abwehr man in Madrid—about the landings four hours before the first wave was to hit the beach. There was no answer in Madrid at 2:30 A.M. when Garbo was authorized to send his message. By the time he raised Madrid, at 8:00 A.M., he was able to include additional information that the Germans would be bound to pick up from the troops on the beachhead the first day.

Before noon on D-Day, Garbo sent Madrid what purported to be the full text of a directive issued by the Political Warfare Executive warning against any statement about further assaults or any speculation on alternative assault areas. Then, on June 9, Garbo sent a long report describing how, together with his three best agents, he had reviewed and reassessed the military situation in England. The message summarized and confirmed previous descriptions of military formations and landing barges in southeast England and concluded that the Normandy assault, though on a large scale, was clearly diversionary. Its purpose was to draw as much of the German reserve as possible to the Normandy coast and keep the Germans there while the major Allied strike was made to the north closer to the heart of Germany. Garbo said he had learned that, of 75 divisions in England, only 20 to 25 would go to Normandy, leaving 50 to make the major strike at the Pas de Calais which, Garbo pointed out accurately, was already being softened up by intensive bombardment from the air. He concluded that the present invasion was a trap designed to induce a hurried redisposition of forces that would open the way for the major Allied thrust on the Pas de Calais.

It was established that the deception was still working when Bletchley picked up this summary of Garbo's message that Madrid sent to both von Rundstedt's headquarters and to Berlin:

Message received at 2230 hours on June 9, 1944. V-man Alaric network Arabel reports 9th Army from England.

After personal consultation on 8th June in London with my agents Jonny, Dick and Dorich whose reports were sent today, I am of the opinion, in view of the strong troop concentrations in South-east and Eastern England which are not taking part in the present operations that these operations are a diversionary *maneuver designed to draw off enemy reserves in order then to make a decisive attack in* another place. *In view of the continued air attacks on the concentration area mentioned, which is in a strategically favorable position for this, it may very probably take place in the Pas de Calais area, particularly since in such an attack the proximity of the air bases will facilitate the operation by providing continued strong air support.*

After the war, the German records showed "diversionary" and "another place" underlined. It was also noted on the message: "confirms the view already held by us that a further attack is to be expected in another place (Belgium)." Jodl underlined in red "in South-east and Eastern England." A green heiroglyph in the upper left-hand square of the message indicated that Jodl showed it to Hitler and the initials "erl" (erledigt) indicated that it was seen by Hitler himself.

Hitler acted. On June 9, he had succumbed to von Rundstedt's demand for reinforcements in Normandy and ordered five infantry and two Panzer divisions of the 15th Army to move south to Normandy. By Saturday, June 10, after initialing Madrid's summary of Garbo's assessment, Hitler had countermanded his own order. All seven divisions were ready to move when von Rundstedt, after receiving a call from General Keitel at Hitler's headquarters, told them to stay on the Pas de Calais.

Even this windfall might not have been enough to save the thinly held Allied beachhead. The 2nd SS "Das Reich" Panzer Division had already been ordered to Normandy from Toulouse. On June 12, Hitler ordered an SS Panzer corps of 35,000 men and two SS armored divisions to leave the Russian front and move to Normandy. Panzer and infantry divisions were being ordered to the Normandy battlefield from Brittany, from the Netherlands, from Bordeaux, from Poland and Hungary, from Denmark and Norway.

On June 11, Lt. Col. Ken Downs led the four men of the advance party of our OSS intelligence detachment ashore at Omaha Beach. The next day he reported to Col. Monk Dickson, First Army G-2, who in England had raised objections about receiving raw intelligence directly from the OSS. Now, he waived all objections and asked that all available intelligence be sent from London immediately. There were 36 messages from London, and Downs, with his signals officer, his deputy Trafford Klotz, and two GIs, labored all night in a tiny blacked out tent without lights or telephone, working by flashlight and candlelight, to decode the messages.

For three days and three nights Downs's little team did nothing but work on codes and cyphers. The initial messages traced the movements of the 2nd SS Panzer Division (Das Reich) and the 189th Reserve Division towards the battle area from the South as well as other convoys of reinforcements moving towards Normandy from the east. There were messages from Chartres, Melun, Orléans, Le Mans, Vannes, Paris, Spain, Algiers, Berne, and London.

Transportation across the channel was so tightly scheduled that Col. Dickson would not authorize bringing additional personnel over and refused to entertain the suggestion that we bring over men by our own means and support them independent from Army headquarters. The larger OSS special force detachment for resistance support was on hand and with their help, by June 16, Downs caught up for the first time with the intelligence messages that our agents had risked their lives to get.

Then came the big storm. On D plus 13 the Normandy coast was suddenly hit by the worst storm in 40 years. A raging gale built up waves six to eight feet high. The engine rooms of landing barges were swamped. Three days later when the storm abated, 800 ships had been driven ashore, floating piers and the artificial Mulberry harbor had been wrecked. The 600,000 troops ashore would soon be short of supplies. In three days the storm had destroyed more vessels than all the German guns, mines, and bombs in the Normandy campaign. Worse still, it had slowed down the rate of Allied build-up. It took two weeks for the rate of daily tonnage unloaded to get back to where it was before the storm struck. The storm had also grounded Allied aircraft, presenting the Germans with a unique opportunity to bring in their reinforcements and sweep ahead in the build-up race.

It was here that the delay which the air force and the resistance imposed on Panzer divisions and troop trains coming to the beachhead counted. Montgomery's headquarters made an assessment that German motorized elements had moved an average of only 45 miles a day, about a quarter of what they could do under favorable conditions. In many parts of France and Belgium—the Ain, the Ardennes, the Auvergne, the Vercors, Haute-Savoie, Limousin, Chalons-sur-Saône—resistance bands engaged German forces, and by the last week in June we were making massed daylight drops of arms to them from England.

When I made my first visit to the beachhead with Colonel

Bruce on June 25, most of the OSS detachments had been consolidated in a farmhouse near Carentan. The coastal area had been so thoroughly evacuated and the lines in the closely confined bridgehead were so tight that there would be little or no active support from the resistance for the advancing Allied troops. But the resistance quickly proved itself as a source of accurate tactical intelligence. Donovan had argued staunchly but to no avail back in London that experience in Tunisia and Italy had shown OSS officers could be most useful in producing tactical intelligence for commanders of divisions and regiments. SHAEF had limited OSS detachments to Army and Army Group headquarters.

Downs now had 50 French officers under his command. He got permission to place them with divisional and regimental G-2s where they proved to be enormously useful in getting and cross-checking information from Norman farmers and villagers who were overrun. This resistance role had originally been seen as incidental, but it proved to be a major contribution in the bocage country. For centuries, Norman farmers had enclosed each plot of arable land, pasture as well as orchard, with hedgerows. These fences, half earth, half hedge would be one to four feet thick and three to fifteen feet high. The invasion planning had studied the beaches and coastal terrain and developed special training and equipment for it, but there had been very little preparation for the advantage which these hedgerows gave the defense, perhaps because the planners counted on moving through the flat, open country around Caen to outflank the bocage on the Cotentin peninsula. At great risk, French civilians would move forward and return with information on German dispositions and movements on the flanks and behind the lines. The OSS staff would brief and debrief them. Both OSS intelligence and resistance staffs turned to launching numerous infiltrations immediately behind the German lines with quickly recruited native agents. They would work their way back with whatever information they could gather. More than one hundred such missions, all hastily improvised, were carried out, frequently with better results than carefully planned operations.

At the beginning of July, we had 14 Sussex teams in place

behind the lines and had heard from 12 of them. Eighty-seven reports had been received by direct radio or "Klaxon" (radio communication from agents to planes), and been disseminated. Twenty-two intelligence messages from the Brissex teams had been disseminated.

Eight additional teams were in England briefed and ready to go. In the first week of July, new teams were sent to Rennes, Dreux, Laval, Angers, and Alençon, all centers that led into our expanded bridgehead and commanded important crossroads in the area of the intended breakout. Three additional teams were dropped at transportation centers farther back at Troyes, Epernay, and Bourges.

These teams needed assistance. A single observer could not effectively cover the entire sector assigned to each team. For this reason, one of the tasks assigned to the advance Pathfinder teams had been the building up of a nucleus of informants at each point for which a Sussex team was destined. The Pathfinders succeeded in most cases in locating at least one reliable local contact through whom the teams could build up small *réseaux* of their own, but a good deal of organizing had generally to be done by the agents after arrival. Some were very successful in this respect. The observer of team Vitrail, for example, quickly organized a rather small but proficient group of six specialized informants, two of them railway station employees, one a railway engineer, the fourth an employee of the Préfecture, and the two others employed at different airdromes. The Vitrail team at Chartres, an observer and a W/T operator, was very active, established an efficient network, and sent during the month of its operation 14 intelligence messages on enemy troop movements, airdromes, bombing targets, and results of bombings. He was shot on 27 June. His W/T operator went to work with another team.

Team Jeanne at Orléans was the most productive of the Sussex teams, sending in 170 messages, of which 127 contained intelligence. The work of this team was repeatedly complimented by SHAEF. Its reporting was concise, its encipherment perfect, and the transmission, according to the operators at Station Victor, was the best. The observer had a network of 80 people working for him, always evaluated his sources, and, if possible, verified the information personally. Among the items sent in were the code routes of the German army across France and accurate reports on the V-1 flying bomb. During the first weeks of operation, the observer suffered from a return of malaria and worked with the aid of hypodermic injections—41 in all.

With the fall of Cherbourg to Allied forces, the OSS was directed to concentrate on the development of intelligence in the area bounded roughly by Avranches-Domfront-Périers-St. Lô. Four of our Sussex agents already behind the lines were ordered to move into that area. Other agents were infiltrated through the lines. It was here that we mounted our best intelligence operation from Normandy. It was called the Helmsman plan. Overrun FFI resistants were briefed on tactical intelligence targets and flown over to England, whence they were parachuted back into France at points about fifty miles behind the enemy lines. These agents then had the job of recruiting sub-agents, briefing them on required tactical intelligence, and sending them back to the Allied lines with what information they could pick up along the way.

Jack Hayes, an SOE organizer, parachuted into the Avranches region, succeeded in recruiting and sending back 28 sub-agents just before the St. Lô breakthrough, and provided excellent reports on German artillery placements, tank units, troop dispositions and the condition of strategic bridges.

OSS officers like Bert Jolis and John Mowinckel undertook the hazardous missions of going forward into towns like St. Lô, not sure whether they would be dodging German or American artillery fire, in order to contact FFI leaders, get their reports, and assign intelligence tasks. A Sussex agent overrun at Alençon got a commendation for valuable reports on installations and tank movements valuable to the breakthrough at St. Lô and Avranches. The most valuable Sussex messages targeted the bombing of munitions dumps and bridges and alerted Montgomery to the movement of the Panzer Lehr Division to attack the British and Canadian armies at Caen. The failure to take Caen by July 1 was the big disappointment of the invasion. It was the key to moving east to the Seine and on to Paris. For that reason Hitler was determined to hold it and concentrated his tanks there. Until Allied forces broke through Caen, mobility for armored warfare and the airfields needed for the tactical air forces would be limited and the Allies would remain vulnerable to a German armor drive that could split the Allied forces and imperil their slender foothold on the continent.

The remarkable thing was that a force of 1500 men on the east coast of England was holding down 22 German divisions, more than a quarter of a million of Hitler's best troops, who only had to cross the Seine to break Montgomery's back and possibly push us all back into the sea. This little force of 1500 men was operating wireless deception equipment, tending dummy boats, planes, and tanks, and lighting fires to animate phantom embarcation camps for the Germans to see at night. How long could this fantastic ruse continue to succeed?

The Germans were concentrating their tank forces against Montgomery around Caen. Still being told that Patton had an army group ready to attack north of the Seinne, Rommel now told von Rundstedt to expect Montgomery to make a thrust toward Paris in conjunction with a landing by Patton between the Somme and Le Havre; Allied armies could be expected up both banks of the Seinne with the objective of seizing Paris. This expectation was encouraged in every possible way—with intensive aerial reconnaissance between the Seinne and the Somme, a British naval feint at Boulogne, smoke screens off the eastern coast of England, and heavy wireless traffic to resistance forces in Belgium and the Pas de Calais.

The great attempt to break out of Normandy came not at Caen where the Germans, with 6 Panzer divisions, and 250,000 men, were well prepared to keep Montgomery from reaching the Seine and Hitler's V weapons, but at St. Lô where the Germans had only 2 Panzer divisions. On July 25, General Omar Bradley unleashed operation Cobra with 140,000 artillery shells and 2,700 planes dropping 4,200 tons of bombs. On July 30, Granville was taken; on July 31, Bradley's forces were in Avranches; and on August 1, the 4th

Armored was over the narrow bridge at Pontaubault. Brittany lay open before it. On August 3, Rennes, 60 miles from Avranches, and with 10 main roads radiating north, south, east and west, was liberated.

At this point, the Allied forces got perhaps the biggest payoff for the thousands of man years of talent that had been put into reading the coded messages sent out on the German Enigma machines. It might also have been the biggest payoff for all the blood and anguish that had been invested in SOE, the OSS, and the French resistance. Since D-Day, the slashing of phone wires and the cutting of telecommunications cables had been a prime sabotage target. The Berlin-Paris cable had been cut and kept out of action for days at a time. A sabotage attack uprooted the land lines and the switching center of the cable and phone system around Le Mans where the German Seventh Army had its headquarters. This made land line communication unavailable or so uncertain that messages between Hitler, the High Command, and the German generals in Normandy were forced into the air where we could read them.

As Patton's XX Corps raced toward the Loire and his XV Corps dashed toward Le Mans, General von Kluge and Hitler conducted a strategic debate that Bletchley revealed day by day to Churchill and Eisenhower, Montgomery and Bradley. Hitler ordered von Kluge to pay no attention to Patton's breakthrough but to collect four of the Panzer divisions from Caen and to retake Avranches in order to divide the Americans at the base of the Cherbourg peninsula and roll them back into the sea. The next day, von Kluge spelled out to Hitler how withdrawing the Panzer divisions from Caen would expose the whole German force in the west to the prospect of being surrounded. In reply, Hitler said he recognized the dangers that von Kluge had pointed out, but insisted that the situation called for bold action and that the risks had to be taken. On August 5, Bletchley reported that von Kluge had told Hitler that his orders would produce only disaster. Hitler responded with his final order to proceed. This drama, played out over four days, provided ample time to formulate a lethal counterstrategy. Hodges's First Army would move down toward Mortain to protect Avranches, Patton would send troops back north and west from Le Mans, and Montgomery would move south and take Falaise. The trap was sprung.

At daybreak on August 7, the German Panzers roared into Mortain and several miles beyond it before Pete Quesada's fighter-bombers and Bradley's artillery started to pound them. That evening, von Kluge reported that his attack had ground to a halt and half his tanks were gone. Hitler came back with an order that the attack be pressed regardless of risk. The Panzers guarding Falaise were to be committed to the attack on Avranches, which was defended by seven American divisions. Von Kluge signaled General Eberbach that Hitler had ordered three of his Panzer divisions from Falaise to join the attack on Avranches. When Montgomery's Canadians, with heavy air support, launched their attack on Falaise, one of Eberbach's Panzer divisions had left for Avranches and the others were preparing to leave. Von Kluge cancelled the movement to Avranches and told Hitler that the Allied attack on Falaise made the German attack on Avranches impossible. In reply, Hitler ordered a new and stronger attack—with several corps to be commanded by General Eberbach—on Avranches on August 11. Eberback replied that he could not proceed before August 12. On August 10, von Kluge signaled that he was on the verge of being surrounded, because Patton was moving north.

Patton, with his XV Corps strengthened by Le Clerc's 2nd French Armored Division, was closing in on Alençon. On the 13th, Le Clerc had taken Carrouges, and the 5th Armored Division was closing in on Argentan. Suddenly at 11:30 A.M. Patton's operations tent received a telephone call from Bradley's staff. Patton was ordered to halt his forces forthwith and to withdraw any elements that might have slipped across the Anglo-American boundary at a line running south of Argentan. Patton pleaded that he be allowed to continue his advance, but to no avail. He kicked and squealed and to the day he died believed that if XV Corps had not been stopped it would have reached Falaise in a day or so and the German

Seventh Army would have been surrounded. During the additional week it took Montgomery to take Falaise, some 30,000 German troops escaped to defend the fatherland on the Siegfried line and the Rhine, where we would lose twice as many men as we had lost in Normandy.

11. Action in the Capitals

ON THE EVENING of July 20, Goebbels announced that a plot to assassinate Hitler had failed. What he did not say was by what a narrow margin it had failed. Virtually the entire top command in the west was either committed or sympathetic or at least had listened to the conspirators and their plan to finish off Hitler—and none of them had blown the whistle.

Generals Stülpnagel and von Falkenhausen, in command of occupation forces in France and Belgium, Speidel, Rommel's chief of staff, and General Boineburg-Lengsfeld, Commandant of Paris, were all staunch, active, long-standing members of the conspiracy. Rommel and Rundstedt had listened to the plotters with sympathy and at least flirted with them. Von Kluge had committed and uncommitted himself to them more than once and it was hard to tell where he stood at any one time. His headquarters on the Russian front had been a center of the conspiracy and several attempts to kill Hitler had been launched there. At all the top military headquarters in the west, von Rundstedt's, Rommel's, Stülpnagel's, and von Falkenhausen's, colonels and officers of lower rank were busy furthering the conspiracy and pushing their superiors to act against Hitler. Speidel talked freely to commanders of Army Divisions and Corps about the conspiracy and he seems to have gotten the commitment of some like von Schwerin and Schweppenberg to use their forces against the Nazis at the right moment.

Just before he was wounded, in mid-July, Rommel himself sounded out Panzer commanders Eberbach and Dietrich and, according to his aide, got assurances that they would execute his orders even if they contradicted Hitler's.

Inside Germany, Abwehr chief Canaris had persuaded Hitler that the presence of millions of foreign workers required a plan to deal with them if they rioted or revolted. General Friedrich Olbricht, chief of staff at the headquarters of the Home Army inside Germany, had developed the emergency plan, called Valkyrie, not so the Home Army could suppress a possible revolt by foreign workers (that was merely a cover for the Home Army to take over security in Berlin), but so the Home Army could be used to suppress the Nazi party and the Gestapo and seize power throughout the German domain. The code word Valkyrie had only to be promulgated and army units would protect or take over all public facilities, and the command post of the Home Army would have power to impose martial law with complete authority over all other services, including the SS. So lax and ambivalent was the atmosphere within the higher ranks of the Wehrmacht that when General Fromm asked Colonel von Stauffenberg—a leader in the conspiracy—to be his chief of staff and deputy in command of the Home Army, von Stauffenberg told Fromm quite openly of his views. Fromm listened and said his own ideas were quite similar, but that the matter must rest there.

Carl Friedrich Goerdeler, former Mayor of Leipzig and an early opponent of the Nazis, had toured the Russian front and directly solicited the support of Field Marshall George von Kuchler, commander of Army Group North, and von Kluge, as commander of Army Group Center, while General Henning von Tresckow, chief of staff at Army Group Center, was perhaps the moving spirit of the whole effort. Field Marshal

Fritz Erich von Manstein, commander of Army Group South (U.S.S.R.) and Gen. Heinz Guderian, Inspector General of Armored Troops, had listened to the plotters with apparent sympathy.

At the High Command, Gen. Erich Fellgiebel, in control of communications, and Gen. Edvard Wagner, First Quarter-master General of the Army, were totally committed. After the plot had failed, Hitler was convinced that Fellgiebel had been using his communications channels to send information to the Allies, that Wagner was sabotaging the supply of his armies, and that Col. Freiherr von Roenne, in charge of foreign intelligence for German armies in the west, had been deliberately feeding him falsified assessments of the strength, disposition, and intentions of the Allied armies—and there is good reason to believe that they were.

Every German officer who was approached had to struggle with a dilemma between his obligation to humanity, his country, and his Führer. This was easily resolved by men like von Tresckow who declared early on to his colleague Fabian von Schlabrendorff that "duty and honor demanded that we bring down Hitler and the Nazis to save Europe from barbarism." Men like Rommel, von Rundstedt, and von Manstein had to overcome not only their revulsion at the idea of assassination, but also the fact that they had taken an oath of personal loyalty to Hitler.

According to Speidel's memoir, Rommel, Stülpnagel, and von Rundstedt had agreed on a plan for armistice negotiations with Eisenhower and Montgomery. They would offer to evacuate German occupied areas in the west and withdraw all German forces behind the Siegfried Line in return for a cessation of the bombing of Germany and the beginning of peace negotiations. Allied radio stations would explain to the German people the military and political situation and the crimes of their leaders. On the Russian front, fighting would continue as necessary to hold a reduced front along the Vistula, the Carpathians, and down to the mouth of the Danube. Hitler would be arrested and tried, and a new government would be formed under Ludwig Beck and Goerdeler. This proposition didn't stand a chance of being considered let alone accepted but the fact that it was formulated by the commanding generals in France tells us something about their desperation and desire to get rid of Hitler.

If Washington had acted at any time on Eisenhower's April plea to clarify unconditional surrender, would the conspirators have acted earlier? Would the German generals in the west have come up with a more realistic proposal? If Eisenhower and Dulles had been allowed to encourage the plotters and soften up the German population, military and civilian, would the conspirators have gotten enough support in Berlin and the provinces to pull off the Valkyrie scheme? We don't know. We do know how close the conspirators came to pulling it off. Washington's failure to exploit this opportunity can be attributed to a political judgment that the Germans had to be brought to their knees in the field no matter what the cost, to Roosevelt's ''Dutch stubbornness,'' and to a reluctance to offend Russian sensitivity and take any chance that Russia would make a separate peace with the Germans. The Russians had no such hangups. Since early in 1943, General von Seydlitz and other generals taken on the Eastern Front, had formed ''The Free Germany Committee'' and had been signing proclamations that the Russians delivered to German troops. In January of 1944, officers in German uniform began infiltrating German lines to get letters from Seydlitz and his colleagues to German commanders still faithful to the Führer. These emissaries had been trained at a special Russian camp. Early in July when more than 20 divisions and 300,000 men were surrounded at Minsk, General Müller of the Twelfth Army Corps put out an order instructing his troops to stop the pointless bloodshed. He told them that the Russian command had promised to care for the wounded, to let officers retain their daggers, and to allow all ranks to keep their decorations. Later on, Müller and fifteen fellow generals of Army Group Center signed an attack on Hitler and appealed to officers of Army Group North to desert or disobey Hitler's orders.

After the bomb that was supposed to kill Hitler went off, von Stauffenberg, in the late afternoon of July 20, took over direction of the Home Army, proclaimed martial law, and sent out orders for the occupation of centers of communication, the relief of concentration camps, and the absorption of SS forces into the army and the arrest of local Nazi leaders.

A fierce battle was fought by teleprinter and telephone from Berlin to Prague, from Munich to Hamburg, from Vienna to Paris. The arrests ordered were carried out for a while in Munich and Vienna. In Hamburg, where the Gauleiter and the Army commander were friends, they sat together and joked about who would arrest whom as orders and counterorders arrived. In Berlin, Goebbels had been placed under arrest by an officer not in the conspiracy who was carrying out orders from Home Army headquarters. A telephone call from Hitler himself got the arresting officer to release Goebbels and turn his troops against the revolt. This enabled Goebbels to get out a 6:30 announcement that Hitler was still alive.

It was in France that the revolt came closest to succeeding. At La Roche-Guyon, Rommel's old headquarters on the Seine, von Kluge deliberated an hour and a half about responding to a telephone call from Beck urging support of the putsch. How would he proceed? The V-1 attacks could be stopped. He could order surrender to Montgomery or Eisenhower. At about 8 p.m. a teletype from Keitel came in saying that the Führer was still alive. von Kluge promptly dropped any idea of joining the coup attempt. Less than an hour away by car, in Paris, General Stülpnagel had acted on the teletype message von Stauffenberg had sent him from Home Army headquarters. By 10 p.m., 1200 members of the Sicherheitsdienst, the Nazi security outfit were under arrest in Paris. When von Kluge heard this, he stormed at Stülpnagel and advised him to get into civilian clothes and disappear. The statement attributed to von Kluge on that occasion—"If only the swine were dead"—is a fitting epitaph. Since a clandestine meeting with Goerdler at Smolensk in 1942, he had been on the fringes of the conspiracy, in sympathy with its aim but constantly changing his mind about active cooperation. At 10:30 p.m., Hitler was talking live on the radio, and within days both von Kluge and Stülpnagel were dead.

If the plot had succeeded, von Kluge as Commander in

Chief West was prepared to order immediate cessation of V-1 attacks on England and to establish contact with Allied field commanders to seek an armistice. Five days earlier, on July 15, Rommel had written Hitler that "the unequal struggle is nearing its end. . . . I must beg you to draw the proper conclusions without delay." Now, Rommel, shot from the air by a Spitfire while touring the front, lay unconscious in a Luftwaffe hospital at Bernay.

Donovan and Dulles had seen immediately the political implications of the failed putsch. Donovan in a memo to Roosevelt said: "a good deal of benefit to the Allied cause can result, as this attempt at revolt should help to undermine the will of the German Army to keep up the struggle. Obviously, an attempt is being made in Germany to play down the importance of those who were alleged to be in the plot, and therefore our tactics should be just the opposite. . . . This attempt to overthrow Hitler was largely engineered by men who desired a western orientation of German policy, even though apparently they received no encouragement from the West, and acted on their own initiative entirely. The next attempt to overthrow the Hitler regime from the inside is likely to come from an eastern-oriented group, possibly after a part of East Prussia is occupied and a German government à la Seydlitz is installed there. It is probable that the failure of Beck and his friends will still further increase the influence of Russia in Germany and somewhat decrease the influence of the West. Russia has throughout played a more realistic policy in dealing with the internal German situation than has either the United States or England, and it is possible that, from now on, the Seydlitz Committee will increase in importance amd have a larger scope of action. This is a development we should not underestimate, particularly now that the western-oriented dissident group in Germany, in and outside of the army, has received a serious, if not a fatal setback."

Two days later Dulles came up with specific proposals:

"Never during the course of this war has the Allied propaganda had such an opportunity to strike at the heart of

the Nazi war effort. In answer to the lies of the official German propaganda, it should be emphasized to the German people 1) that the attempted revolution was the first major attempt to overthrow the Hitler regime since its inception; 2) that a large number of leading generals and members of the General Staff, as well as many younger officers, were apparently back of the attempted plot; 3) that it is more than likely that the Chief of Staff of the German Army, Zeitzler, and others of this rank were involved because they were of the opinion that it was useless to continue the war and to sacrifice more German youth for a hopeless cause; 4) that a group of prominent civilian leaders were ready to take over the government after the military government had cleaned out the Nazis; 5) that the new government had intended to bring peace to the German people as quickly as possible; 6) that now the time had come for every German to do his share to overthrow the Nazis, to end the war, and to save for Germany whatever can be saved.

"A special broadcast might well be addressed to German soldiers and workers giving directions how each of them could contribute to peace by disobeying orders, staying away from work, returning home to their families, etc. So far, Russian propaganda has been particularly astute in making use of this opportunity. In this connection, the recent appeals of the committee, Freies Deutschland, to the German people, especially to the German soldiers and workers are outstanding examples. Up to now, we have had nothing as effective to offer."

Next day, Donovan sent these proposals to Roosevelt:

"A subtle, psychological approach may help the Anglo-American military forces. The following points might be suggested to high Wehrmacht circles:

(1) Unconditional surrender unalterably remains the Allied policy, but German military leaders must, in the

face of inevitable and rapidly approaching military defeat, consider the future of their country.

(2) In both the East and the West Germany faces the choice of making each German city an Aachen, Warsaw, or Budapest, or of facilitating the entry of Allied armies and the orderly transfer of authority to occupation forces under conditions which would spare unnecessary destruction, facilitate the distribution of food and raw materials and a resumption of economic life and make possible the orderly evacuation of prisoners and foreign workers.

(3) Wehrmacht officers who contribute to such a constructive policy, assuming they are not marked as war criminals, would be treated with consideration due their rank and according to the services which they render in the liquidation of the Nazi regime and the forces which have supported it."

While the Allies talked only of "unconditional surrender" and bombed the German people, the U.S.S.R. had no part in the bombing and sedulously refrained from joining the "unconditional surrender" policy. Germans captured by the Russians on the Eastern Front were sent back to Germany to spread the communist gospel. "Free Germany" committees began to form in secret on the Eastern Front and to a limited extent in Germany. On the Moscow radio, The Free Germany Committee broadcast: "The Soviet Union does not identify the German people with Hitler. Our new Germany will be sovereign and independent and free of control by other nations. Our aim is: A free Germany. A strong, powerful, democratic state which has nothing in common with the incompetence of the Weimar regime. A democracy which will suppress every attempt of a renewed conspiracy against the liberties of the people or the peace of Europe."

The Moscow radio gave a great deal of attention to the July 20th conspiracy, using captured General Walter von Seydlitz as head of the Association of German officers to call for renewed attempts for a Free Germany. Of this Allen Dulles said:

"And what came from Washington and London? The attempt on Hitler's life was dismissed as of no consequence. Churchill suggested that it was merely a case of dog-eat-dog."

A little encouragement to those Germans ready to risk their lives to free Germany of Hitler could have brought peace before the Russians had crossed the Vistula and before the western Allies had advanced beyond Normandy. This could have avoided many thousands and perhaps millions of casualties, in gas chambers as well as in battle, and could have saved the freedom of millions of people in Eastern Europe.

12.   On Patton's Flank

THE TROOPS in Normandy didn't have much time to think about the failure to seize the political advantages implicit in the July 20 plot. They still had to fight their way out of the German vise. No one fought with greater speed or more panache than General George S. Patton and his Third Army. That he could move so swiftly and so daringly was in no small part due to his refusal to worry about any German threat to his flanks—and to the protection his flanks were given by our resistance forces. The original Overlord plan had called for the Third Army to break out of Normandy and sweep into Brittany, whose ports—Brest, Lorient, St. Nazaire, Nantes, and St. Malo—were considered critical for supplying Allied troops on the Normandy beaches. But the original plan had to be shelved. The German defenses in Normandy proved too strong for any swift breakout. Meanwhile, the Breton maquis could not be kept down much longer. Stiffened German resistance in Normandy was bought at a price— stripping Brittany's defenses of seasoned German soldiers and making the maritime province an inviting target for the French resistance and its eager forces. For weeks we in London had been more concerned with holding down the profile of the local FFI than in harassing the Germans. If the policy of restraint worked anywhere—and God knows it did not work well—it succeeded in Brittany to the extent that the French did not soon challenge German power on the open field. But they did focus on transportation, cutting rail lines, blocking roads, and so on. Most of the troops Rommel brought into Normandy from his six Brittany divisions arrived on foot, cart, or bicycle, not by train or truck.

Resistance operations in Brittany after D-Day must rank among the most brilliant and successful of the war. Months earlier the Gestapo had liquidated most Allied "circuits" there. But the Bretons are a sturdy and fiercely independent people who had built up an active and well-organized resistance movement without much Allied help. What they needed from us that spring and summer were weapons, communications with the Allied Command, and officers able to dovetail their activities with Allied needs.

SHAEF had decided to hold back our OSS Jedburgh teams. With their operations in Normandy all but impossible because the Germans had cleared everybody out of the landing areas, Brittany became the most promising territory. Jedburghs could work with the resistance there to soften up the enemy and tie down or delay German troops.

On June 5, an advance unit of Jedburgh teams, a squad of radio operators, and the advance party of one of the two French parachute battalions attached to the British Special Air Services (SAS) landed northeast of Vannes. Their orders were simple: Make contact with the resistance and cut all communications between Brittany and the rest of France. They quickly set up two bases, one south of the Breton coast near Guingamp, called Samwest, the other further inland at Saint Marcel, dubbed Dingson. Two days later, on June 7, the SAS moved farther inland, dropping 18 separate parties of three to six men between St. Malo and Vannes. Trained rail cutters, they were to begin "disconnecting" rail communications. On June 9, the base camps were reinforced. A

Jedburgh team and 50 SAS troops were sent to each base. Commandant Bourgoin parachuted into Dingson to take command of all French resistance forces in Brittany and raise a full-scale revolt—to be unleashed at a time and under circumstances of London's choosing.

A day later we sent in another six Jedburgh teams to help organize pickups of arms drops and to shape the resistance. The Jedburghs arrived none too soon. Days later 2,000 maquisards had gathered at each of the two camps, clamoring for arms, ammunition, and uniforms, and, of course, attracting German attention. On June 18, the Wehrmacht moved in to crush the insurgents. But it was already too late for that. The Breton resistance fought its first pitched battle against the Germans at Saint Marcel, and fought all day long. By nightfall the resistance had learned that most basic of all guerrilla lessons: avoid open battle wherever possible, move in only to support regular troops when they arrive, disperse when combat is unavoidable. The Breton resistance dispersed. That it could do so without being chopped to pieces, as other FFI forces had been earlier in the war, was a tribute to German uncertainty and weakness, to the growing strength and self-confidence of the indigenous Breton soldiers, and to the efforts of the SAS and the Jedburghs. More important, perhaps, the battle was a major contribution to slowing the flow of German soldiers from Brittany into Normandy. And, indeed, all through June the Germans had to fight their way out of Brittany to reach the front.

By then we had eight Jedburgh teams operating in Brittany who had quickly established contact with resistance leaders. They reported that 31,500 Bretons had been mobilized, but that fewer than half of them were armed. Most of the men and guns were on the south side of the Breton peninsula in Morbihan where 9,000 men had gathered, 7,000 of them with guns. Another force of 10,000 men had been mobilized in the Finistèrre Department at the tip of the Breton peninsula near Brest, but only 3,500 of them were adequately equipped. Clearly, getting the men of Brittany—and those waiting in other parts of France—properly armed and equipped had to receive top priority. It did. On July 1, SHAEF set a target date for arming 30,000 Breton resistants—August 5. That meant getting more Jedburghs into Brittany and more sorties flown over it. During the first half of July we managed to stuff another ten Jedburgh teams onto the peninsula. Their tasks were detailed and varied: They were to select possible landing grounds, explore the possibility of sea operations, pick a "free dropping zone" where aircraft could unload supplies, organize groups of 2,000 men into units of 100 each, and, finally, make sure the FFI avoided offensive action until the signal was given. Bringing in the needed arms was tougher. We flew all the sorties we could manage, but their number was restricted. Montgomery had put a limit on supply flights in order to veil our Brittany intentions a little, and not make them too obvious to the Germans. As a result, 13,000 Bretons were still unarmed by August 1.

All during July we kept in constant radio communication with Brittany. On July 12, we stressed the need for secrecy in the arming of FFI troops. On July 17, we reiterated the necessity for keeping guerrilla action in check. It was "no go" until we said so. Meanwhile, the resistance should cut cable and railroad lines. We radioed a list of rail and telephone links that were to get top priority. On July 28 and July 30, London radioed two more warnings against any premature uprising. Large-scale action was to be avoided until the agreed upon message for "D-Day Brittany" had gone out over the BBC.

The situation outside Brittany was much harder to control, as we have seen already. FFI units were ready to rise, fight the Germans, and protect the advancing Allied flanks. As early as June 20 Churchill had started that ball rolling—and precipitated hurried conferences and demands for more information from both SHAEF and Special Forces HQ—with his trenchant minute to the Minister of Economic Warfare:

> *"The Maquis has started open guerrilla warfare and is in temporary control of certain areas of southern France. The Germans are reacting strongly with fully armed troops. Every effort must be made to supply the Maquis at once with rifles, Bren guns, Piat guns, mortars and bazookas*

*with ammunition, and whatever else is needful to prevent
the collapse of the Movement and to extend it. What is
being done about this? Have you any difficulty in getting
men to repack containers with the right sort of weapons?
Could General Wilson help from North Africa? Pray tell
me if I can help you to accelerate action."*

(Initialled) W.S.C.

Those initials had a special magic. They got immediate action. Churchill's personal confidant on matters involving liaison, intelligence, resistance and the French, Major Morton, went at once to see Ike's chief of staff, Bedell Smith, and Major General Harold R. Bull—as G-3, the head of operations. On Wednesday, June 21, 1944, Morton summed up the results of his conversations with the Americans in a memo to Churchill. Bedell Smith, he reported, "will do everything he can to prevent the Maquis in south-eastern France from being destroyed in detail by the German Armed Forces. A daylight sortie of 300 American bombers escorted by fighters will try to drop arms and other necessities to the Eastern Maquis tomorrow, 22nd June."

But Morton added one note of caution:

*"General Bedell Smith does not believe that under present
conditions the Maquis could coalesce rapidly to control a
large part of the country. If and when ANVIL [the proposed
landings in the south of France carried out in August] takes
place the situation will change. At least the Maquis will be
very useful and must be kept going for that purpose. At
best their contribution might be of high importance. The
more arms the Maquis is given now, above the level necessary to maintain resistance and morale, the more unarmed Frenchmen will join them. This will entail a demand
for an even greater effort to arm and feed them. Such a
continued process would rapidly result in an unjustifiable
dispersion of effort from the main battle."*

On the same day, June 21, Lord Selborne, charged with ministerial responsibility for Special Operations Executive (SOE) sent a detailed reply to Churchill's memo of the day before. Some 33,000 maquis had been mobilized in areas outside Brittany, but only 13,000 were armed, even though we had dropped enough weapons to equip 100,000 men. The trouble was drops had been made in other parts of France or the Germans had snatched the supplies.

Selborne urged Churchill to arm and equip the 20,000 waiting FFI as quickly as possible:

> *"To meet this commitment we have been promised by SHAEF for Thursday, 22nd June, or as soon as possible thereafter not less than 180 American heavy bombers with fighter escort to drop arms and ammunition to those areas where the need is greatest. This will arm some 10,000 more men and provide about 2.5 million rounds of Bren and Sten ammunition. The new arms will consist mainly of Brens, rifles, and some Bazookas. This help is urgently required since these bands may be forced to disperse unless we can support them soon. We are hopeful that this operation will result in such a strengthening of resistance in these areas that they will be able to withstand any but a major enemy attempt to liquidate them. This is unlikely at present."*

Morton's estimate of 300 planes the next day proved too optimistic. Lord Selborne's figures were more accurate. On June 25, at four in the morning, 180 B-17s took off with fighter escort to drop supplies to the target areas, already the scene of heavy fighting between the Germans and poorly armed FFI forces. Flak downed one bomber, a German fighter another, two more planes ran into engine trouble and had to turn back. The rest dropped more than 2,000 containers to the resistance forces. Dubbed Operation Cadillac, it was the first daylight mission, precursor of many more to come. In the short June nights, we could not afford the cover of darkness and had to risk flying during the day.

The need was clearly urgent. In central France west of the Rhône, heavy fighting had raged since D-Day. Southeast of Limoges a maquis uprising had stopped enemy traffic cold immediately after D-Day. But the FFI could not keep up the pressure. Its supplies were soon exhausted. In the Vercors, as we have noted, the entire population was embattled. Strong FFI units had proved very effective in disrupting traffic southeast of Dijon. In the Ain, west of Geneva, and in the Haute-Savoie to the south, large areas had been liberated by mid-June. But weakened FFI troops now faced powerful German counterattacks.

Less than three weeks later, on Bastille Day, July 14, General Doolittle mounted an even more ambitious air-drop operation. An awesome armada of nine wings—349 planes carrying supplies and escorted by 524 P-51 and P-47 fighters—took off from nine airfields. Two wings headed for the embattled Vecors plateau and dropped close to a thousand containers crammed with guns, ammunition, and supplies. A third wing flew southwest of Chalon-sur-Saône to deliver over 400 containers. The remaining six wings dropped 2,500 containers to resistance forces in Corrèze, the Cantal, Lot, and Haute-Vienne.

On August 1, the B-17's took off again, five wings of 36 planes each to parachute supplies to five targets. One wing returned to the Chalon-sur-Saône area to resupply the FFI which had used the equipment dropped earlier to good effect. They had cleared out the Germans from a strategic area commanding communication lines running north and south between Lyon and Dijon and east and west between Nevers and Geneva. Other wings flew west and south of Geneva and into the Haute-Savoie.

American daylight sorties flown from England, however, were only one part of the massive Allied effort to keep French resistance forces armed and supplied. From June until the Anvil landings in mid-August, the RAF flew a steady stream of equipment in from England, as did other Allied planes based in North Africa. Together, they brought in another 4,000 tons in a six-week span.

Direct OSS involvement in Patton's planning went back to early June, the week before D-Day. Two OSS detachments were assigned to General Patton's headquarters at Huntsford, England. One OSS group supervised resistance operations in France and the other coordinated OSS intelligence activities with the intelligence activities of the Third Army. A New York architect named Robert I. Powell, affectionally known as Rip, commanded the resistance staff with the rank of Lt. Colonel. He worked closely with operations, G-3. Major Edward Haskell headed the OSS intelligence unit and reported to Patton's G-2, the hard-driving and scholarly Colonel Koch. Both OSS detachments had kept close tabs on resistance activities and brought detailed information about FFI units, their leaders, strength, location, arms code names, signal plans, and communications facilities. OSS officers labored long and hard to keep that data as current as possible.

Powell and Haskell brought their detachments to France the week after SHAEF established the August 5 target date for arming the Breton FFI. OSS operational headquarters were set up with Patton at Néhou on the Cherbourg peninsula in Normandy. Powell had followed Brittany developments closely from the beginning and he quickly realized that the greatest contribution the OSS could make to Patton's planned sweep was to convince Koch and his boss that the Breton FFI was tough, resourceful, and reliable.

How well he succeeded became apparent toward the end of July when General Koenig visited Patton's headquarters. He wanted to discuss final arrangements for calling out the Breton resistance when Patton turned the corner into Brittany. During the talks Koch pointed out that while keeping their 15th Army intact east of the Seine, the Germans had been draining Brittany of their mobile forces. The Germans had drained their garrison to a crust of two divisions and immobilized elements of three others. Given the spirit and strength of the Breton FFI and the arms that had been flown to them in recent weeks, it now seemed feasible to overrun Brittany much faster and with fewer Allied regular forces than anyone had believed possible. In fact, Koch suggested it could be done in ten days with two tank and two infantry divisions.

Back in London, a Brittany War Room was set up at Etat-Majeur des Forces Françaises de l'Intériur (EMFFI) headquarters on Portland Square. Three messages were drafted for broadcast over the BBC to each of the five departments in Brittany. One would signal "go" for guerrilla warfare, a second would signal for sabotage action against industrial targets, and a third would call for "interdiction" of rails, roads, and telecommunications. Soon after Koenig's visit, Rip Powell showed up in London to lay out Patton's needs and expectations for the Brittany campaign. He stayed for several days to help work out instructions for our field teams behind enemy lines before returning to his Special Forces detachment in France. By August 2, all the preparations for calling out the FFI to engage in guerrilla activities—but not all-out warfare—were completed. Messages made that point to all those in Brittany in radio contact with London. We also needed volunteers able to pass through enemy lines with tactical information, and familiar enough with the local terrain to act as guides for advancing Allied soldiers. In asking our people in Brittany to find such agents we were specific as to what we wanted from them: data on fortifications, troop and armor concentrations, artillery and automatic weapons emplacements, oil and munitions dumps, command posts, identification of enemy units, and the location of the most promising targets for air attack.

With American armor rolling·swiftly toward Dinan, EMFFI decided to beef up its own forces in Brittany—as distinct from the indigenous resistance—by sending in more men from England. Several Special Air Service Units and an OSS Operational Group were selected. Their mission was two-fold: to help in keeping reins on the local FFI and to protect essential public works and strategic lines of communications we would need after clearing the Germans out. Plans called for sending a squadron from the 3rd SAS Parachute Battalion east of Brest to hamper enemy movement along the roads around the port and eventually inside the port. Also, the squadron was to guard the Morlaix trestle and the Plougastel-Daoulas viaduct against German efforts to blow them up. A squadron from the 2nd SAS regiment was to go southeast of Redon and block German forces moving up from the St. Nazaire and Nantes area, as well as protect the electric installations at Pontchâteau. Finally, a French Operational Group, trained by the OSS and attached to us, was to prevent destruction of a trestle east of Guimiliau.

On the night of August 3, General Koenig's Brittany War Room on Portland Square became the most crowded place in London, as we gathered round to listen to the BBC messages calling for general guerrilla action in all five Breton departments. Koenig had already put together a staff to direct FFI operations in Brittany and had sent them off. Colonel Eon, a battle-tested regular in the French army and chief of the FFI for Brittany, was in command of this 25-man team. Colonel Passy, tired of his desk duties and again longing for action, became Eon's chief of staff and went out to direct the battle in the territory he had organized. Eon, Passy, and their people, dropped in central Brittany near Guingamp and were met by members of the Jedburgh team "Frederick." A vast communications network was quickly established with direct links from Colonel Eon's HQ to Patton's, to London, and to the resistance leaders in all five departments. The FFI mission in Brittany had been firmed up the previous week. It included seizing and holding the high ground north of Vannes and protecting the railroad from Brest along the north coast of the peninsula, as well as more general assignments, such as providing guides and information, intensifying guerrilla activities, protecting communications lines from German attack, and containing or mopping up enemy groups.

The high ground north of Vannes was captured the day the message went out. Six thousand FFI resistants stormed onto it. At the same time, Rennes, 60 miles southwest of Avranches, was captured. Throughout Brittany a force of 20,000 armed men was ready for action, while tens of thousands of others provided invaluable intelligence, cleared highways and byways, and guided our troops.

Passy was tremendous. He would gather all maquis leaders together as he traveled from area to area and with his great prestige among them and the detailed knowledge acquired in four years of hovering over maps and messages, he laid out with the greatest precision and clarity the assigned task of each maquis group. Around Tréguier and Paimpol there were 2,500 Germans. Patton's Task Force A took Tréguier and the FFI moved in to to hold it. Patton's unit moved on to take Lézardrieux and Passy moved an FFI force to take Paimpol.

Major John Rees, the ranking American with the Aloes mission, brought back a report that squares with my impression of the Passy I knew in London:

> *Above all he was a Frenchman and anything he might do that could be of benefit to France he did. *** Never once did he depart from this military mission and any question of politics that arose he always replied that he was there in a strictly military role and that any political differences would just have to be straightened out later and that the job for the Frenchmen to do, primarily, was to help the Allies liberate France. At all times he was absolutely tireless; there were many times when he went without sleep for two and three days straight. As far as personal courage goes he was above reproach and he never asked any member of his staff to do any job that he would not have cheerfully undertaken himself.*

By August 5, the FFI had liberated Vannes and St. Brieuc on opposite coasts of the Peninsula. French volunteers streamed through porous German lines to brief advancing American units about enemy troop concentrations and fortifications. FFI units took up their role as "flankers" for the Americans, while at the same time guarding the rail lines. They also protected roads and bridges between St. Brieuc and Morlaix. The stone viaduct at Morlaix was held by Bernard Knox's Jedburgh team Giles, beefed up by 100 SAS troops. Brittany was liberated in less than a week. German forces unable to escape, holed up in the port cities of St. Malo, Lorient, St. Nazaire, and Brest. We could afford to do without them now.

Plans were being developed in London to prepare for the post-Brittany sweep across France and for the role other French resistance forces would play in that drive.

The arming of the resistance in central France, it turned out, was split-timed with Patton's advance. As he paced impatiently about his headquarters near Cherbourg, Patton had taken occasion to make it clear to David Brech and Rip Powell, and to General Koenig on his visit to France, that he had his eyes on Metz, that he intended to go to the east as far and as fast as he could, and expected the tactical air squadrons and resistance forces to cover his open flank to the south.

On August 8, as Patton swung his Third Army eastward beyond Avranches, Rip Powell was told to organize resistance forces along the way into a screen to protect the advancing Americans' right flank. Strong German formations remained in the south. It was up to the FFI to slow their movements in combat and to keep regular Allied forces informed in detail about all enemy movements. Powell and the FFI had drawn a rough assignment. Patton moved so fast he was hard to keep up with. Already his armor pointed toward Angers and on to Orléans. For us that meant inserting Jedburghs and flying supply sorties just ahead of the Third Army to reception points near Patton's rapidly extending right flank. Six Jedburgh teams were dropped along the Loire to help organize and direct local resistants. Others were redeployed.

Delaying the Wehrmacht, however, was only one of the tasks assigned to the FFI flankers. They were to mop up cut-off or isolated German units so that Patton need not bleed his own troops for that task. They were to cut every kind of communications—road, rail, cable, telephone—provide intelligence, and, perhaps most important and most difficult, preserve bridges and other vital installations for later Allied use. As August wore on, there was no holding back the French forces. They occupied lightly garrisoned towns or teamed with Third Army units in doing so. FFI troops helped the 4th armored division capture Chateaudun near Chartres, and by themselves liberated Blois and five towns in the Orne; 1,000 prisoners were taken during those operations.

On August 16, we learned that the FFI had proclaimed "general warfare" from the Eure department southeast of Le Havre down to the Cher river south of the Loire. German losses were reported as heavy. In order to facilitate battlefield coordination, resistance leaders from the area of Patton's advance came to a meeting in Rennes and later to one in Orléans. As a result, the FFI screening operation became more formalized. First 3,400 men guarded the Nantes-Angers line. As Patton's drive picked up speed across France's midsection the screen was strengthened, totalling 6,000 men by the time the Third Army hit Tours. It was double that when the flank stretched to Bourges, about halfway across France and the point where Patton wheeled his armor hard left to drive north. The day Paris fell, the Third Army was in Troyes, southeast of the capital. The FFI screen was coalescing into a force of 25,000 FFI troops, made up of eighteen different resistance groups, defending Patton's southern flank.

Casey at the Research Institute of America

Casey in uniform, with his daughter, Bernadette,
and his wife, Sophia

Casey in England

Casey being awarded the bronze star by Admiral Harold R. Stark

Field Marshall Bernard L. Montgomery and
General Dwight D. Eisenhower in Normandy, July 26, 1944

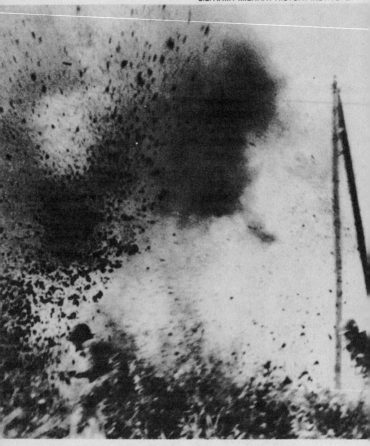

American paratroopers dash through a field amid bursting
German artillery fire at Arnhem, October 9, 1944

Lt. General Omar N. Bradley, General Dwight D. Eisenhower, and
Lt. General George S. Patton in Belgium, February 5, 1945

Casey standing in front of a picture of William J. Donovan at a dinner honoring veterans of the OSS in San Francisco, 1982

13. Dragoon

IN THE SECOND week of August, I was ordered to go to Algiers to exchange briefings with OSS officers attached to General Patch's Seventh Army that would be invading Southern France. From there I was to go to OSS headquarters in Italy and then join Ed Gamble's OSS detachment as it moved north from its landing area on the Riviera.

The liberation of southern France was like one of those swashbuckling movies of the 1930's—the kind Douglas Fairbanks used to make. Only this time it was for real and the only movie-like thing in it was Douglas Fairbanks, Jr. He wore the uniform of a Lt. Commander in the U.S. Navy, as he stood on the prow of a fast PT boat slicing through the waves of the Mediterranean off the coast of San Remo. Two British gunboats steamed on either side of Fairbanks' and several other American boats. It was the night of August 14, 1944. On the coast, guns barked out to sea. Telephones jangled in various Wehrmacht headquarters. It was a part of John Bevan's deception scenario for the landings in southern

France. So also was an air attack far to the west over Marseilles. It was impossible to conceal from the Germans a flotilla of 1200 ships converging from southern Italy, North Africa, and Corsica; but it was possible to deceive them as to where it would strike.

Around 2:00 a.m., five Dakotas swept across the port city and dumped 60 rubber dummies out the tail gates. Parachutes opened automatically. When they hit the ground at La Ciotat, 18 miles east of Marseilles, the sound of gunfire crackled through the night. German troops grabbed their gear and ran for the beaches to beat back the expected invasion. A short while later, several C-47 transport planes flew near the shore further to the east and dropped a small hailstorm of wide tinfoil strips. Germans manning radar screens saw a phantom air fleet approach. At the same time, Lt. Buckley, who had taken MacArthur off Corregidor and won fame as a PT boat commander in the Pacific, led a small group of PT boats in a dash to shore in a mission similar to Fairbanks': He was to trick the Germans into believing he headed an invasion fleet. On radars not knocked out by earlier bombing, his flotilla registered strongly enough for the Germans to report all over southern France that the Allies were attempting a massive landing east of Marseilles.

In fact, the real invasion fleet had been steaming on a course to Genoa for several days. The first ships had left Italian ports as early as August 10. In the following days others sailed out of Algiers and Corsica. On the night of the 14th, some 1,200 ships loaded to the gunwales with 200,000 troops and supplies had veered west of Genoa and approached a strip of French coastline barely 40 miles long. Six assault divisions were to land at nine points between Cavalaire-sur-Mer, 30 miles east of Toulon, and Agay, 8 miles east of St. Raphael at the western tip of the French Riviera.

The armada nearing the beaches was one of the best-briefed attack forces of the war. Intelligence had been meticulous, down to the location and condition of every last pillbox or pylon, and more than half of it had been gathered by OSS agents operating in southern France. Yet the invasion very nearly did not come off.

Churchill never liked the idea and opposed an invasion of the south when it was first broached at the big three conference in Teheran in 1943. He wanted to strike much further to the east—through the Balkans and into Austria. Politically that was sound. It would have kept the Russians from "liberating" eastern and half of central Europe. Certainly the iron curtain would not have dropped in the middle of Germany. Strategically the British favored dispersing the enemy and forcing him to spread his power thinly. The American approach was to pour maximum strength into France and crush the Germans there. Moreover, General Marshall, the U.S. chief of staff, was adamant about Marseilles. He wanted to capture the port and use it as a troop and supply funnel into France. Understandably, the Russians, for their own political needs, backed the Americans, who won the day at Teheran. The Allies would make two landings in France about the same time, one across the English Channel, the other on the Riviera beaches.

But the British were not convinced yet. Montgomery insisted on expanding the scope of the Normandy invasion. To do this, he needed more landing craft, which made the southern operation, then codenamed Anvil, impossible. Anvil, therefore, had to be postponed. And during the postponement debate flared anew about doing it at all. Disagreement continued up to a week before the invasion as thousands of American and French soldiers began to board ships. Churchill pleaded with both Eisenhower and Roosevelt to scrap it. The British Joint Chiefs even radioed General Maitland "Jumbo" Wilson, Supreme Allied Commander, Mediterranean Theatre of Operations, to ready a sudden shift of the invasion force to Cherbourg, Brest, and other Breton ports.

Churchill lost the decision but never his distaste. It found expression in his selection of code names, a prerogative Churchill lovingly reserved for himself and usually exercised with care. But sometimes he seemed to reveal too much. The attack on southern France was first named Anvil for the hammer of Overlord to beat against. When security reasons dictated a change of name, it was called Dragoon, and Churchill would say that he had been dragooned into Dragoon.

But British opposition had not hampered the gathering of intelligence from southern France, nor delayed the organization of resistance forces to help the invasion armies once they had landed. It did, however, throw a proportionately larger share of the task our way so that intelligence for Dragoon became more of an independent, or at least semi-independent, OSS operation than any other so far. This was largely due to Henry Hyde's activities out of the OSS post in Algiers.

Complementing Hyde's Algerian effort was Gregory Thomas's operation in Spain. Thomas was OSS chief for the whole Iberian peninsula and he had assigned Frank Schoonmaker the task of organizing a Spain-based French mission. Schoonmaker began to put agents across the border from Bilbao and Barcelona and with them to build intelligence chains in central and southern France. By October 1943 he had ten such chains active, all of them producing important and reliable intelligence. Six months later, in May 1944, there were 15 chains with 1,400 agents churning out much of the raw strategic intelligence pouring into Allied Forces Headquarters from France.

But since Schoonmaker worked in the relatively hostile environment of Franco's Spain and began later than Hyde, his intelligence was never as good or as timely. For the most part the "Spanish" recruits were Frenchmen who had escaped across the Pyrenees and were anxious to join the Allied cause. To facilitate their return to France, Schoonmaker had set up a forging operation in Barcelona to turn out needed credentials. The OSS did not have any radio facilities in Spain, so communications proved a major problem. It was inadequately resolved through personal contacts, mail, letter-drops, and couriers traveling back and forth between France and Spain. The role of these couriers grew more important as the invasion neared and the nature of the desired intelligence changed. Through 1943, most reports sent to Algiers from southern France were of a general strategic nature: the location of airfields in the Lyon-Clermont-Ferrand-Avignon triangle, the condition of the Rhône bridges, the construction of submarine pens at Bordeaux, the capacity of railroad repair shops, the bombing damage done rail yards, etc. But as the Germans strengthened their Mediterranean fortifications, greater detail was needed about such items as camouflaged artillery emplacements, pillboxes, casements, anti-tank walls, and underwater obstacles like mines and blockships. A rapidly expanding Allied intelligence network was able to report accurately on these enemy installations and to accompany the reports with appropriate drawings.

Clearly, drawings could not be radioed to Algiers but had to be taken out by pouch. From the south that meant taking them across the mountains into Spain. The material itself was crucial: scaled drawings, sketches, and map overlays provided details not visible from the air and made it easy to distinguish fake from real defense installations.

In the spring of 1944, the Gestapo began to close off the Pyrenees. Border crossings became more difficult and more hazardous, though, of course, they still had to be made. It was decided, therefore, that intelligence circuits operating under OSS Spain's direction had to be equipped with radios and transmit as much intelligence as they could directly to Algiers where in the spring and summer most of the planning for Anvil-Dragoon was carried out. Radio operators were dropped to the ''Spanish'' chains during the moon periods of May, June, and July. By D-Day, August 15, 1944, four radio circuits were operating on a daily schedule to Algiers.

Allen Dulles's operation in Berne was a third source of intelligence on the south of France. Dulles had set up his own networks inside France, pushing them down through the Alps of the Haute-Savoie to the coast and further to the east, much to the chagrin of MI-6. Initially, Dulles's agents focused on political information. But by early 1944 that focus had shifted and about half the intelligence coming from Berne was about military affairs, specifically the enemy order of battle. The information was radioed both to London and Algiers and often supplemented what we had learned from other sources.

It was clear by the spring of 1944 that the strongest FFI formations were active in the area of the Anvil-Dragoon mission: the mountains of southeastern France and the Massif Central. From there the resistance threatened major rail and road links between the 1st and 19th German armies, and the supply routes from Germany to southern France that ran from the Saar through Burgundy to the sea. Give the resistance arms and equipment, we argued, and the FFI might well take virtual control of all southern France. And if the FFI couldn't achieve quite that much, it would at least threaten enemy communications in the Dragoon target area and protect the Allied flank in the then projected drive up the Rhône valley. The argument was persuasive enough for the American and British air forces to fly deep penetration supply missions and to fly them, as we have seen, during the risky daylight.

By early August the French and German assessments of the situation in the south coincided. General Blaskowitz, in command of the German Army Group G, reported to Berlin that resistance forces had grown from guerrilla bands into an organized army at his back. Moreover, it was an army too strong for his forces to destroy and at the same time hold coastal defenses. Blaskowitz thus conceded that his lines of communication were vulnerable at all times, both the lines up the Rhône valley into Germany and across the Carcassonne gap running between the Bordeaux area and the Mediterranean beyond Toulouse and linking up the German 1st and 19th armies. True, the Wehrmacht could still defeat the FFI in pitched battle, but it no longer controlled its own communications. German units no longer dared go far from their garrisons. The FFI ruled during the night and much of the day.

In the last week of July, Henri Zeller, the FFI commander for southeastern France, flew to Algiers to report the de facto FFI occupation of the south. Most of the smaller German garrisons, he said, were ready to surrender to the first Allied uniforms they saw. Larger units equipped with tanks and artillery could still carry out terrible reprisals, but had to huddle in their quarters at night. No isolated German car was safe on a southern road. Few truck convoys made it from one place to another intact. Every second one could count on being attacked.

De Gaulle, still in Algiers, was impressed. He gave Zeller the Anvil-Dragoon plan—the French were privy to this invasion secret—and asked him to study it. Zeller was appalled at the slow pace of the contemplated attack. Grenoble could be reached much more quickly than 90 days after the invasion. And if it was not, the resistance, already over-exposed in many places, might well face annihilation. French control of mountain ranges allowed much faster Allied progress. De Gaulle promptly dispatched Zeller to Naples where General Alexander Patch had established 7th Army headquarters prior to the invasion.

Patch, like other American generals from Marshall on down, had his eye on Marseilles. He and his staff wanted to go ashore at Sète, west of Marseilles, because its beaches were perfect for a landing. From there, Patch hoped to drive the 7th Army up the Rhône, cut off Marseilles and at the same time threaten Toulouse and Bordeaux further inland. But Sète was out on a spit of land with a sea inlet behind it that would have made progress difficult if not impossible. And Sète's port facilities were too meager to handle the needs of so large an invasion force. With that plan scotched, Patch selected landing sites between Toulon and St. Raphaël, with most of the troops going ashore near St. Raphaël. But he still hoped to wheel west and take Toulon and Marseilles, secure his right flank on the Var river near Nice, and only then drive up the Rhône toward Lyon and Vichy. Estimates of German resistance and of logistical problems in supporting so large a force from offshore, before the port facilities of Toulon became available, led Patch to the conclusion that he would need two months before starting to drive north up the Rhône— and another 30 days after that before he could reach Lyon and Grenoble.

When Zeller arrived in Naples he urged Patch to tear up his timetable and write a faster one. The FFI controlled all roads and had the Germans bottled up in their garrisons east of the Rhône valley. Light columns, Zeller argued, could streak up the "Route Napoléon"—the road Napoleon had taken to Paris on his return from Elba in 1815—and make it to Grenoble in 48 hours, to Lyon in four days. A force of 1,500 to 2,000 men supported by armored cars and cannon would draw enough FFI support as it streaked up the Route

Napoléon from a baseline between Aix en Provence and Le Muy just north of St. Raphaël to seize Digne, Sisteron, Gap, and other mountain towns to Grenoble and beyond. The thought was not new. Zeller had urged it in a cable to London on July 18: "Success of landing is certain if made in general direction of Route Napoleon with Main effort on Grenoble." With his armada about to sail, Patch remained noncommittal, but Zeller's advice would prove sound and prophetic after our landings.

Meanwhile, the invasion stood before us. Even as the ships were at sea the pace of intelligence operations was stepped up. Right up to the landings, information was radioed to General Patch's command ship where Colonel Quinn and his G-2 staff pored over the messages and fitted them into the mass of details they already had. Each unit commander had a set of maps with artillery positions, machine gun nests, bunkers, pillboxes, and mine fields marked, and those roads that could carry jeeps and two-and-a-half-ton trucks and tanks were also identified. The communications system we had set up was ingenious. A "blind" network had begun to broadcast weeks earlier to cover the heavy increase of radio traffic during the landings. From July 13 to August 9, dummy broadcast circuits operated 24 hours a day. For the next six days, August 10 to 15, actual traffic was inserted into the continuous stream of dummy messages. That allowed Patch to relay urgent queries quickly to agents in critical areas and to receive answers just as speedily.

Among them was the answer to a special request radioed just 36 hours before the invasion: a quick check on antiparachute pickets at Le Muy, the main area where American parachute and glider troops were scheduled to land. We had known for more than two weeks that the Germans were sinking large stakes connected by barbed wire at 5-foot intervals in open spaces suitable for such landings. At the same time we learned that the agent sent by Special Projects Operation Center to prepare the reception for the airborne forces had been captured by the Gestapo. Those twin events had triggered the hasty departure of a paratroop officer fluent in French, Geoffrey Jones, for the Le Muy area where he was to clear dropping grounds for General Robert Frederick and his First Airborne Task Force of 10,000 men. Frederick was to block all roads leading to the beachhead and to attack the defenses of Fréjus, adjacent to St. Raphaël.

Now, in response to the request from Patch's command ship, one of Hyde's agents went on a bicycle tour of the target area. He bicycled from Cannes to Hyères, a grueling 60 miles, and then cabled Algiers the latest information about defense emplacements, the calibers of their guns, the coordinates marking their position, and whether they were occupied or dummies. The information was promptly radioed to Patch.

The next afternoon, Jones heard the BBC broadcast signalling that the invasion was set for the next morning, August 15th. He had the resistance groups spring into action. They worked all night to dismantle pylons and other obstacles on the landing grounds. French gendarmes protected them from the Germans by pretending that the resistants were their prisoners. The FFI was thus able to travel safely to different sections of the target area. Early on the morning of the 15th, Jones took a small group of maquis to Fayence where they destroyed a key German radar station, helping assure complete surprise for the airborne landings. Later on the 15th, he took five gendarmes through German lines to brief General Frederick—whose airborne attack had been a smashing success—on German strength, the conditions of roads and bridges, the location of electric power lines, and other field data.

The landings themselves had gone well. The first airborne troops hit the ground at 2:15 A.M. The second wave followed at 4:15. Shells and bombs plastered the target beaches beginning at 7:10, and by 8 o'clock the first troop-laden landing craft crunched into the sand. Much of the credit had to go to intelligence for making this the best-briefed invasion of the war. As Bill Quinn, Patch's G-2, reported afterwards: "D-Day dispositions (of German troops) confirmed advance information in every particular." And Patch himself praised the "extraordinary accuracy" of data OSS agents had submitted. A G-2 memorandum went further: "Intelligence provided for operation DRAGOON (ANVIL) was probably the fullest and most detailed of any provided in a series of combined operations commencing with TORCH. . . ."

Events now overtook Patch's original plans for a cautious, careful campaign to conquer southern France. Time frames began to speed up and on occasion our advance resembled a blur. Patch had intended to send General de Lattre de Tassigny's First French Army slugging toward Toulon and Marseilles. General Truscott's 6th Corps—the 3rd, 36th, and 45th divisions—was to protect the French right flank and hold off German reinforcements trying to reach the beachhead. General Frederick's airborne troops were to move east down the Riviera to guard Patch's forces against a German counterattack from Italy, a real possibility. Plans called for Toulon to fall by D plus 20, Marseilles by D plus 40 to 45. Then de Lattre and Truscott would wheel north and drive up the Rhône valley where the main German forces were concentrated.

Within 72 hours of the landing, the plan was outdated. Frederick's airborne troops spread out quickly across a wide area and hit all the strategic spots doing it. By August 18, his men had captured the pivotal Le Muy and spun a protective sceen above the beachhead. Other units had probed north as far as Draguignan and captured the German LXII Corps headquarters and its commander, General Ferdinand Neuling.

Geoffrey Jones got some of his men into Nice where they ambushed a German command car and brought back a bloodied knapsack full of papers. When Jones and his make-shift staff sifted through them, they found maps and plans outlining a German withdrawal to fortified positions on the Italian border, and field orders for the next four days to carry them out. It was a coup that allowed Allied forces to operate with much greater certainty. Patch could follow up his advantages north and west, and Frederick could pursue the retreating Germans east toward Italy. As Frederick did, it was easy to deceive the enemy into thinking that backup Allied troops landing on Riviera beaches were headed for Italy.

General Truscott sensed the expansion of his own mission

and moved swiftly to exploit the opportunity. He put together a mobile striking force under the command of his deputy, General Butler. "Task Force Butler" included tank, cavalry, infantry, and artillery battalions, and a company each of tank destroyers and engineers. Butler assembled his forces at Le Muy on August 17. The next morning he struck out for Sisteron, 65 miles northwest. On August 19, Troop B of the 117th Cavalry joined forces with an FFI battalion, and, aided by a few tanks and U.S. infantry units, captured a force of 600 Germans on the road to Sisteron. As the day waned Troop A of the 117th pushed into town unopposed. Within 36 hours the Allies had raced halfway to Grenoble, the plus 90 objective. It was a dramatic clincher to the case Zeller had made to Patch in August. The Americans were quick to pay Zeller his due. On the night Sisteron fell, SPOC fired off a cable telling Zeller his "Plan Faisceau" was in operation. As a gracious gesture, Patch had named his speeded up plan after one of Zeller's code names. More importantly, to help his force move as quickly as events dictated, Patch asked Zeller's help: "Please have the FFI block enemy movements to the south of Lyon and harrass the enemy retreat on all routes during the night. Major air support will be given the operation during the day. Faisceau's representatives must make contact as early as possible with Allied columns and provide them with guides."

General Butler arrived in Sisteron some hours after Troop A and set up his headquarters. A cup of scalding coffee in one hand, a cigarette in the other, Butler stood poring over detailed maps of the French mountains that lay ahead of his men. He wondered how strong German formations were along the winding roads that ran alongside the Route Napoléon itself—the Route Nationale No. 85—when a young British officer importuned to see him. Butler wasn't interested, but when his visitor insisted, he curtly asked him who he was and what he wanted. His name, the man replied, was Francis Cammaerts, and he could tell the general the number and location of FFI units in the mountains up ahead who were eager to help his advance. Cammaerts could contact them by radio and courier and they would act on the general's instruc-

tions. Butler didn't take his eyes off the maps. He said he
wasn't interested in private armies. He had a battle to direct.
Cammaerts was dismissed and left. Cammaerts was stunned,
and so were some of Butler's staff. This was not the reception
he had deserved or expected. He was urged to go and see
General Patch. Perhaps someone on his staff would remember who Francis Cammaerts was, and be interested in how
he could help.

SOE had sent this schoolmaster turned guerrilla leader into
southeastern France in mid-1942. Moving through a quadri-
lateral that ran south from Lyon and Grenoble and through
the departments of Ardèche, Var, and Rhône, all the way to
the Swiss and Italian borders, Cammaerts had organized 200
resistance groups of 15 to 20 men each. As each group grew
and became too large and unwieldly to handle easily, it was
split. Such slow, careful organization had worked well for
two years prior to D-Day. But after the Normandy landings,
resistance numbers swelled, and so did the number of arms
the Allies delivered to them. London eventually radioed orders to the guerrillas to integrate into a unified military command under General Koenig at EMFFI. Colonel Zeller would
act as local commander and Cammaerts would be senior Allied liaison officer.

Guerrilla action increased dramatically. Down in the
Drome, between Valence and Avignon, Cammaerts had 2,000
men keep the Route Nationale No. 7—the major highway from
the Riviera to Paris—mined continuously for weeks after the
Normandy landings. Further southeast in Provence the FFI
shut down the Route Napoléon, N-85, completely. This forced
German troops called north to Normandy to use secondary
roads through the mountains, often no more than cart routes,
where they were exposed to ambushes and landslides. Cammaerts, together with Zeller, had fought the Germans in the
Vercors. For more than two months after Overlord, the FFI
in Cammaerts's territory needled, harrassed, ambushed, and
punished the enemy. By the time Dragoon was launched, the
maquis were battle-tested veterans. Most of the time the field
commanders did not know how much help they were getting
from the French.

Neither did Cammaerts. On August 13 he had fallen into German hands and been thrown into prison in Digne. His escape from certain death was the stuff of romantic fiction. Cammaerts had a Polish courier, Countess Krystyna de Skarbeck, née de Gyzicka, known as Christine in the resistance. As soon as Christine learned of Cammaerts's capture she visited a French gendarme with good contacts to the Gestapo. She explained that her "husband" was among the prisoners taken by the Gestapo. Could the gendarme help her to see him? He could. There was a Belgian Gestapo employee worried about his future, with the Allies only days away. He was definitely bribeable. For two million francs, then about $50,000, he agreed to spring Cammaerts. Christine quickly had an operator radio the terms to Algiers where the intelligence services sprang into action. That night a plane flew low above an agreed-upon dropping point and dropped a container with thick bundles of French banknotes amounting to two million francs.

Time was crucial. It was possible the Gestapo had not yet discovered how big a fish they had captured in Cammaerts. Once they did, the best he could hope for was shipment to a German concentration camp. Christine, therefore, hurried to see her Belgian Gestapo man. Cucumber-cool, she bargained hard and as if all the power were on her side. They sat in a Digne cafe. The Belgian nervously sipped a vin blanc, Christine drank coffee. The Americans, she said, will be in Digne in a day or two. Nevertheless, she would give him the two million francs if he got Cammaerts and two companions released. If he were harmed, the maquis would treat the Belgian as a war criminal and hang him. She leaned forward and added with emphasis: "They'd hang you with pleasure." The Belgian knew that and needed little further persuading. He had already learned that Cammaerts and his friends were to be shot the next day. He had gone to their cell, ostensibly for "interrogation," and had kept the key. He promised to walk them out at dawn before the Gestapo commandant arrived.

Christine found a car, no easy trick in war-time France, and drove to the agreed-upon rendezvous. Light fog still hugged the ground though the sun was beginning to burn it

off. She had given the Belgian a million francs down, the rest
on delivery. A shopping bag on the seat beside her was stuffed
with five bundles of bank notes, a rubber band around each
one. She lit a cigarette. Finally, she saw four men hurrying
up to the car. Cammaerts and his friends got into the black
Citroën. Christine handed over the money. The Belgian disappeared. Everybody kept his part of the bargain. British officers of Special Operations Executive protected the little
Belgian and arranged for his safe passage to Australia later
on, presumably with some of the money. What happened to
the rest is anybody's guess. The war still had nine months to
run, but the deal was prophetic of many more to come, as
the little cogs in the German terror machine sought to bargain
for their postwar lives with the lives of their prisoners.

Cammaerts shrugged off Butler's snub in Sisteron and
hitched a ride to Patch's headquarters where both the 7th
Army commander and his G-2, Colonel Quinn, rolled out the
red carpet for him. And despite Butler's lack of interest in
"private" armies, the FFI was not dissuaded from providing
information, clearing roads, and guarding the flanks of the
American advance. Local FFI leaders all the way from Sisteron to Grenoble and beyond to Bourg and Mâcon knew they
had to keep roads open, remove obstacles, attack smaller
German units and warn the Americans of larger enemy concentrations ahead. Everything was done to allow the 7th Army
to move forward as swiftly as possible. Communications were
simple and direct. When the local FFI heard the jangling of
rolling tanks, the leader would step out waving. The U.S.
tank commander was briefed on what lay ahead, on what the
FFI could do and not do, and on how to contact French units
with local couriers. Finally, the French assured the Americans that they would be shadowed all the way along the roads
by FFI troops.

The OSS unit attached to the 7th Army was under the
command of Colonel Ed Gamble with Major Nathan Went-
worth as his deputy. They had the usual frustrating time of
trying to convince field commanders like Butler to make
greater use of the resistance and local forces. But at least they

were listened to at 7th Army Headquarters where Colonel Quinn, the G-2, was always a warm friend and priceless ally.

I flew into an airfield near St. Raphaël on August 17, and went by jeep to Sisteron. By the time I roared out of Sisteron in a huge truck, Troop A of the 117th Cavalry had entered Gap, 45 miles south of Grenoble. Troop A had found a large German garrison afraid to come out and surrender to the FFI. When American tanks crunched into town, the Germans almost shouted with relief. As the U.S. tanks rumbled to a halt and hatches were opened, the amazed Americans saw German soldiers walk over with their hands up.

I saw hundreds of them as we took the truck up N-85 toward Gap. Poles in German uniforms guarded them with a handful of American GIs riding shotgun. Unable to handle the more than 1,000 prisoners, Troop A had discovered the Poles pressed into Wehrmacht service who were eager to act as military policemen for the Americans. The GIs gave them yellow armbands to wear and sent them south with their prisoners. We encountered other armbands—those of the FFI—in virtually every village we passed. Men cheered. Women and children waved flags and handkerchiefs. Repeatedly FFI soldiers assured us that the road ahead was clear. Elements of Task Force Butler had wheeled west of Gap toward the Rhône and units of the 36th Division were already roaming beyond Grenoble. Our advance was becoming a German rout.

When our truck clattered across Grenoble's cobblestones, we asked around for Gamble's whereabouts and were directed to a magnificent château on the outskirts of town that commanded stupendous Alpine views from its tree-shaded terrace. Gamble was living up to the OSS code of grabbing the best available accommodations. This time it included a first-rate chef whose art we sampled that night with another new arrival—General Donovan—who had flown up to a captured airfield nearby and driven into town in a jeep. Over fine French cooking and several bottles of excellent Burgundy the château caretakers had managed to hide from the Germans, we spent a long evening talking over what was ahead. The Wehrmacht was clearly pulling out of southern France, hoping to get through the Belfort Gap before Patch and Patton linked up and cut them off.

Grenoble was alive with FFI, SOE organizers, Jedburghs, and OGs coming into town from all directions to celebrate its liberation, greet this vanguard of Patch's army, and talk about what should be done next. OGs who had dropped into the Vercors and retreated eastward to join the Oisans maquis came in, as did maquis leaders of the Republic of Vercors who had retreated to the south and west. Lt. Leon Ball, who was attached to an SOE mission, drove all the way from Annecy to Grenoble with a French flag flying from his car. He had a plan to use the FFI of Savoie and Haute-Savoie to contain the remnants, some 5 to 10,000 strong, of the German 157th Division that was caught in the mountains between the Isère river and the Italian border.

The most important man who came south to meet the American spearhead was Col. Richard Heslop, who had organized resistance in the Ain and the Jura, the region just north of the area for which Cammaerts was responsible. Posing as a salesman for a Marseilles jewelry firm, he had gone into France as head of a mission with Owen Johnson, an OSS radio operator, and Jean Rosenthal of the French-Swiss fur and jewelry house. Their job was to assess and support resistance in five Alpine departments, Ain, Isère, Savoie, Haute-Savoie, and Jura. Under the code name Xavier, Heslop became a legend in the mountains. When he died a few years ago, he left instructions that his ashes be scattered from an airplane over the land on which he had made so powerful an imprint.

The next day in headquarters established by Col. Johnson, commander of the advanced tank force, Donovan, Heslop, Gamble, and I looked at the maps with Johnson and some of his staff. Johnson's unit had its neck stuck out a good 50 miles ahead of the rest of Patch's army. But by now it was clear that the two German armies in southern France would have to scramble to get through the gap between Patch's Seventh Army, somewhere between Mâcon or Dijon on the east and Patton's Third Army near Auxerre and Nevers on the west, and make for the Belfort gap to get back to Germany. The task of the FFI of the Ain and Jura would be to push the retreating Germans to the west. Johnson was ready to push on to Besançon and Belfort. Heslop said the maquis of the Ain was ready to protect the road and clear any road blocks or small forces interfering with the rapid progress of Johnson's tanks. The maquis could guide and guard the Americans north to Ambérieu-en-Bugey and Bourg, where they were likely to run into a German garrison too strong for the maquis to handle. In the event, Johnson's tanks bypassed Bourg to the east before the Germans could react, but the Germans then stiffened to defend the Belfort gap.

The main body of the German 19th Army was retreating along the Rhône Valley and being cut up by the FFI of the Drôme and Ardèche. Two OG teams that had been sent in from Algiers late in July had succeeded in blowing the suspension bridge between Montélimar and Viviers so that it lay in the river and cut all barge traffic. They had also blown a railway bridge on the west bank south of Viviers. The special force unit attached to the Seventh Army under Col. William G. Bartlett, and a Jedburgh team dropped in June, reported that several thousand maquis of the Ardèche were holding the hills west of the Rhône right up to the valley, and were shepherding toward the valley the German forces that had been holding to the Sète, Nimes, and Arles areas, as they tried to force their way north. The FFI of the Drôme had engaged the retreating Germans north of Montélimar for 36 hours while General Butler wheeled west to Montélimar. On a Rhône valley road from Montélimar, 2,000 German vehicles were destroyed or taken by a combination of American armor, American air squadrons, and the FFI. By August 28, the German 19th Army was no longer a fighting force and the road to Lyon was open.

On August 26, Donovan and I were off again. We were to drive to an airfield where we would meet Allen Dulles. The three of us would fly back to London on a plane specially sent out to fetch us. Dulles and Donovan had not seen each other for almost two years. It was a warm and happy reunion for them. It was my first meeting with Dulles with whom I would work closely for the rest of the war. The DC-3 took off at mid-morning and we flew along the Loire, south of the retreating German armies. While I worried about German fighters slipping down to attack our defenseless plane, Dulles brought us up to date on the aftermath of the July 20 plot against Hitler and outlined what he thought we should do to exploit the opportunities that even its failure had left us.

The involvement of so many senior and junior officers in the plot had turned Hitler fanatically against the whole German military class. The Abwehr was stripped of independent status. Admiral Canaris, its head, was in a concentration camp. Himmler had taken command of the Home Army, the spearhead of rebellion. He and Kaltenbrunner were rounding up thousands of suspects. Gestapo informants swarmed through army headquarters looking for "plotters." The Nazi salute was replacing the military one in the Wehrmacht. Regular army officers had to give up their sidearms before seeing Hitler. The army grew more and more outraged at Nazi actions.

Dulles was convinced that domestic opposition to Hitler was spreading, despite the bloody suppression of the July 20 plot. We should do everything in our power, he argued, to fan the flames of discontent. Our propaganda should reach local commanders and create conditions that would allow them to surrender before the long arm of the SS descended. Himmler was already scanning lists of 50,000 suspected anti-Nazis and recently had obtained names of those slated for top posts in the Beck-Goerdeler government (that was to have emerged from a victorious coup). Dulles talked with intensity and unshakeable conviction. He sensed a breakdown of the German social order that exceeded anything we had visualized from England (and he was right, as we would learn directly when we sent agents into Germany just months later). He was full of praise for the tilt of Swiss neutrality and for the excellence of Swiss intelligence. And he wanted to work more directly and more closely with other OSS units from his Berne headquarters. An OSS base on the French side of the Franco-Swiss border was set up in the fall to help him accomplish this.

As we flew over the Channel and saw the white cliffs of Dover shimmer in the sunlight, we were full of hope and exhilaration. The end seemed much nearer than anyone had dared hope weeks ago. Unhappily, the hope proved illusory.

14. France Liberates Itself

BACK IN MY office in Grosvenor Street, I dug into an accumulation of documents and cables. Events had moved so swiftly in the last ten days that it was hard to catch up. France had virtually liberated itself. German resistance had been squeezed into pockets south and east of the Seine, while Model's disorganized armies were streaming north towards home. Paris had fallen the day before. Negotiations for the Germans to leave Bordeaux were almost complete. The FFI had liberated Toulouse. Tours and Orléans were in Allied hands. And across France, Jedburgh teams and Operational Groups and British SAS units had joined FFI forces to harass and encircle a demoralized German army.

In many villages and cities, even in whole departments, the FFI had risen and chased the Germans out as the Allied armies approached. Sometimes it had been a popular uprising, much broader and deeper than the organized resistance. Indeed, the huge area south of the Loire and west of the Rhône, as well as Paris, were liberated entirely by the people

178

and the FFI, albeit aided by the threat of approaching Allied armies.

Orders for the FFI to move against the larger cities in the southwest—notably Toulouse, Bordeaux, and communications centers like Limoges, Poitiers, and Châteauroux—came out on August 17, two days after the Dragoon forces went ashore on the Riviera. The FFI and factory workers at Tarbes in the Pyrenees, about as far from Allied forces as it was possible to be that day in France, drove out the Wehrmacht and forced the Vichy militia to surrender. News of the Tarbes action spread quickly and on August 18, the FFI sent an ultimatum to the German garrison in Lourdes. On the 19th, some 340 Germans surrendered to fewer then 200 maquis. At nightfall, the FFI marched into Pau and the Germans rattled out of town in 80 trucks headed for Bordeaux. The whole southwest blazed with tricolor flags, and village streets echoed with cheers. The Germans scrambled north.

In Bordeaux, a tense drama began to unfold. The maquis wanted to prevent the Germans from destroying Bordeaux's harbor and bridges. Leaders of the wine trade got busy. The German port commander, a reserve naval officer, had been in the wine business in Berlin before the war and knew most of them. He agreed to pressure General Nake, the German army commander in the city, not to blow up key installations. Nake went along but insisted on scuttling three ships to block the entrance to the harbor. It was the best deal they would get and it was quickly approved. With bridges and port facilities apparently safe, attention shifted to keeping marauding FFI units from action that could trigger German reprisals.

But the situation was too fluid for anyone to be safe from surprises, especially given the secret and delicate nature of the negotiations. Thus Roger Landes, chief SOE organizer in the Gironde, knew nothing of the talks between Bordeaux city officials and the Germans, and when a German approached him with yet another plan, he was interested. Franz Stahlschmitt was an anti-Nazi sergeant who had defected and wanted to blow up German explosives before the Wehrmacht could use them to destroy the port. He had obtained copies of German orders—issued before General Nake opened talks—to destroy bridges across four rivers, the Garonne, the Dordogne, the Isle, and the Lot; clearly a much more ambitious program than merely taking out Bordeaux. Landes was unsure about Stahlschmitt's sincerity. He had other agents try to bribe him; he also had him followed. But Stahlschmitt refused the bribes and made it clear he wanted only FFI protection. Landes was finally convinced. On August 22, Stahlschmitt obtained keys to the bunkers where the explosives were stored. Walking in around 10 p.m., he laid a fuse, lit a match, and left. Twenty minutes later, a huge blast shook Bordeaux. The debris was scattered for blocks around.

Two days later, on August 24, Nake and French officials agreed to publish the terms of their agreement and warned the local population against committing sabotage or attacking German forces. A second agreement fixed the time for the Wehrmacht withdrawal from Bordeaux. Early in the morning on August 28, the last German troops pulled out.

The pattern was repeated across the southern belt of France. Often it was hard to tell whether the FFI had driven the Germans out or simply moved in after the enemy left. The last ten days of August in France were utter pandemonium. Towns fell like nine-pins. Tulle, Limoges, Ussel, Brive-la-Gaillarde, Auch, and Le Puy were occupied on August 20, with the FFI in control of Montauban, Toulouse, Castres, and Bergerac the next day. A force of 150,000 German soldiers began the pell-mell rush north, hoping to escape from the pincer forming between Patton's sweep east and north, and Patch's drive up the Rhône.

As the scope of the German rout became apparent, more and more FFI formations took to the field and the many groups we had sent out from London in the preceding months played a growing role in coordinating their activities. They did this even though it grew progressively more difficult to supply them. Lines were too fluid to risk drops. By the time our planes were overhead everything had shifted far afield. But the Jedburghs had become sufficiently established to operate without any help from London. As Patton swept east and north and the Germans tried desperately to get between the 3rd and 7th U.S. Armies, our OSS units worked closely with the FFi in organizing a screen for Patton's advance and in knocking out communications and other facilities the fleeing Germans needed.

Meanwhile, the one clear aim both Ike and Bradley had in the rout was to bypass Paris and leave its capture for some later time. They feared a bloody battle for the capital and the staggering job of feeding and supplying the city. A SHAEF study had concluded such a commitment would be equivalent to maintaining eight fighting divisions in the field. In order to keep his troops on the move, Ike had planned to push Montgomery across the Seine near the open sea, capture the V-1 launching sites on the Pas de Calais, and then have two corps race to Amiens, 91 miles north of Paris. Bradley's armies would sweep east of Paris and cross the Seine at Melun, then slam to Reims 87 miles northeast of the capital, and finally swing west to meet Montgomery's forces and cut off Paris and any Germans still there. It was a leisurely plan. Eisenhower expected to shut the Amiens-Reims trap door sometime in October.

The only fly in that ointment would be an uprising in Paris. SHAEF accordingly ordered Koenig to keep the resistance in check, but that was an order de Gaulle had trouble swallowing. Under no circumstances did he want the communists to liberate Paris, yet they were the one group he did not control. He therefore told Jacques Chaban-Delmas, his 29-year-old military delegate, to keep the lid on until he, de Gaulle, took it off. Passy was told to refrain from dropping arms that might fall into communist hands.

But how long could the communists be kept down? They had 25,000 men under arms. The Soviet embassy in Switzerland sent a stream of couriers with instructions. Other orders came directly from Moscow by wireless transmitter including one naming Henry Tanguy, known as Colonel Rol, military chief for the capital. Chaban-Delmas, for one, was convinced the communist-dominated Military Action Committee, COMAC, would stage a street uprising, no matter what the cost in life and blood. It was an opportunity the communists could not afford to miss and one the Allies could scotch only by quick action. In early August, with Allied armies still mired in Normandy, therefore, Chaban-Delmas arranged to catch a Lysander to London and plead with Colin Gubbins of SOE and with anyone else who would listen, all the way up to General Ismay, Churchill's chief military advisor, that the Allies could and had to walk into Paris. If they didn't, Paris would be destroyed as communists fought Germans in the streets and the Wehrmacht systematically demolished the city. When it was over, the communists would control the rubble. Chaban-Delmas reached no one in a position to change Eisenhower's plans, and returned to Paris a deeply discouraged man.

Then events took over and forced everybody's hand. The first radio messages arrived in London on August 19. The Parisian police had responded to German orders that they disarm by launching a general strike that was joined by other municipal workers. Food supplies grew suddenly short. The Germans threatened bloody reprisals, but already a force of 20,000 FFI troops was inside the capital. The next morning, August 20, the first radio messages told of street fighting. General de Gaulle flew from Algiers to France to take personal charge. He promptly urged Ike to shift his plans and send troops racing to Paris. If the supreme commander balked, de Gaulle warned, he would order General Le Clerc's 2nd Armored Division to attack Paris on its own. For a while, Eisenhower ignored both plea and threat.

But not for long. On the 21st, a resistance leader named Roger Gallois ran into a 3rd Army patrol. He had been sent by the communist military commander in Paris, Colonel Rol, and with the agreement of the German commander General von Choltitz, one of whose officers accompanied him, to plead for quick Allied action. The two men were taken to see our Rip Powell. After satisfying himself that Gallois was the real thing and not a plant, Powell took him to see Colonel Koch, the 3rd Army's G-2, then Patton himself. Patton was brusk. He was in France to destroy Germans, not capture capitals. But then he relented and sent Gallois to Bradley's headquarters at Laval.

Even while Gallois bumped down country roads in a jeep, a blizzard of radio messages hit London. Something had to be done to equip the FFI in Paris. Special Operations Executive officers in Baker Street swung into action. Chuck Heflen's B-24 squadron at Harrington was ordered to load containers of arms and ammunition. Plans were drawn up for a fleet of 130 planes to drop 200 tons of arms over Paris: in the Bois de Boulogne, the racetrack at Auteuil, the Esplanade of the Invalides, even on the larger squares and courtyards. But only Ike could flash the final green light.

When Gallois arrived at Bradley's HQ he ran into Colonel Lebel, the senior French liaison officer to General Sibert's G-2 section. He told the French officer that Allied troops had to slam into Paris fast to avoid the threatened slaughter of perhaps hundreds of thousands of Parisians. Sibert listened, was convinced, and drove to Ike's advance post where he quickly briefed Eisenhower and Bradley on the Parisian crisis. It was now the evening of August 23. Already, gunfire crackled through Paris. Ike decided to scrap his plans. Le Clerc could make the dash for Paris. The next afternoon, Le Clerc's men were fighting in the southern outskirts of the capital. When Captain Dronne reached City Hall, he flung open the hatch of his tank. The men waiting on the steps struck up the Marseillaise. Liberation was only hours away.

News spread quickly and the more adventurous Americans made plans to ride into their ''home away from home'' right behind Le Clerc's division. Colonel Bruce packed Ernest Hemingway in a car and set out to retake the Ritz bar. Mike Burke, Harry North, and Moe Berg were not far behind. John Haskell did them one better. He picked up a phone in Rambouillet, then already in Allied hands, and dialed a friend in Paris. He'd be there in a day or two, he said, and hung up. The English and the Americans have made a career of cursing the French telephone system, and still do in the 1980s, but it functioned admirably during those confusing days. Ken Downs and John Mowinkel rode into Paris in a radio-equipped command car. On the way they picked up Col. Arnould, chief of SOE's most important network in northern France. Once in the city, Arnould took them to his headquarters in a convent near the Santé Prison. Nuns served them tea. Downs grew itchy to hustle up a situation report for headquarters.

Arnould gestured to one of the nuns who brought the convent's current intelligence summary. It identified and located every German company in and around Paris. Downs and Mowinkel walked back out into the courtyard where they had parked their car and had their radio man put on the air their first intelligence report from Paris, and it was more complete and detailed than anything they had yet produced.

Having caught up on events in France and moved little pins and flags on the map in our war-room in London I was itching to get off again. In a matter of days London had lost much of its attraction as the center for Allied clandestine activities. We smelled victory in August and Paris was a magnet. Everybody wanted the touch of glamor that early entry would provide. I could just see Bruce's elbow testing the mahogany at the Ritz bar. Accordingly, I got over to Paris as quickly as possible on August 28 in a Dakota that touched down at Le Bourget, east of the capital. I had not come too late to share the general euphoria. Hugs and kisses and drinks and toasts were offered in profusion.

Reality, however, soon intervened. Wally Giblin had arrived in Paris right behind Bruce and had spent less time in the Ritz bar. Bruce sent him out to hunt up office space. Giblin had a practiced eye for good real estate and he soon found a suite in an office building at 70 Champs Elysées just above the Avenue George. Special Operations Executive had its headquarters a few doors down and we were both quickly inundated. Resistance leaders, Jedburgh teams, and Operational Groups poured into Paris from all over, even from areas behind the front lines still under German control. Sorting those out was a full-time job. Colonel Bill Jackson, a national guardsman from Indiana, commanded the OSS detachment with Bradley's Army Group headquarters. In late August he sat in Paris trying to direct operations of men coming in from beyond the Loire, keeping lines open to Rip Powell who worked out of Patton's HQ—no easy task since Patton broke camp daily in his pell-mell rush north—and working with London and Chaban-Delmas's FFI operation now centered in Orléans.

I had barely found a desk in the Paris office before we were off again. Giblin, Jackson, and I piled into a command car, parked free-form style across a sidewalk, and headed up around the Arc de Triomphe and down Avenue Kleber. We got lost behind the Trocadero and finally ran into the Avenue de Versailles and onto Route Nationale No. 10 that led to Chartres. General Sibert, Bradley's G-2, had commandeered one of the narrow-gabled houses on the Cathedral Square and turned the ground-floor tavern into his operational room. It was disconcerting, to say the least, to look at front-line maps placed on shaky easels while the beautiful lines of the gothic cathedral shone through the window panes. With the Cathedral as background I had trouble concentrating on what Sibert and his deputy, a New York lawyer also named Bill Jackson (a nomenclative confusion we solved by calling our Jackson "Indiana Jackson" and Sibert's man "New York Jackson") were telling us about the military situation. The news was still euphoric. Patton's tanks had rattled into the champagne capitals of Épernay and Reims. Third Army HQ was being moved up to Châlons-sur-Marne and Patton was poised outside Verdun. Within a week, 3rd Army tanks would smash across three rivers—the Marne, Aisne, and Meuse—that millions of men had fought and died over in four years of World War I. There was for all of us something eerie about the prospect of such speedy victory on land so blood-soaked. Bradley's people were full of admiration for Patton's boldness and drive but could not hide some anxiety that he would overextend himself and end up isolated and immobile. Weeks later, exactly that happened.

From Chartres we drove to Orléans where Rip Powell had a meeting of top French resistance leaders with our own men. Weeks earlier, Patton had aptly summed up the purpose of the meeting while pacing impatiently in his Cherbourg headquarters: "Let the other son-of-a-bitch worry about flanks." We were now "the other son-of-a-bitch." Patton's motto had been spectacularly successful. He had driven 600 miles from Nantes in Brittany to Commercy in Lorraine, leaving his exposed flank to tactical air squadrons, the FFI, and a few patrols of 3rd Army infantry and motorized cavalry to protect. Moreover, even Colonel Koch, Patton's confident G-2, had begun to worry about the threat posed by the German 1st and 19th armies on their retreat north from the Mediterranean coast and the Bordeaux area.

The problem, as Powell saw it at that meeting in Orléans, was in the route the retreating Germans were taking. Most of the 1st Army was marching along a corridor that ran through Bourges, which is about 40 kilometers from the Loire. The Loire crossings would put the Germans on flat, open country where they would be fairly impervious to FFI ambushes. The terrain offered the still lightly armed French little protection. The trick, therefore, lay in blocking any German effort to reach the Loire bridges to the north and force them to cross further south at Nevers and Decize. That would put them into the rolling Morvan country and make them more vulnerable to hit and run attack. More and more Germans were moving out of Bourges toward Nevers but still, a disturbing number were crossing in the north at Gien and Cosne-sur-Loire, putting them on a line to Langres. Once at Langres, the Wehrmacht would sit astride the major highway to Nancy, Metz, and home to Saarbrücken. Clearly, the FFI screen would have to be extended to contain the troops already across the Loire. Patton had ordered all bridges across the Loire and Allier cut in order to bottle up as many retreating Germans as possible.

Philippe de Vomécourt, a leader of the French resistance, picked up Powell's pointer and continued the Orléans briefing. Three FFI armies had formed in the southwest and were harassing the Germans all the way north. The Germans moved only at night. They worried about every pile of rock and every heap of dung. Everything had to be examined and searched for mines. Meanwhile, the convoy stopped and valuable time was lost. Farther down the road, small groups of maquis would gather on hill tops and start small rock slides, fell trees across the road, or fire bazookas at passing tanks. A captured German officer described the mood: "We have the feeling that each fern is firing at us. Every mile we fall under the fire of an ambush. As soon as we reorganize ourselves we attack an invisible enemy and find nothing but ferns."

What made the FFI so dangerous, and so hard to track was

its constant growth and change. The Germans never could figure out what kind of force they were encountering. One day the French could only mount a hit and run attack, while two days later the FFI could stage a far-flung strategic maneouver that forced whole regiments to cross the Loire at Nièvre and not further north, block roads converging on Dijon and interdict access to the Langres plateau. Nor could the Germans compete with FFI mobility. The French thought nothing of forced overnight marches if they had to make them. But they often took advantage of the near miraculous performance of the French national railroads in making trains and rolling stock available to the maquis and not the Germans. The humiliated Wehrmacht had to retreat on foot. De Vomécourt seemed pleased with himself, and with reason.

As August turned into September, time and place began to jumble in my mind. It seemed as if we were in constant motion, driving from one ancient French town to another to attend a series of briefings designed to keep us abreast with swiftly moving events. Back in Paris from Orléans, we drove next to Châlons-sur-Marne where Patton had set up headquarters. He had just returned from a set-to with Bradley and General Bull at Chartres. Patton, Rip Powell told us, was beginning to smell trouble. He was sure Bradley and Ike were siphoning "his" gasoline to satisfy Montgomery's demands for fuel to speed the British drive toward Belgium. At the same time, Patton's expanding flanks demanded our urgent attention. Even if he ran out of gas they would have to be held. We looked at the battle map. Châlons-sur-Marne was 140 kilometers north of Auxerre, a town Colonel Chevrier, commander of the FFI in the Yonne, had just captured. Bill Colby's Jedburgh team was moving along the Yonne river south of Auxerre and reported sighting large German formations heading east after crossing the Loire around Nièvre. The problem for the flankers was to interdict German stragglers who did not just move in platoon but often battalion and regimental strength, before they escaped. The German escape was dangerous because Allied troops had not firmly occupied the territory through which the enemy passed. Holding key towns with FFI troops, however, forced the Germans to stay off the major roads and away from urban areas. By early September, Colby and Colonel Chevrier had pushed the 3rd Army FFI flank south to the Loire, crossed the river at Cosne-sur-Loire and east on a line to Clamecy and Avallon, thus forcing the Germans to ford the Loire where we wanted them to. Patton's orders to blow key bridges had also been carried out.

Further southeast, meanwhile, General Truscott's 6th Corps and General de Lattre de Tassigny's 1st French Army continued their drive up the Rhône toward Lyon, long a center of resistance activity. The French carried themselves with more spirit and cockiness there than elsewhere. Lyon was the home of the Army of the Alps, which back in 1940 had given the Italians a pasting. Now FFI units converged from all over, many already battle-hardened in the struggles of recent months against combat Wehrmacht units, including some veterans of the tragic battle of the Vercors. By September 1, plans for encircling and capturing the city, had been completed. FFI and regular French army forces would attack Lyon from the right bank of the Rhône while Truscott's Americans approached on the left. Inside the city, FFI irregulars were to sabotage German formations, blow up cars and tanks, and disrupt staging areas. H-hour had been set for 6 a.m., Sunday, September 3. But again the French could not wait. Lyon had erupted the previous night, and the Germans blew up all but two of the city's 28 bridges across the Rhône before moving north.

In the days that followed, FFI forces cleaned out the German escape hatches across the Loire and captured key road hubs. The Germans recognized their hopeless position by blowing up the bridge at La Charité-sur-Loire that they had been using as a major Loire crossing.

To the north and west the FFI was moving to firm its hold on Lorraine. On September 14, Gilbert Grandval, FFI chief for the province, cabled London announcing his attack on Nancy and asking the 3rd Army to hasten its advance. He was short of guns and ammunition and said ''at least send us some tanks. Vive de Gaulle. Vive la Lorraine. Vive la France.''

On the 15th, Grandval sent his joyful message to General Koenig: "Mon General, I have the honor and joy of informing you of the liberation of the capital of Lorraine. The people of Nancy are awaiting with calm and order the arrival of the Allied armies. In this splendid hour, their thoughts are turned towards the man who during these last four years, has shown them the road to honor and liberty. Vive de Gaulle! Vive la France eternelle!"

15. Antwerp and Arnhem

THE HOPES of August ran high. Paris was free. Allied armies were closing on the German frontier and had punched across the Belgian border. The enemy retreated in disarray. The British and Americans lunged for Liège, Brussels, and the Scheldt River. Perhaps the war would be over in a matter of weeks, certainly before the onset of winter. Then came the twin debacles of Antwerp and Arnhem. There was, for us, bitter irony in both. As much as anything else, they were the result of a failure to utilize fully the resistance capability in Belgium and to understand and act on intelligence from Holland.

What added to the bile of Antwerp was that with the port intact in their hands, the Allies failed to cross the Albert Canal and race 18 miles across a narrow peninsula to the sea and thus safeguard the Scheldt estuary, the basic prerequisite to using Europe's best port. It was winter before the first Allied ship could pull up to an Antwerp dock.

It should not have happened that way and the Belgian resistance had done all it could to see that it did not. Things had been difficult for the Belgians. Their country was ill-suited for guerrilla warfare, so most of the resistance was concentrated in the cities. In London it had a low supply priority. Air drops were tricky because the Germans concentrated fighter and anti-aircraft strength in what was essentially an air corridor for raids on the Reich.

Despite handicaps of geography and supply, Belgian resistance had grown into a potent force by the time we needed to use it. Belgium had 15 resistance groups. 54,000 of the resistants were in one "Armée Secrète." There was also the"Armée Blanche," named the white army to distinguish it from the black worn by the SS and Belgian collaborationists. The white army was similar to the French FFI and charged with similar tasks: to cut communications, divert and harass German forces, and act only when London gave the orders. London retained operational control, as it had with the FFI, while a Belgian, Major General Ivan Gérard, was in command. In addition, there was "Groupe G," an intelligence and sabotage outfit directed by several University of Brussels professors. The savants applied their academic training to identifying promising sabotage targets, checking them out with Special Forces HQ in London, then selecting specialized resistance teams to attack and destroy them.

Since D-Day especially, the "Armée Secrète" had given a good account of itself. The statistics for the months after the invasion give an idea of just how active the Belgians were: 1,100 rail cuts; 80 derailed trains; 800 railroad cars, 176 locomotives, 79 railroad bridges, 35 pumping stations, 27 watering points, 25 railroad turntables and 15 rail signal boxes destroyed or damaged; 200 telephone and 100 cable lines severed; 20 telephone exchanges sabotaged; 11 waterway lock gates, 15 barges, three boats, and two floating cranes destroyed or damaged.

One of the more spectacular Belgian attacks reads like a film script. The resistance discovered the Germans had hidden 36 tank cars loaded with fuel in a tunnel. They hijacked a locomotive, found two freight cars, loaded on explosives and quicklime, and hitched the cars to the engine. The dynamite train puffed down the track toward the tunnel. A hundred yards from the tunnel mouth the engineers opened the throttle and jumped for their lives. The blast rocked the mountain and the massive fire burned for three days despite desperate German efforts to put it out.

The Belgians also used technological skills to make up for a lack of supplies. Take "crabs" and "aspirine" as examples. "Crabs" were sharp, four-pronged gadgets that when thrown into the street always landed with one point up ready to puncture a tire. One underground factory turned out 500 of them a day. "Aspirine" did little for headaches but a lot to motors. Chemical pills, they knocked out engines when put into gasoline tanks. "Aspirine" tablets are credited with giving 50 German Panzers engine trouble and delaying their passage to the Normandy beaches in June.

During August and September more supplies and weapons were sent into Belgium. Two drops made over the Ardennes dumped 50 tons, as much as we had dropped in all the months before D-Day. Resistance became bolder and more open as the Allies neared the Belgian frontier. The advance was spectacular. Within a week, most of the country was liberated. As Hodges's First Army and Dempsey's Second British Army sped north, the Armée Secrète played the same role the FFI had in France: It protected the advancing Allied flanks, provided guides for Allied columns, and helped mop-up operations in overrun areas like Mons, Namur, and Charleroi. Behind enemy lines, the resistance protected key installations like bridges, roads, and harbor facilities from destruction. The retreating Germans looted and burned Belgian homes and shot some of their prisoners. But this last wave of terror did little to dampen the spirit of resistance. Liberation was too close. When it came, feelings exploded. The Allies marched into Liège on September 2 and met a forest of British, American, and Belgian flags and streamers. The capture and preservation of Antwerp was the resistance's crowning achievement, and, moreover, a caper with all the elements of a Hitchcock thriller. The port had been a major objective of Allied strategy from the beginning. Antwerp's harbor facilities would end the Allied supply problems that had grown steadily worse as one port after another was destroyed. Brest and Cherbourg lay in ruins, so did the Channel ports. The Belgian resistance had pondered ways of saving the harbor facilities on the Scheldt river, 50 miles from the sea, long before the invasion. It had set up a planning committee in 1943 that operated out of the Colonial University in Antwerp. The committee had quickly formed a separate "save the port" command and put a regular Belgian army officer, Lieutenant Urbain Reniers, in command. He was given a list of six minimum objectives:

1. *The docks along the Scheldt were to be kept free of every obstacle.*
2. *Access along the river was to be kept open to assure Liberty ship passage through the channel.*
3. *Piloting staff was to be recruited.*
4. *Bridges, tunnels and locks were to be protected.*
5. *Electricity-generating installations were to keep functioning.*
6. *Stocks of essential supplies were to be built up and key industrial enterprises—especially oil refineries—were to be protected from German efforts to destroy or dismantle them.*

Next, a group was formed to implement these objectives. "Le Comité Clandestin de Coordination de la Resistance d'Anvers" was to assume responsibility for civil resistance and support of armed resistance groups. In July 1944, this committee had become firmly enough established to give Reniers the military command over the varied armed resistance groups in the city—roughly 3,500 men. Edouard Pilaet was named Reniers's assistant, while Eugene Colson, a merchant marine officer, was put in charge of forces operating in the immediate port area of the city that comprised 26 miles of docks, locks, water towers, and other facilities. Clearly, his would be the key group. He had assembled all the specialists: merchant seamen, pilots, employees in the harbor master's office, dock workers, ship maintenance crews, and harbor policemen.

Colson wasted little time. He put one of his men in every German harbor office, where they filed minute reports on enemy plans, both for the defense and for the destruction of the port. Methodically, the Nazis went ahead with preparations to blow up the harbor before the Allies arrived, and just as methodically men more familiar with the installations than the Germans noted and reported every move. Countermeasures were planned or taken almost instantly. Special crews were chosen and trained to handle German mines, booby traps, and other explosives. Preparation of borings along the wharves were quietly sabotaged, with care taken to make them look like accidents; the same technique was applied to the manufacture of steel containers for explosives. Combat squads were formed to protect anti-destruction crews. Men were assigned to guard bridges and seize tugs. Everyone would go into action when the time was ripe.

But for all resistance efforts to keep a low profile in Antwerp, the Gestapo did get wind of their preparations. On August 25, the day Paris fell, the Germans cracked down on the key coordinating committee. The chairman and other top members were arrested. Communications between London and Antwerp were interrupted and not reestablished until September 3. But the Gestapo had moved too late. The resistance would not be denied, not with the Allies beginning their final drive to the Belgian frontier and Canadian units already beyond Dunkirk.

On August 26, the Belgians defiantly destroyed two cement plants turning out special cylinders for use in mining Antwerp harbor. The next night, the central railway pumping station at Antwerp Dam was blown up, putting 60 locomotives out of action and preventing the Germans from shipping hundreds of resistants to the Reich. Clearly, Belgian boldness was growing by leaps and bounds—and in direct relationship to the speed of the Allied advance. Monty's 21st Army Group jumped off from the Seine on August 29th. On the 31st, the British Second Army was in Amiens, while the U.S. First Army reached the Belgian border. In Antwerp, the resistance celebrated by blowing up the signal box at the "Central Station" completely disrupting German troop movements in and out of the city.

The second phase of saving the port now began. Electric cables were cut to make sure that drawbridges would remain closed and that the Germans would be unable to create a "wall of flame'' at the key Fruissachans lock. Demolition charges were removed from two tunnels. Barges loaded with dynamite were seized by resistants who disarmed the crews and thus frustrated German plans to blow up harbor installations.

Brussels fell on September 3rd. That morning the BBC finally sent the long awaited action message to Antwerp. Armed groups scampered to wharves, tunnels, bridges, and other installations slated for demolition. By afternoon, all resistance forces were at "battle stations." Among them was an officer in the Belgian army engineer corps named Robert Vekemans only recently released from a German prison camp. He knew that the Allies had reached Tournai, fifty miles southwest of Antwerp. He decided to reconnoiter the southern approaches to the port. Once past Aalst, the Allies faced the twin problem of crossing the Willebroek Canal and the Rupel Stream at Boom, about ten miles south of Antwerp. At Boom, Vekemans found the Germans had mined the two major bridges across the canal and river. Guards in the lookout house atop one of the bridges had an unobstructed view that would spot approaching Allied tanks early enough so that the bridges could be blown. Poking around, Vekemans found a 19th century toll bridge—the Pont van Entschodt—spanning the Willebroek Canal about half a mile east of the other two bridges. Although the Germans had mined and guarded it, buildings blocked the view south. What's more, the explosives had been put in place carelessly and could be dismantled easily.

If Vekemans could flag down Allied tanks before they came in sight of the guards on the bridge house, he could lead them to the Pont van Entschodt undetected and overpower the guards before they blew up the bridge. Once across, the tanks could wheel west and surprise the enemy at the Boom bridges from behind. Buildings along the canal and in town would give the tanks cover. With the bridges in Allied hands nothing could stop the Allied rush to rescue resistance fighters in Antwerp.

The next morning, Vekemans sat at a cross-roads café at Breendonk, about four miles beyond the spot where the first British tanks could be seen from the bridge house at Boom. Luckily, no German troops were nearby, and the café windows gave him an unobstructed view of the road south. When he heard the crunch of the first tank he was outside and flagged the vehicle down. The British listened to Vekemans's story. It sounded plausible enough. But would the 19th century bridge hold the weight of a Sherman tank? Vekemans emphatically said it would. The tank commander radioed his C.O. for approval, got it, and sent two tanks and a staff car to the bridge. They surprised the German guards, barreled across the span before the demolition charges could be set off, cut the wires, got the rest of the tank squadron across the canal, and moved down the other bank to the first of the two Boom bridges. Vekemans forced the surprised Germans at pistol point to show him the demolition firing point. As he cut the leads, the other Boom bridge exploded—too late to slow down the British advance.

In Antwerp, Colson's men had not been idle. By one p.m., on September 4, they held the vital Bonaparte Lock and the Kattendyk Lock. Hours later they had captured intact the Royers Lock, the Strasbourg Bridge, and the Albert and Leopold Docks. Finally, with Allied tanks already in the city and most of the Germans digging in on the other side of the Albert canal, Colson's teams won a bitter fight over the valves before the Germans could open them to let the Scheldt flow into Antwerp's sewer system at high tide. If they had succeeded, the city would have faced a major health hazard.

Despite Allied failure to take full advantage of Antwerp's fall, the port's capture with all its facilities intact must rank as one of the most amazing feats of the war. Three factors combined to make it possible. First, the British 30th Corps performed an epic feat of tank warfare that caught the Germans off guard and unprepared. In seven days the English tanks raced 240 miles north, a blitzkrieg the Germans believed impossible. Second, the 1,500 man dockside Belgian resistance force was able to stop German demolition efforts— at the high cost of 150 dead. And finally, Vekemans's ingenuity at Willebroek Canal bridge robbed the Germans of the time they would surely have otherwise had to overcome Colson's forces and destroy the port.

With so much going for the Allies, the blunder that followed was doubly painful. The British failed to secure the northern bank of the Albert Canal and the Scheldt river so that shipping could pass safely from the sea into Antwerp harbor. The move was so logical that on the night of September 4th, only hours after the port had been secured, Reniers and Colson sent a force across an Albert Canal bridge. They expected prompt British support of Edouard Pilaet's unit and were flabbergasted when the British refused to secure the bridgehead. Pilaet had to withdraw his men as the entire Allied front came to a standstill. The reason: Field Marshal Montgomery, hardly a visionary man, had dreamt a more distant dream.

The post-mortems of that dream make for grim reading. The history of the 11th British Armored Division, the division poised to strike across the Albert Canal, says: "Had any indication been given that a further advance north was envisaged these bridges (across the Albert Canal) might have been seized within a few hours of our entry into Antwerp." Later, Bradley would write Ike that "had Monty cleared the Scheldt as SHAEF suggested he do . . . we might have been spared the famine that immobilized us in October." And Lt. General Horrocks, Montgomery's Corps Commander, whose troops took Antwerp, commented that "if I had ordered Roberts (the 11th Armored Division commander) to bypass Antwerp and advance for only 15 miles northwest, in order to cut off the Beveland isthmus, the whole of this force (82,000 men of the German 15th Army) which played such a prominent part in the subsequent fighting, might have been destroyed or forced to surrender."

What happened? The cautious, methodical Montgomery, a general who had moved through the war one careful step after another, was suddenly filled with the vision of ending the war with "one powerful and full-blooded thrust toward Berlin," as he wrote Eisenhower the day Antwerp fell. His eyes were on the bridges across the Rhine in eastern Holland. As a result, he missed the easy opportunity of sealing off what was left of the disorganized 15th German Army and thus open a port which could have supplied a drive to the Ruhr before winter set in. Eisenhower, 400 miles away at his Normandy HQ, failed to insist that Monty clear the banks of the Scheldt.

The Germans got a much-needed breather that they used to triple their forces in the west to 70 divisions.

But in early September few foresaw the shape of things to come. The speed of the Allied advance had blinded all of us to the mistakes made and the obstacles still ahead. In Rotterdam, the Hague, and Amsterdam, the normally placid Dutch were swept into premature celebration. They were sure their own liberation was now only a matter of days away, not a full eight months during which 15,000 Dutchmen would die of starvation. In March 1942, Special Operations Executive parachuted two agents into Holland, who were arrested. The Abwehr chief in the Netherlands used them against London. The SOE radio operator was a man of courage. With the Abwehr leaning over his shoulder, he gave the agreed upon signal—an error in the 16th letter of his text—that he was operating under enemy control. London ignored his security check. The operator fiddled with the code and inserted a series of letters to be stricken from the message. The letters spelled out the word "caught." The cipher clerk in London unfortunately did not catch it, despite three or four repetitions.

The results were predictable. Over the next 18 months, SOE contacted an expanding network of fictitious resistance fighters. More than 50 agents, several thousand guns, and hundreds of thousands of rounds of ammunition were dropped to reception committees the Abwehr had organized. Not till the end of 1943 did one of the captured SOE operatives manage to escape and reach London. His report was met with utter disbelief. All the SOE agents could not have been seized! When the story was finally verified, the blow to Dutch morale was terrible. All but five of the agents were executed, but not before many of them had implicated thousands of others. In London, the Dutch government-in-exile was convinced an enemy agent had infiltrated SOE headquarters. It took a Dutch Parliamentary Commission of Inquiry after the war to establish that the disaster had resulted from inefficiency, errors of judgment, and a sloppy disregard of fundamental security requirements.

Meanwhile, reestablishing a functioning opposition in Holland took time, patience, and effort. Colonel Somer, selected for the task, needed months to get back to Holland. Reestablishment of contact with London—and confidence in that contact—took much longer. One of the perils of working outside an occupied country in support of the resistance within it, is a tendency to see the resistance only in terms of those groups dealt with directly. SOE's blundering in Holland blinded us to what was really going on there. The resistance differed from France's and Belgium's but was no less fierce. Dutch patriots hid 25,000 Jews facing deportation. They provided shelter, food, coupons, and money for 250,000 Dutchmen living underground to avoid deportation as forced laborers.

Perhaps the most dramatic moments came in April and May 1943. Late one Thursday afternoon, the Germans announced that all members of the Dutch army who had seen action against the Wehrmacht would be sent to Germany as forced laborers. On Friday morning, the entire country went on strike to protest. The Nazis were unable to break the strike for weeks, and ended it in May only after shooting 150 people pretty much at random.

As the months passed, the silent war grew increasingly bitter and grim. Contact with London remained sporadic. The SOE debacle had sown too much distrust on both sides. As late as June 1944, the Special Forces HQ report to SHAEF carried this passage about Dutch resistance: "Attempts made during the past months to establish a working contact with Netherlands resistance movements failed, resulting in the arrest of the agents employed. A further approach is being attempted during the current moon period, but it would be unwise to hope for considerable results at this stage."

Nevertheless, the process of building resistance forces and coordinating them with London operations continued. Queen Wilhelmina's government-in-exile set up a Netherlands Force of the Interior, known as B.S. for Binnenlands Strydkrachten. B.S. gathered together the three main Dutch resistance organizations, Knockploegen (Fighting Squads); Raad van Verzet (Council of Resistance); and Ordedienst (Order Service) and all were put under command of Prince Bernhard. During the summer after the invasion, their ranks were swelled by 10,000 new recruits. Communications improved, too. In August, we dropped 15 tons of supplies into various parts of the country, and 7 agents, who managed to stay out of the Gestapo's clutches. Contacts were made with more resistance groups and soon London was pinpointing targets for sabotage action. Early in September, we sent an OSS mission to Holland, codenamed Melanie. Van der Stricht and Jan Laverge set up Melanie headquarters in the town of Eindhoven.

Then, on September 8, the Germans revived Monty's dream of a quick strike north. About seven p.m., two thunderclaps were heard in London. The first V-2 rockets had landed, one in Chiswick, the other near Epping. Hours later, the Dutch resistance radioed London giving the exact launching pad location outside the Hague. Air strikes, they warned, would have only limited effect. V-2s would rain on London until Holland's west coast was occupied or its communication lines with Germany were cut off.

The day after the first rocket fell, September 9, London asked Montgomery about liberating Holland. Still smarting from Ike's rejection the week before of his plan to strike at Berlin, Monty was quick to resubmit the idea for an airborne attack on Arnhem coupled with a 70 mile ground thrust across five waterways (along a single road) to join the paratroopers. This time Ike agreed, perhaps because of the audaciousness of the idea and because of the specifics of the plan that Montgomery's earlier talk of a "full-blooded thrust" had lacked. Certainly the plan was out of character. Bradley commented later that he would not have been more surprised if the teetotaling Montgomery had come in dead drunk.

The Arnhem operation was to be launched on September 17, a week after Ike approved it. Though his approval letter had emphasized the importance of opening the port of Antwerp to Allied shipping, it was clear that so ambitious an operation had to delay that goal still further. Already, the Germans on the northern bank of the Scheldt had won a six-day reprieve in which to regroup and dig in. They had also been regrouping elsewhere—near Arnhem, as the following week's massive intelligence reports would reveal. But field commanders from Montgomery on down refused to adapt their plans to the ominous news, choosing instead to believe what they wanted to believe.

There were other pressures to move ahead with the airborne assault. Two U.S. airborne divisions that had not been in action since Normandy and one British airborne division were ready. Plans to use them in France had been cancelled no fewer than 18 times because ground forces had moved ahead so rapidly. Their commanders were desperate for a piece of the action and Montgomery's plan seemed the best way to get it. In Washington, General Marshall supported the air strike, hoping with Montgomery that this was the way to finish the war quickly.

The Dutch government-in-exile in London was just as eager, convinced liberation was at hand. It decided to call for a rail strike in Holland to coincide with the attack and thus block the flow of German reinforcements. The Dutch Railroad Administration, heavily criticized for carrying Jews, Dutch workers, prisoners, and confiscated property to Germany, saw a chance for vindication and supported the strike plan. On the day of the attack, September 17, Dutch Prime Minister Pieter Gerbrandy went on the air to call on Dutch railroad workers to walk out. He brimmed with confidence. When one of his aides warned that it was easier to call a strike than to call it off should Monty's attack fail, Gerbrandy replied, "Don't worry. We'll be back in Amsterdam by next Sunday."

His optimism was as foolish as Montgomery's and ignored Dutch intelligence. Colonel Somer had made good use of the months since Normandy. He had revitalized intelligence networks to the point where General Crerar, in command of Canadian forces, would call them the best in Europe during the last winter of the war. Somer had 1,000 agents collecting information, drawing maps, writing reports, and manning more than a score of radio transmitters. By September, he had laid out the disposition of German forces in Holland down to the last company and gun emplacement. Moreover, in the crucial week before the attack, the flow of vital information was stepped up. All of it should have discouraged even an imprudent commander. Monty and his generals should have pondered the fact that barracks near Arnhem could house 10,000 men, and that thousands of others could be lodged in the town. Heavily wooded cover made aerial photographs ambiguous and the photographs did not warrant the conclusion that only a few tanks and several thousand soldiers would meet the invaders. Fresh doubt was cast by Dutch intelligence reports of large numbers of SS troops and tanks in the Arnhem vicinity. The concentration was large enough, some intelligence officers argued, to indicate that the 2nd SS Panzer Corps, pulled out of Normandy before the rout, was being reorganized. A young British officer, Major Brian Urquhart, later Deputy Secretary General of the U.N., took that view. He had examined all the available aerial reconnaissance pictures, and had spotted some tanks on or very near the drop zone at Arnhem. Worried, he took them to the commander of Montgomery's airborne troops, General Sir Frederick Browning. Urquhart's concern was brushed aside and he was told to take a rest.

Still the warnings multiplied. On September 15, Dutch intelligence located the 9th Panzer Division near Arnhem. Bletchley decoded a message that General Model had set up headquarters at Oosterbeeck, 4 kilometers west of Arnhem—between the drop zone for the British airborne division and the critical bridge at Arnhem. Remnants of the German 15th Army had regrouped and were moving east toward what would be Monty's left flank after the drop. Ultra reported German concern about a possible Allied thrust from Eindhoven into Arnhem. On the 16th, SHAEF issued a report locating both the 9th and 10th Panzer Divisions at Arnhem. At Monty's 21st Army group headquarters the warning was discounted. The Second British Army, in fact, studied the same pictures Major Urquhart had seen and concluded they showed no tanks on the ground. Worried by the ominous news and SHAEF's assessment of it, General Bedell Smith, Ike's Chief of Staff, and Kenneth Strong, his G-2, drove to Brussels from Paris. German Panzer formations, probably equipped with new armor, were close enough to Arnhem to endanger Montgomery's operation, they warned. Monty and his staff ridiculed the warnings and the two Americans returned to SHAEF with grim forebodings.

Montgomery would not be denied. He listened to nobody and to nothing that cast doubt on his plan. Hitting the Germans before their retreating units had a chance to regroup, he believed, was more important than careful intelligence and preparation. Moreover, he was determined to cross all water barriers between his forces and the Ruhr, turn the Siegfried line, and break out into the North German plain. And do it all in one blow. Intelligence officers at all levels—divisional, regimental, and battalion—gave short shrift to information about growing German strength around Arnhem. Intelligence on terrain, roads, and anti-aircraft defenses was uniformly bad, yet no one consulted the Dutch or asked them what they knew. If the British had, some of their blunders might have been avoided—such as dropping troops six miles west of the bridge at Arnhem and virtually on top of two SS Panzer divisions, just as Major Urquhart had predicted. Meanwhile, Lt. General Sir Brian Horrocks's ground troops who were supposed to be "rushing" to the relief of the airborne soldiers, were mired in a 20,000 vehicle traffic jam on a single road north. The rosy prospects of winning the war in 1944 faded in the cannon fire of Tiger tanks.

Despite the fact that the British were almost willfully ignoring their intelligence, the Dutch people aided the Allied forces to the limit of their capabilities. The railroad strike was 95 percent successful, with workers walking off the job in defiance of German threats to shoot strikers. The whole rail system ground to a halt for several days until the Germans could bring in enough experienced personnel to run the trains. The Germans made good on their threats, too, by shooting strikers in public in different parts of the country. But the executions only hardened the Dutch will to resist. The 30,000 workers stayed out for weeks. The rail administration arranged for them to get paychecks, including a Christmas bonus. Some of it clearly was hazard pay. Rail lines were sabotaged every night. During the actual battle around Arnhem, the yards at Hertogenbosch, west of the airhead landing sites, were destroyed.

The Dutch resistance went all out to aid Allied airborne soldiers fighting a battle doomed from the start. The Germans had concentrated too much heavy armor and too many troops for the British to handle. A few days before the assault we had dropped a special team that included OSS personnel into Overijssel province to coordinate resistance and airborne activities. Four other teams with similar objectives were dropped with the "First Allied Airborne Army"—the official title for the three divisions used. It paid off. The resistance men provided valuable tactical intelligence which would not otherwise have been available.

But their attempts—and those of Montgomery's airborne army—were not enough. On September 25th, the ninth day of battle, ammunition and food ran out. All the efforts to resupply and relieve the beleaguered paratroopers on the northern shore of the Lower Rhine had failed. About 2300 men of the First British Airborne Division were ferried across the river, another 6000 fell into enemy hands, and the resistance managed to hide 500.

Montgomery would claim later that his operation had been 90 percent successful. After all, he had carved a 60 mile salient into German-occupied Holland, despite the traffic jam and the presence of more Nazi soldiers than he had expected. The trouble was that the salient went nowhere.

Horrocks, who commanded the force charged with racing 70 miles to relieve the airborne forces at Arnhem, has written that Montgomery competely underestimated the opposition when he started his orders by saying that the disorganized German army was struggling back to the fatherland. "Why," he lamented, "did I receive no information about the German formations which were being rushed daily to our front? Looking back, I believe that the fly in the ointment was General Brereton's powerful Allied Airborne Army in the U.K. By now it was bursting at the seams, having had no fewer than 16 operations cancelled at the last moment owing to the rapidity of our advance. It is probable that the Arnhem operation had already been decided upon at the beginning of September, and the powers that be were not risking another cancellation at the last moment. Back in Washington, General

Marshall was urging Eisenhower to use this immensely powerful force in one great operation to finish the war in 1944. So Patton's two flanking thrusts on the right and my 30th Corps on the left were halted. This was a great pity; if those transport aircraft which had been sitting in the U.K. doing nothing could have been used to supply us both, the war really would have been over in 1944. The fortnight's delay before the complicated Arnhem operation could be launched proved fatal, for the enemy was growing stronger every day.''

Montgomery did not give up easily. Though he had to pull back from the Arnhem salient, he clung to his dream of striking deeply into Germany's heart. On September 23, when the battle at Arnhem had all but been lost, Ike had ordered the 21st Army Group to open Antwerp as "a matter of urgency." Nothing happened. On October 9, two weeks after the debacle in Holland had been sealed, Eisenhower wrote his British subordinate:

"Unless we have Antwerp producing by the middle of November, our entire operation will come to a standstill. I must emphasize that of all our operations from Switzerland to the Channel, I consider Antwerp of first importance."

It took another week before Monty gave in to his commander-in-chief's orders and agreed to clear the northern bank of the Scheldt. Six weeks later, on November 28, 1944, with a dripping fog hanging over Antwerp, the first Allied ship sailed into the harbor. The Belgian resistance had delivered the miles of first-rate dock facilities precisely 85 days before. During that time the Germans had more than tripled the force available to hold the Siegfried line. Patton had to battle till November 22 to enter Metz, which could have been taken in the first days of September. Hodges needed a little less time to take Aachen, marching into Charlemagne's city on October 21. Lightning Joe Collins's VIII Corps had reached Aachen by mid-September.

16. Stalemate

EUPHORIA HAD ruled Paris in September. The British Joint Intelligence Committee pronounced the war all but won and we all believed the end was near. It took the cold winds of October for the twin debacles of Antwerp and Arnhem to sink in, and with them the realization that we faced another winter of war and the shedding of much blood. Naturally enough, I suppose, a period of griping and discontent set in that eroded the Allied cohesion. We grumbled about the failure to seal off the 15th German Army and open Antwerp. We shook our heads in disbelief at the dismissal of Dutch intelligence during the Arnhem operation. And we argued vehemently about whether Ike should back Patton in a drive for the Saar or Montgomery in a thrust to the Ruhr.

If Eisenhower had only decided one way or the other, the war might have ended six months before it did. Certainly Roger Hesketh argued that point then and in a final report he wrote for SHAEF on the "grand deception." Garbo, MI-5's brilliant Spanish double-agent and his fictitious espionage network, had lost none of his credibility. Yet when the Germans asked him whether Ike would put his chips on Patton or Monty, Garbo had to fudge. If he had not, the Germans might have moved strong forces to meet either phantom threat, Patton in the south or Montgomery in the north, weakening one flank or the other and leaving it vulnerable for the decisive breakthrough.

Ike's failure to decide, or rather his decision to opt for a slow and massive drive along the entire front, gave the Germans valuable time to regroup, and they performed miracles in beefing up their depleted ranks. Hitler had moved with astonishing speed and firmness even as his regime tottered from internal revolt and both the eastern and western military fronts reeled. In July and August alone, he formed 18 new divisions, moving the bulk to stiffen the Russian front. Meanwhile, he garrisoned the Siegfried Line with 140 fortress infantry battalions that had seen only rear echelon duty. In addition to the still high-quality troops he sent to Russia, Hitler began forming so-called ''Volks Grenadier'' divisions in August, mostly made up of young boys and old men, with the first of 25 such divisions moving into the line on the Western Front by mid-September. Even submarine crews were brought up as infantry units.

It was a difficult situation to assess. Hitler had begun to scrape the bottom of the barrel. Cripples and children of 15 began to show up in prisoner-of-war cages. Interrogators suddenly confronted near-sighted and middle-aged men who had spent the war keeping books before being put in uniform a few weeks earlier. Some were deaf and had served under officers able to communicate in sign language. Others had rotten stomachs and served in units fed special food. But they were fresh cannon fodder and we did not know just how quickly they had been moved up. None of these changes in front-line strength showed up in aerial photographs or radio messages, certainly not enough to indicate the dimension of what was happening.

The fighting had taken on a desperate, slogging, stalemate quality. It took three weeks to conquer bloodied Aachen, the last eight days spent in house-to-house fighting. German troops, forced to sign pledges that they would never surrender, hung on to Channel ports like Calais, Boulogne, Dunkirk, Ostende. Their fanatic resistance made the price of capturing these ports now too high. In Lorraine and in the mountains of the Vosges, Patton and Patch were running into the same phenomenon: small gains were costing too much and both generals had begun to feel the supply pinch. The lost opportunity on the Scheldt estuary cost Canadian troops, Royal Navy Ships, and RAF planes dearly as they continued efforts to open Antwerp.

For the OSS, the mood of the day had swung too suddenly. It was not that disaster struck us, but only that Allied momentum was lost and we did not know how to go about restoring it. Neither we nor the other clandestine outfits were able to contribute much to this new war of attrition on the fringes of the Reich. So together with everybody else, we began to establish ourselves in Paris, a magnet for those with even a little pull. The OSS had already staked out posh offices with balconies overlooking the Champs Elysées and commanding a sweeping view from the Arch of Triumph to the Place de la Concorde. Others tried to do as well. Every last WAC secretary and staff lieutenant dredged up the most overpowering reason why orders had to be cut for them to go to Paris. Once they arrived, their London tasks, generally obsolete anyway, were forgotten. The OSS began to take over one hotel after another, and it seems to me now that in a matter of weeks we had filled the nearby Elysées park and Gallia and Powers hotels. As a naval officer, I was entitled to bunk down at the Royal Monceau, the U.S. Navy billet. It turned out to be the only hotel around with hot water. As cold October days descended, I suddenly acquired a lot of friends who wanted to shower in my bathroom.

Work, what there was of it, tended to be routine. We engaged in cleaning up loose ends. We had more than 300 agents to repatriate, for example. Jedburgh teams, Sussex agents, and other groups we had parachuted into France drifted to Paris. There were so many, we had to set up a center at the Cecil Hotel where Bill Hornaday ran a staff of a dozen men arranging for papers and transportation back to

England. A final report in October toted up the list and found we had sent back 321 British, French, and American agents.

Tom Cassady, our liaison man with Vichy before the U.S. entered the war (who had also been active in Algiers after his exchange as a diplomatic prisoner in Baden-Baden) came up to Paris to handle another chore—decorations and letters of commendation and gratitude to the hundreds of resistance leaders, agents, couriers, and families who had provided safe houses for our people. He asked Bruce to get him a French-speaking secretary to help write citations and commendations. Bruce sent Evangeline Bell, his own secretary. Several weeks later Cassady told Bruce that while Miss Bell was extremely capable, her mind seemed elsewhere. Much to Cassady's embarrassment, Bruce replied in his calm, matter-of-fact way, "Well, perhaps we should send her back to Washington. I'm going to marry her soon anyway."

It was that kind of time. Soon after the 7th Army came under Ike's command, having linked up with Patton's forces on the drive up the Rhône, Bruce and I drove to 7th Army headquarters at Vesoul in northeastern France. Ed Gamble commanded the OSS detachment assigned to Patch and took us to see a divisional commander, General Dalquist, in his trailer. Dalquist greeted us cordially, saying, "Bruce, where are you from?" Bruce replied: "Sir, I'm from Virginia." Dalquist looked at the eagles on Bruce's shoulders, snorted, and said: "Hell, I mean what regiment." Clearly he figured a Colonel ought to command something more substantial than an OSS theater.

He lost Gamble for his pains. We brought him back to Paris to command OSS headquarters and made Cassady chief of Secret Intelligence in the French capital. Most of the work dealt with keeping ties open to SHAEF and servicing our detachments with the various U.S. Army commands. They also kept an eye on small OSS centers established at Bordeaux, Annemasse on the Swiss border, and Monaco. Finally, there was counterespionage work. Paris was full of people hiding out, most of them fearful of the Gaullists and the Allies. But some were on the lam from our Russian friends, and we did our best to protect them, no easy task.

Bert Jolis had recruited several Russians who had defected from service with the Germans and was training them for future missions behind enemy lines. One of them was brought to a Russian repatriation camp—I no longer recall the circumstances—and then taken to Le Bourget for the flight back to Russia. On the way, the man, knowing what awaited him at home, managed to get "lost" and found his way to Jolis's headquarters at St. Germain en Laye. Jolis took him to the home of Anatole and Lydia Tolstoy who agreed to harbor him. One day, Mrs. Tolstoy returned home and found her guest gone. Neighbors said a van had drawn up, several men had broken into the house, dragged out her "guest," kicking and screaming, put him in the van, and drove away. He was never heard from again. There would be other Russians, thousands of them, who disappeared in similar fashion as the war wound down, and especially after it was over.

Nor were our French allies easy to deal with at that time. De Gaulle, engaged in a fierce power struggle with the communists, distrusted all Anglo-Saxons in general and all the French who had worked with them; in fact, Gaullists took a jaundiced view of all foreigners not at the front battling Germans. Thus, Colonel Petit-Romans found himself in a Lyon jail, apparently the reward for his brilliant leadership of the Ain maquis. Another resistance leader almost faced court-martial for wearing a British uniform. Four top SOE field chieftains, Frenchmen who had worked diligently against the Nazis all over France, were invited to leave their homeland. General de Gaulle personally told two of them, Starr, a British subject, and Landes, a Frenchman, to get out. But at least these men did not face death or prison.

At most army headquarters, OSS units were either liked or tolerated. Colonel Dickson, the First Army G-2, was an exception. He never wanted "raw intelligence" and decided his units could get their own tactical information without our help. The OSS detachment was banished from his command. But both Colonel Koch at 3rd Army and Colonel Quinn at 7th Army enjoyed having the OSS around and always gave us a warm welcome when we came down from Paris or over from London. At Bradley's Army Group HQ, OSS talent had been integrated into General Sibert's G-2 operation. Lyman Kirkpatrick was his order-of-battle expert and a principal briefer at Bradley's staff meetings. Charley Kindelberger had come over from London to advise on German supply and transportation capability and help select communications targets for the Ninth Tactical Air Force to disrupt. Pat Dolan rose to chief enemy ''morale underminer'' at the front, while Hubert Will advised on counterespionage.

While we were thus waiting to move into the Reich and had run out of major targets in France, our networks were still operating in and behind German-occupied pockets, reporting on ammunition trains at Belfort or oil cars bunched at Strasbourg. These targets were plastered by Allied planes. More importantly, however, we were left to clean up what the Germans had left behind. Mostly this work consisted in checking out rumors and reports through agents on the scene and getting their fresh information to the troops. In some ways this proved harder than it had been before and during the invasion. The Germans had become more cautious, their terrain had shrunk, and we could no longer give such clandestine operations our full support.

After the Americans had crossed the Moselle and moved into the Vosges mountains in eastern France, the going got steadily tougher, and greater ingenuity was required to move agents back and forth. We sent a French forest ranger and a young priest to Bruyères, for example. The priest wore clerical garb and had a cover story that he was hurrying to give last rites to the ranger's desperately ill sister in the next village. The Germans believed him and let the priest move back and forth freely. He set up a chain of subagents who sent information back by couriers. One of them reported seeing sixty 105 millimeter field guns, more firepower than we had encountered between the Mediterranean and the Moselle. The report sent tremors up to divisional, corps, and army headquarters—and back down again to Captain Justin Greene who commanded the OSS unit attached to the 36th Division. Would he confirm the report quickly, please. Greene tried. He had four agents captured and two shot without nailing down the information. Days later the Germans did it for him with authority, laying down a terrifying barrage. Unfazed, Greene found girls willing to cross lines and talk to German soldiers, bringing back unit identification and other information. A local businessman organized a group of retired French artillery officers for Greene who operated along the Meurthe river, east of Lunéville and southwest of Strasbourg. As military specialists, their work was invaluable. They drew 10 overlay maps with 170 pieces of intelligence on them—details of German artillery positions, machine gun and anti-tank emplacements, mine fields, and, incredibly, the field of fire for each German battery. When the 36th smashed across the Meurthe, it moved as if it were on drawing board maneuvers.

One of the boldest and most picturesque OSS adventures of those weeks involved a five-man mission dropped early in September to the maquis of Confrançon, a small village near the Swiss and German frontiers where roads from Dijon and Besançon joined the main Paris-Basle highway. Their task: develop intelligence networks in eastern France, an area Patton was then expected to reach first. The unit commander was Wally Booth, an OSS Lt. Colonel booted out of Spain in May for too diligently shoveling French and Spanish agents into the French Mediterranean coast. Mike Burke, famed at the time for his football prowess at the University of Pennsylvania, was his deputy. Two regular French army officers assigned us by General Koenig and Lieutenant Walter Kuzmuk rounded out the team. Kuzmuk had jumped into Normandy with the 101st Airborne and he owed this assignment to his supposed knowledge of Russian. Shortly before taking off from England, Booth had seen intelligence about Russian deserters working with the Confrançon maquis.

They found the Haute-Savoie swarming with Germans withdrawing from the west and south. The Confrançon maquis numbered 200 well-armed and well-organized men who worked together with 700 men in German uniforms. These were the "Russians" Booth had heard about in England, only in fact they were Ukrainians. Like so many vignettes of the war, this one had a shooting script quality. In August, a German major and thirty SS officers rode into the area on horseback with the 700 Ukrainians, then in German service, and 87 German non-coms walking on foot behind. They were to destroy the maquis. But the Ukrainians had had enough. Their ranking officer, a major named Hloba, secretly met with the maquis to arrange for an ambush. Several nights later, the Ukrainians struck. A pitched battle followed, in which the entire German cadre was wiped out. For several weeks this force of 900 seasoned troops had harassed Germans retreating up the twin roads from Dijon and Besançon that ran on either side of Confrançon forest in which the maquis operated.

It had not taken long, of course, for the story to get back to the Germans. About the time the OSS mission arrived, reports came in that the enemy was massing troops near Luxeil-les-Bains, more than 100 miles to the northeast. By mid-September a German major general moved into the forest with 4,000 soldiers equipped with artillery and tanks. For three days the Germans and the Franco-Ukrainians fought one pitched battle after another. Maquis mortar, machine gun, and anti-tank fire kept the enemy from sweeping through the wooded hideout. Outnumbered four to one and their ammunition exhausted, the maquis were close to giving up. Fortunately, the German general didn't know it, and the next day broke off the engagement, pulling his troops out of the region. Villagers swarmed into the streets, singing, cheering, and kissing.

By this time it was clear that Patch, moving up from the south, would reach the Vosges before Patton could strike far enough east. Booth had a problem: how to get word to Patch's forces not to attack the Ukrainians. Leaving Kuzmuk behind as liaison—it turned out Kuzmuk spoke Polish, not Russian, and it was a stroke of luck that the Ukrainians understood his Polish well enough—Booth and Burke set out to contact advance 7th Army units. Fording the Saone they reached the command post of the 117th Cavalry Reconnaissance Squadron, an isolated unit miles ahead of the main force. Charles Hodge, a hard-bitten Wall Streeter, was in command, having joined the Essex Troop of the National Guard because he liked to play polo and couldn't afford his own ponies. Hodge looked on Booth with some skepticism, especially upon hearing the story of the 700 Ukrainians. What happened next had touches of a Preston Sturges movie. Booth wanted to radio his commanding officer in London. Hodge asked for his name. "Colonel Forgan," Booth replied. Hodges was, in civilian life, a partner in the Wall Street firm of Glore, Forgan. "What's his first name?" Hodges asked. "Russell," Booth said. Hodge now figured he had Booth because Forgan's first name was James, though everybody called him Russ. "What are his initials?" Hodges pressed. "He signs his name J. Russell Forgan," Booth answered. "O.K., you're cleared. Add to your message that Charlie Hodges wishes he were here."

Booth was summoned to 7th Army headquarters and charged with leaving an enemy force astride its lines of communications. The incredulous Booth had to spell out the details of Ukrainian heroics. That got him out of this jam but the Ukrainians into a new one: He was told the U.S. had agreed to turn former Red Army units over to the Russian authorities. Patch's G-2, Colonel Quinn, saved Booth from apoplexy by a sleight of hand. He simply enrolled the Ukrainians in the French Foreign Legion where they could continue fighting the Germans. I do not know if they were able to stay in France or were ultimately repatriated to face certain death.

During these weeks of stalemate, frustration, and often comic confusion, I moved around almost continuously. I had to deal with the constantly changing OSS staff arrangements. So I would spend a few days in London, a couple in Paris, swing to our missions in Belgium and Holland, and then tour OSS attachments assigned to Bradley, Patton, Simpson, Patch, and Devers. Though nominally still chief of the OSS Secretariat in the Eisenhower theater, others were coming in to support my work and take over parts of my job. Charlie Bane and Walter Lord were handling the London Secretariat efficiently and with dispatch. Howard Cady had set up another Secretariat for Bruce in Paris, his new base of operations. Ed Gamble ran France for him, and Lester Armour, England. Bruce was scheduled to return to Washington at the end of the year with Forgan due to succeed him as OSS head in Europe. The Haskell brothers, Joe and John, had left OSS, Joe to command a tank regiment and John to head up an armored strike force that was to seize documents and equipment in captured German cities. Both assignments were more likely to boost a West Point career than continued service under Donovan. We did not lack for replacements, though, and the men who came over to take the jobs said something about the personnel OSS attracted: Gerry Miller, a Detroit investment banker, succeeded Joe Haskell as chief of our Special Operations (SO) and as U.S. co-commander of the joint British-American Special Forces Headquarters (SFHQ). Alan Scaife, a member of the Pittsburgh Mellon clan, took over from John Haskell as Acting Chief of Secret Intelligence (SI).

By mid-October, my constant travel and occasional trouble-shooting had given me a clear idea about what had happened to OSS capability in the last six to eight weeks. Everybody had hustled to Paris. London was denuded. Neither office was really functional. OSS detachments with the armies in the field had little work to do, because contacts with the resistance and the local population either were non-existent or had to be rebuilt. In short, we had staff and organization but few functioning agents, no air lifts, and no communications on the continent. Back in London, our staff had to "ungear" from France and start thinking about penetrating Germany. Meanwhile, however, we had no way of reaching the Reich.

At least none that was clearly visible from the top layer of the organization. But peel that off and there were operatives scattered through Grosvenor Street who kept a purposeful eye on the fatherland. Paradoxically, most of this "private enterprise" intelligence could be found in the Labor section, little noticed during the prelude to Overlord. But the section had been built up by an astute and clever Chicago labor lawyer named Arthur Goldberg. Beginning in 1942 in New York, he had contacted and recruited trade unionists who had fled Hitler's Europe. In London, George Pratt, former chief trial counsel for the National Labor Relations Board, had organized an OSS labor desk. Gerhard Van Arkel, the NLRB's general counsel, had done much the same thing in North Africa. I had gotten first whiff of this potential during a PT boat trip across the English Channel to Cherbourg with Goldberg and Jolis. Goldberg told me about the range of recruits and channels of information available in the German refugee communities of England and the U.S.

Unfortunately, Goldberg had been deceived by September's euphoria. He too thought the war was about over and persuaded Donovan to release him from military service so he could return to his law practice in Chicago. But Pratt and his aide Tom Wilson continued to beef up the London Labor desk for missions to Germany. Gary Van Arkel had set up in Switzerland to grease agent border crossings into Germany. Bert Jolis and Dick Watt had established small units on the continent and were scouting for "agent material" and information on what it took to live in and move around Germany. The base was solid enough, the sense of urgency was not, a fact illustrated by our Polish-American project.

In the summer of 1944, Colonel Stanislaus Gano of Polish intelligence had suggested that we train and send Polish agents into Germany. Working from a pool of 2,000 Poles—who had been pressed into the German army or into work battalions and somehow gotten to England—we selected 40 men. That fall they were put in training in a special school we had set up at Bryanston Square in London. Our plans called for giving them six months training and dispatching them into Germany after May 1, 1945! Even the Poles did not seem in any great hurry. The Scandinavian section was the only one in those days operating effectively and efficiently out of London. Men, weapons, and materials were dropped into Norway and Denmark on a near clockwork schedule.

Part of our problem was Eisenhower's lack of interest in our progress—an attitude that filtered down the ranks. Ike and his staff were too frustrated by stubborn logistical problems and the unexpected strength of German defenses to pay much attention to intelligence initiatives. This did not make Allen Dulles's task any easier and added to our own frustration when we met with Dulles, which we did more or less regularly in Paris. Dulles, too, moved around a lot that fall, peddling his line that more attention should be paid to indigenous German resistance. He would travel to France every week to brief Sibert, the 12th Army Group G-2 and Col. Quinn of the 7th Army. He met in Paris with Bruce or Forgan, or Donovan if he were in town, then drive out to Versailles for a session with General Tom Betts, the ranking American intelligence officer at Ike's HQ. What made his job so difficult was the dissemination and wide currency just then given the Morgenthau Plan to dismember Germany and convert it into "a country primarily agricultural and pastoral in character."

Roosevelt and Churchill had leaked the plan to the Anglo-American press early that fall and given Goebbels a field day. He need do little beyond print such proposals as that the Ruhr "should not only be stripped of all presently existing industries but so weakened and controlled that it could not in the foreseeable future become an industrial area" and that "all industrial plants and equipment not destroyed by military action shall either be completely dismantled or removed from the area or completely destroyed, all equipment shall be removed from the mines and the mines shall be thoroughly wrecked." Exhorting Germans to fight on lest their country be turned into "a potato patch" was hardly distorting the truth, and as is so often the case, the truth was much more effective than the biggest lie. Captured letters from front-line troops showed how well Goebbels had succeeded. True, Roosevelt tried to ease the damage during the 1944 campaign by promising not to enslave the German people. But he refused to budge on unconditional surrender, nor was Washington interested in winning bloodless victories by establishing contacts with generals in enemy ranks. Dulles kept talking into the wind—but he kept talking. He knew that many high-ranking German prisoners were ardent anti-Nazis.

During October, Dulles and Gero von Gaevernitz, an anti-Nazi German-American businessman living in Switzerland, came up with a scheme to use these prisoners to finger German front-line commanders willing to help end the war. Junior officers with anti-Nazi sympathies would then be sent across enemy lines as escaped prisoners to contact the "prospects." The idea was fired by the unhappy experience the

Americans had in General von Schwerin, the commander of a Panzer division in Aachen. Despite Hitler's orders for a last-ditch defense, von Schwerin wanted to declare Aachen an open city to avoid destruction of its Romanesque cathedral and other treasures of the age of Charlemagne—and he let the Americans know it. The population cheered. But for three days the American First Army did not react to von Schwerin's offer.

Meanwhile, a tense drama unfolded inside the city. As the hours passed and still the Americans failed to respond, failed even to begin an advance on Aachen, the SS got wind of the plot and denounced von Schwerin to his superiors. He was ordered to relinquish command of his division and report to Army Corps HQ. Von Schwerin stalled. Military police drove to the farm house where he was headquartered. Panzer soldiers took up positions around the stone building behind mounted machine guns. A tense confrontation brewed, but the police backed down when it became clear that von Schwerin's soldiers would shoot to guard their commander. Von Schwerin stalled for another three days. Still the Americans did not come. He gave up and reported to Corps Headquarters where he lucked into lukewarm Nazi investigators who toned the incident down and spared von Schwerin serious punishment.

The battle for Aachen, meanwhile, lasted until October 13 and involved eight days of bloody street-fighting. It should have made von Gaevernitz's case. Had the Americans been alerted to von Schwerin's messages and known what to do about them—they were not and did not—the city might have been spared and thousands of lives saved. General Sibert now gave the Dulles-von Gaevernitz plan full support. Five German generals were found in various camps ready to help launch probes of front-line enemy loyalty. With Sibert and Bradley behind him, von Gaevernitz now proposed his plan to Eisenhower, who sent it on to Washington. Weeks passed before an answer came: No. The project had been considered and rejected.

In November, Eisenhower tried another tack. He cabled the Combined Chiefs that efforts to reduce the German will to resist should be redoubled. The British concurred. Himmler and Goebbels were getting all the propaganda mileage out of the Morgenthau plan and the Allies were doing nothing to sway German opinion or the German generals. The Russians, they pointed out, were doing both successfully, even influencing the thinking of German generals in Allied hands. The British proposed spreading the story into Germany that the Allies would use German productive capacity after the war to rehabilitate Europe and that after unconditional surrender we would impose stable conditions within Germany. The hope was that German industrialists would swallow the bait and work quietly for an early end to hostilities before all their plants were destroyed.

Again Washington said no. The U.S. Chiefs would only authorize "black" propaganda agencies to disseminate such reports so that they could later be denied. At that, there wouldn't be much to deny. The reports "should be done in a manner which does not by implication commit the Allies to permit the" use of German industry to rehabilitate Europe. On this one, though, the OSS was ahead of the British and our own chiefs. We had started needling German industrial channels before the invasion. What got me thinking about it was a U.S. mission sent to Stockholm in the spring of 1944 to pressure the Swedes into cutting back iron ore and ball bearing export to Germany. The talks showed how heavy the German-Swedish business traffic really was. On a quick visit to Washington in 1944 I suggested to Donovan that this was really worth exploring, perhaps we could find a way of tickling the German cupidity nerve by suggesting they could make more money if Hitler lost the war. Donovan liked the idea and told me to go ahead. Drawing on my Research Institute experience, I suggested publishing a weekly business newsletter from Stockholm that would go to German businessmen. Donovan asked who would write it. I immediately thought of Henry Bund, an Austrian refugee who had moved from the Research Institute to the Quartermaster Corps. Within half an hour—things could be done that quickly in Donovan's shop—the Harvard project was born. We had Bund out of the Quartermaster Corps and into the OSS in a week. Two or three months later a business newsletter, blending defeatist propaganda with solid economic information, was available to German visitors to Stockholm and found its way into the briefcases of Swedes traveling on business to Germany. I don't know how much good the letter, entitled "Handel und Wandel," really did, but the investment and risk were low, and it was one way to reach a part of German society potentially hostile to the Nazi cause. Bund wrote the letter from Washington every week. It pretended to be prepared by German interests in Sweden and certainly read that way. It lasted from July 1944 right up to April 1945.

It was, of course, a far cry from the kind of contacts we might have had with the Germans if Washington had only allowed them.

17. Counterattack

THE SURPRISE and power of Hitler's drive through the Ardennes sent shock waves from the Allied high command to GIs stocking supplies in the rear areas. We had accepted the fact that Hitler had reconstituted an army that would put up a tough and costly defense of the homeland. That he could actually force the Allied armies to retreat none of us was prepared to believe. For a week or so, alarm and near panic spread through the Allied forces in Europe.

Nobody expected an attack in the Ardennes. The 80-mile stretch from Echternach on the Sauer to the Monschau river was held by one corps of Hodges First Army, four combat-weary divisions sent there for rest and relaxation. Allied brass were convinced the Germans lacked the punch to mount an effective counter-strike.

But just before dawn on December 16, the Germans opened up with a tremendous artillery barrage. Fourteen inch guns had been mounted on flat-bed freight cars behind the line to pound positions. After an ominous pause, Hodges's tired and frightened soldiers saw the great hulks of Tiger tanks crunch through the fog. Behind them, eerie in the milky white mist, marched row upon row of white-clad Wehrmacht soldiers. The Battle of the Bulge had begun. Hitler had committed 28 divisions, including ten of armor, grouped into three armies to the assault. They were supported by 2,000 fighter aircraft, 80 of them revolutionary jets, the Me-262, and 400 bombers. And Hitler had placed 30,000 tons of ammunition and 6 million tons of fuel at Field Marshal von Rundstedt's disposal.

By nightfall on the 16th, the Germans swept toward the Meuse as if it were that balmy May of victory in 1940, not the winter of defeat of 1944. Dazed, the Americans reeled back. On the 17th, the Germans had cut a wedge out of Allied lines 12 miles deep and six miles wide. On the 18th, the Tigers were across the Amblève. The next evening, the Panzers had ground to within 15 miles of Liège. On the 20th, the Germans were outside Bastogne, and the stage was set for the famous confrontation with Brigadier General Anthony McAuliffe, whose contemptuous "nuts" to German surrender demands made military history.

And only on the 20th did Bradley's command realize that this was a full-blooded offensive. Wires were crossed constantly, commands given and rescinded. It took days of confusion to pull the Allied armies back together so they could prepare a counter-strike. Near panic gripped our forces for a week, a panic heightened by clever German use of psychological warfare. It wreaked havoc behind the lines.

"Operation Greif" (German for "grab") had been ordered by the Führer in person. Lt. Colonel Otto Skorzeny, the scar-faced Viennese adventurer whose exploits in snatching Mussolini and Hungarian dictator Horthy's son had made him a legend, was put in command. Attaching Skorzeny's name to "Greif" gave it extra cachet. So did the capture, two weeks before the Ardennes offensive, of a German order calling for recruitment of English-speaking German soldiers for a special mission. The information was too vague to do much about, but ominous enough to cause concern, and contributed to our confusion when the attack came. Then, several hundred men, some parachutists, others in cars that raced ahead of the Panzers, arrived behind our lines. They wore American uniforms and drove U.S. jeeps. One of the first of these "special unit" soldiers who had been captured said that they had orders to assassinate Eisenhower, Bradley, Patton, and Hodges.

That tore it. A mixture of panic and slapstick seized the rear echelon. Security forces had a field day. Road blocks were set up all the way to Paris. GIs spent hours checking each other out with questions designed to flabbergast any German in American uniform. Who is Lou Gehrig? Betty Grable? What's the capital of Illinois? Where does the short-stop stand, a guard line up in a football team? Woe to the GI who didn't go to the movies or read the sports pages— including one general held for hours by GIs either suspicious or capricious. The fake Americans, though, were hard to catch. They had been well trained, down to striking matches inward, U.S. style, not outward.

One more element added to the confusion—the intelligence failure. The Allies had grown complacent. Ultra had spoiled our generals. They had little use for any intelligence lower than communication intercepts between Hitler and his commanders. At all levels, there had been an attrition in the patience needed to sift and work masses of detail into a mosaic revealing enemy intentions and purposes. Now Ultra failed. In the Ardennes offensive the Germans had decreed radio silence. Vital communications moved over land lines we could not tap. Nor did we have any information from behind enemy lines. There was no FFI in Germany itself whose resources we could utilize. Aerial reconnaissance wasn't much good in that cold, foggy winter. Prisoner-of-war intelligence was limited. The Germans made sure that subordinate unit commanders knew as little as possible beyond their own target, and were briefed on that as late as possible. Precautions against desertion were tightened. It added up to what the post-mortems showed: Neither Bradley nor Montgomery's headquarters had any hard intelligence pointing to German intentions of attacking the Ardennes. Yet a few well-placed agents, say "tourists" marching through the forested hills of the Eifel, or men watching the hundreds of trains pass through key centers like Cologne or Koblentz to well camouflaged and dispersed assembly points in Hitler's thinly populated launching area, could have spotted German intentions and reported on them.

The surprise and heavy casualties caused by the Ardennes offensive were widely attributed on both sides of the Channel and both sides of the Atlantic to a colossal intelligence failure.

At SHAEF and Twelfth Army group, the intelligence estimates emphasized dwindling German strength. The First Army, where the German counterattack hit, was caught off guard, although in a December 10 intelligence estimate Colonel Monk Dickson, First Army G-2, predicted a German counterattack well north of the Ardennes. He did not, however, believe the German counterattack was imminent. When the Ardennes thrust hit, Dickson was in Paris on his first leave since landing in Normandy.

Donovan must have reached for an airplane the moment he heard about Hitler's drive into the Ardennes. He was in Paris a few days before Christmas.

Intuitively, Donovan sensed both failure and opportunity. He blamed Colonel Dickson for the intelligence failure. The successful German surprise had struck the front where the man responsible for reading German capabilities and intentions had proclaimed his reliance on processed intelligence passed down from higher headquarters, and kept Donovan's intelligence staff out of First Army HQ. But Donovan knew too that neither the OSS nor the British were producing enough intelligence from behind German lines. He sensed immediately that getting caught flat-footed in the Ardennes would create for the first time a clamor to get agents inside Germany. Always a swift decision-maker, Donovan acted, and this time I became the target of his action.

A few days before Christmas, when the situation in the Bulge loomed its worst, and Allied confusion seemed rampant, I was named Chief of Secret Intelligence for the European Theater. I was all of 31, but already middle-aged by OSS standards. I was given blanket authority to concentrate all of the OSS's resources on prying fresh intelligence out of the Reich.

My new status had its problems. I was still, officially, a lieutenant in the U.S. Navy, yet colonels and Navy commanders would be reporting to me, and I would be dealing with British and American generals directly. Captain Lester Armour, then the ranking naval officer in the OSS, walked me over to Admiral Stark's office across Grosvenor Square to discuss my protocol plight. We mulled the problem for a while, then Stark and Armour decided that I had best become a civilian again. I was put on inactive duty and sent out to buy some grey suits.

There was not much time to waste that Christmas. The sweep through France and into Germany had all but put OSS out of business in Eisenhower's theater. We had placed two agents into Germany in the fall of 1944, but neither had any means of getting information out. A third man had a radio, but he operated out of Holland and would soon be captured and played back against us. Our British partners and tutors had decided long ago that the odds against agents sent to Germany were stacked too high. Controls were too tight, sources of help too slight. With Bastogne still under siege and the issue very much in doubt, I went to see Sir Stewart Menzies, the head of MI-6's SIS and Sir Gerald Templer (a future Field Marshal and Chief of the Imperial General Staff), then head of the Special Operations Executive German section. Both were highly skeptical that we could get men in a position to operate and sustain themselves in the tightly controlled and hostile Reich. This shook me, but we had to try. The Battle of the Bulge was proving how much punch the Wehrmacht had left. The men who would have to lay their lives on the line were entitled to better information than we had been giving them.

Meanwhile, SHAEF and Bradley's G-2, Brigadier General Edwin Sibert, had an immediate, urgent task for us. No one knew how far the German advance might take the Wehrmacht. We were to establish ''sleeper'' teams, an observer and a radio operator, and put them in the path of the expected German advance. These teams were to give us better and faster information for our counterattack and it is a measure of the near panic that prevailed that we were instructed to lay "sleepers" all the way back to Reims. By the end of December, with the Germans still on the offensive, we had 20 "sleeper" teams in place. Happily, the Germans never got far enough to make their activation necessary.

Early in January, I left London for the front. The Dakota bounced over a choppy Channel and across bleak French fields. The spires of Reims cathedral were festooned with scraps of fog. A staff car took me from the airport to begin a series of talks with Army G-2s and OSS detachments assigned to Twelfth Army Group HQ and the U.S. First, Third, Seventh, and Ninth Armies. It was a journey of several hundred miles along iced roads. Often we could hear the sound of enemy gunfire and see shadowy forms move through the fog. The talks and the trip itself were invaluable. They gave me a feel for how the front had tightened and the situation in the forward areas had changed. There were more roadblocks and controls. Mines made crossing battle lines more difficult. Reliable recruits who knew the country and could move easily among Germans were harder and harder to find.

But the Army intelligence officers all bolstered my own feelings about what we had to do. Tactical intelligence they could get from patrols, prisoner interrogation, and aerial reconnaissance. They needed reports on troop movements well behind the front lines, information, in short, only agents could obtain.

The biggest asset on my inventory list was Joan Eleanor. No, not a sultry agent who coaxed secrets from impassioned SS lovers but a four pound "wireless telephone" agents could use to communicate quickly, clearly, and safely with a plane directly overhead. It had been developed some months before by a brilliant and hard-driving RCA engineer named Steve Simpson, who carried the rank of lieutenant commander in the U.S. Navy. Give him some airplanes and a few men to train, Simpson had said, and he could come up with a communications system German direction finders on the ground could not hear. Within three weeks he had the RCA laboratories working on the device while he studied maps and began his training program for Joan Eleanor, or J/E as we quickly dubbed it. Joan Eleanor was a honey. The agent would be dropped with the compact device in his pocket. It was that easy to carry and to conceal. Small long-life batteries eliminated the need for an outside power supply, the bane of wireless transmission operators sent to Germany. With a J/E the agent could stand in the middle of a field and talk directly to an OSS officer circling in a Mosquito or other high-flying airplane. The agent could have messages repeated to make sure he had gotten them right. He could ask for clarifications on the spot and not wait hours and days to get them. All conversations were recorded aboard the plane and thus a permanent record was kept. The delays and garbles so endemic from coding and decoding operations were eliminated. The OSS officer in the plane could brief the agent directly. Questions could be asked and answered at once. The threat of enemy detection of a message in the air was reduced almost to zero.

Joan Eleanor was first tested in November. Simpson had wheedled three patched-up Mosquito planes from the British for his mission. He had stripped them, installed the needed equipment, and studied the prospects for loading more gasoline to lengthen the range. On November 10, a 27-year-old Dutch engineer named Anton Schrader jumped from an airplane for the first time in his life. He had Eleanor—the transmitting device—stuck in his pocket. He was codenamed Bobbie. Days after he jumped, Simpson tried to make contact with him, and failed. So did a second effort. Both failures were the result of technical malfunctions in the creaking Mosquito. On November 21, Simpson switched planes. He flew over Holland in a second Mosquito. Despite fierce German flak fire, Simpson heard "Bobbie" describe his location and the Panzer regiment he had seen heading toward Arnhem. Joan Eleanor worked. And the quality of intelligence Bobbie provided matched the technological innovation. Another report from Bobbie in early December about a Panzer Division rushing out through Holland should have alerted us to the German mobilization for the Ardennes, but its significance wasn't recognized. Months later, Bobbie was captured by the

Germans and played back. He signalled that he was under duress and this time we recognized instantly that he was under enemy control. I needed all the encouragement I could get. Equipping planes for spy flights proved difficult and burdensome; so was finding pilots willing to fly as deeply into the Reich as we wanted them to, and planes able to do it. The OSS was once again embroiled in a shootout with other parts of the armed forces. This time we were at odds with the 492nd Bombardment Group of the 8th Air Force. The unit had flown our agents into France during the spring and summer. But since September, the planes of the 492nd had been flying regular supply and bombing missions. One squadron had been detached from the Western Front and sent to Italy to fly with the 15th Air Force. John Bross, named OSS executive officer in London that fall, negotiated with the Air Force for return of the 492nd's planes to parachute missions. Progress was slow. True, they had agreed to drop Bobbie over Holland, but not much more. A new commanding officer and his green crews had little experience and less interest in dropping men blind into enemy territory. The generals drew lines on maps. Their planes would not drop anyone north of Stuttgart or west of Munich. If we were to accomplish our tactical mission, we had to fight the bureaucratic battle first. We did. It took two months to win it.

After returning to London from my swing along the front, and after completing my own "inventory" of OSS assets and liabilities, Russ Forgan and I flew back to France. We wanted guidance from SHAEF on just what observations from our agents would be most useful. An appointment was set up at Versailles for us with General Betts, Eisenhower's American deputy G-2. Our jeep rattled up the cobblestones and across the courtyard of the magnificent palace. Too much fog, I thought, too much grime. The building's beauty shone only fitfully. We were taken into Betts's office. It looked like a movie set. The floor-length French windows revealed a snow-packed park below. The room was large. The walk to Betts's desk was interminable.

Once we were seated, though, Betts briefed us briskly and in no-nonsense fashion. Eisenhower had decided to clear the west bank of the Rhine before attempting to cross the river. The Allied advance had stalled, going was tough, and German resistance in the homeland was fierce. Still, SHAEF felt that Bradley and Devers at 12th Army Group HQ and the generals in the field had the situation in hand—well enough, at any rate, for SHAEF to get busy preparing the next step: storming the river. Crossing the Rhine was to be the big operation. Preparations were to be extensive. Overwhelming force would be used. The assault would rival Normandy in breadth and scope. There were to be no salients or spearheads. A broad front strategy, Eisenhower reasoned, would keep Hitler's forces spread out thin. Intelligence for such strategy had to focus on reinforcements moving up behind the lines and on shifts of individual divisions from one part of the front to another. Target areas for the OSS, Betts said, should be the Ruhr and Frankfurt. We should put agents at road and rail centers leading to both regions since Montgomery would attack the Ruhr while Bradley's forces pointed south and east of Frankfurt. After the briefing, Betts offered us a drink and wished us well. As we walked through the dusk to our car I wondered where we would get the men we needed, men who were ready to go into Germany and who were trained to stay alive and function there.

Back in London I pondered the problem some more. We had no time for any extensive selection and training process. We were down to recruiting non-communist German refugees and anti-Bolshevik Russians, as Bert Jolis was doing in Paris, or sifting through anti-Nazi deserters and prisoners of war, or emigré Poles, Dutch, French, and Belgians. I had watched this operation on my visit to Bari the previous summer and on my recent visit to Henry Hyde's 7th Army OSS detachment at Lunéville. It was slow work and the pickings were often slim.

Joe Gould, a labor organizer and former President of the Screen Publicists Guild, had spent months in London among refugees with diverse left-wing political backgrounds, including communists. He had found seven men willing to go to Germany. They were all family men in their thirties or forties. But some had been contacted through CALPO, a Free

Germany committee that took the same political line in western Europe as did Moscow's Free Germany committee, and the link was troublesome. Some in the OSS counseled strongly against using agents with communist ties. They would be more interested in a Soviet-dominated, communist-run Germany than in saving Allied lives. Donovan, however, adhered to a policy of working with anyone who might help win the war. We decided, therefore, to use all seven of Gould's recruits.

The Poles, French, Belgians, and Dutch would have to pose as foreign workers. The initial problem, however, was not their survival but their availability. Relations with the French intelligence service under Jacques Soustelle had been strained since September. The French haggled about the degree of control they would continue to exercise over agents they made available to us for work in Germany. But since the French weren't giving us any men anyway, the argument was largely academic. Soustelle was busy fighting communists in France and in helping de Lattre's French First Army. Our needs came last. In early January, therefore, I moved to end the fruitless bickering with Soustelle. We set up a French desk of our own in London manned by Harold Haviland, fresh from his work of drafting cover stories for the "sleeper" teams on the road to Reims. He was soon able to have a working arrangement with Soustelle, whose early opposition to our efforts had been softened by the shock of the Bulge. He proceeded to give us French agents we could train for missions inside the Reich. It took the same kind of horse-trading with the Belgians and the Dutch to get us needed manpower.

I gave George Pratt—who had served as chief trial examiner for the National Labor Relations Board before coming to the OSS—responsibility for setting up an organization for dispatching agents behind enemy lines and got it staffed with a team of pros. It was called the Division of Intelligence Procurement, a good bureaucratic term that could mean anything we wanted it to mean.

I prepared a directive to crystalize our purpose and procedures and define priority intelligence objectives and the kind of agents we would need to gain them. Our first priority, I specified, were missions to report on troop movements through rail centers. Selection and pinpointing of bombing targets came next; then obtaining industrial information on production schedules, plant sites, and technological innovation; and then finally discovering Nazi plans for last ditch resistance and postwar underground activity as well as the potential for indigenous anti-Nazi resistance. OSS field units attached to the advancing armies were instructed to search for agent material and were assured of full support from London for deep penetration missions. Cover, briefing, air drop, and communications capabilities would be provided. These instructions I applied broadly to everybody except Henry Hyde's detachment with the 7th Army. Hyde's operation was special. He had made his unit fully self-contained. It had its own operational intelligence, cover, and briefing capability, thanks to an Austrian adjutant in the German army he plucked out of a POW camp. Hyde had his own men forge documents and forage for clothes. Bill Quinn, the 7th Army's G-2, was so pleased with Hyde that he gave him most things he needed, including planes to drop agents. Though he was nominally under my command after the North African OSS unit blended into Eisenhower's theater, I had the good sense to leave him alone. I give myself credit, still, for realizing instantly that Hyde knew what he was doing so well that I only had to define intelligence objectives and give him all the support he needed or wanted. There wasn't much of that either. I did control the air lift and made sure Hyde got his share. Occasionally, Hyde or one of his agents came to London to pick up radio equipment or get help in printing forged documents. That was it.

Hyde prepared everything with meticulous care, and chose, equipped, and shipped out agents with confidence and dispatch. He figured that disgruntled POWs were his best agent source. And after clearing the use of prisoners with Donovan—who agreed, provided Patch and Quinn did, too, which they did, enthusiastically—he set to work. He found a brick and stone barracks in Sarrebourg in Lorraine and converted it into a prisoner-of-war cage. Next, he assigned three refugees from Nazi terror to work the camps. Peter Viertel was the son of a leading Viennese theater director, Berthold Viertel, and after the war blossomed into a leading American screenwriter and novelist. Walter Muecke carved out a postwar career in New York real estate. Peter Sichel came from a family of well-known German wine merchants. No one could have asked for three more polished performers or more dedicated professionals. They sat hunched for hours sifting military and personnel record cards of prisoners or discussing individuals with their interrogators. Anyone with anti-Nazi identification—a Socialist past; a spell in a punishment battalion; Austrian, Czech, or Polish nationality—became a possible recruit. Sometimes our trio dressed up in German uniforms and had themselves inserted in the POW cages to talk with prisoners. More often they would interview captured Germans without subterfuge. But their purpose was always to find out just how strong a man's anti-Nazi feelings were and what he was prepared to do about them. Once his activist outlook had been established, he would be asked if he were interested in returning to Germany to help bring this senseless war to an end. Germany had lost the war, Viertel, Muecke, or Sichel would explain earnestly, and both sides really wanted peace. Hitler, however, was a madman who blocked all sensible efforts to end the bloodshed and was as much their enemy as he was ours. If they went to Germany they would not be traitors, but builders of a new German future. Their pitch worked beautifully. Every so often they brought Hyde in to deliver the clincher. As good an actor as his German-speaking front men, Hyde delivered his arguments in polished English. The combination was dynamite. Before the OSS 7th Army was finished, they had recruited 40 agents and sent them back to Germany without one being fingered as a double-agent or letting us down.

Once an agent was selected, the serious business of readying his mission began. The new agent was taken to a nearby safe house where he signed a contract with the OSS. He was to keep his mouth shut and not betray any secrets. In return, he would get an agreed-upon compensation for his services. Usually, there was an under-the-table agreement to reward the man for good work by helping him and his family in the postwar period. The carrot was backed up by a stick: Treachery would not be forgotten in a world where the Allies, not the Germans, ruled.

Next came a relatively brief training period. The recruit was taken to a ''Joe'' or agent house, given khaki fatigues and combat boots, and put to work. He attended classes on identifying German weapons and insignia, for example, and usually revealed how little he knew of procedures and weapons used outside his own unit. Parachute training was rudimentary. By the time an agent was ready to go, Bill Quinn would specify information he wanted about a unit behind the lines, a bombing target, or a town or village.

Captured German staff maps of the area were hauled out and spread on a rough-hewn kitchen table. Aerial photographs were studied to find an open field or a clearing in the woods as a dropping point. Usually the zone was not too near a town and was linked to a river or lake or some other landmark easy to identify from the air.

Meanwhile, the OSS infrastructure swung into action. George Howe—in peacetime a distinguished architect who had designed Donovan's farmhouse in Berryville, Virginia— had set up a print shop in Strasbourg to forge papers and stamps for 7th Army agents. He also grew expert in developing cover stories. The hardware Howe—or sometimes, in more difficult cases, Willis Reddick's printshop in London— produced covered the gamut. The agent was given the dog tag every German soldier wore around his neck, his pay book, travel orders, train tickets, and ration stamps. All of them were carefully crafted to dovetail with his new identity. A visit to our lovingly built-up stock of German uniforms and other paraphernalia followed. The agent would get a uniform, have his picture taken to complete the documentation process, and would rehearse the cover story until he would blurt it out when awakened from a deep sleep. All the details of his recent and not so recent past had to stand up to fierce questioning. Finally, aerial photos were studied once more to select a home address—in a bombed out building difficult to check on.

Most of these turned POWs were sent on "tourist" missions. At first, we pushed them through enemy lines for quick trips and had them try to return the same way. But this proved too risky. The chances of getting shot or blown up by mines doubled, for one thing. For another, cover stories did not hold up as well. If the agent belonged at the front, somebody in the area should have known him. Later, we parachuted the men about 50 miles behind the lines. There they had time to develop their new identities and give their forged orders greater credibility. That eased their return.

In London, the agent material we had—Poles, Belgians, Dutchmen, Czechs, Germans, Russians—usually called for an identity and cover story as a foreign worker or as a German civil or military official. With three million foreign workers in Germany, an observer need not speak too much German. His past could not be easily checked. He could get into war industries or work for the military. We could concoct for him the foreign worker's passport and the work permit he would need. It was easier to provide and harder to check a foreign worker's documents than the identity card, police registration, labor registration, food and clothing ration stamps, travel permits, housing registration, driver's license, and draft exemptions of a German civilian.

When we had a German or an eastern European recruit, the best cover was that of a military officer or civilian official. We knew a great deal about the Gestapo and the Todt organization. This cover provided a reason to travel and to have access to military and industrial installations.

By the end of January I could see daylight. We would be able to deliver, I figured, in the next three to four months.

18. The Penetration of Germany

By THE END of January, Allied confusion over the Battle of the Bulge had begun to abate and the psychological shock had faded, but some indecision remained within the high councils of SHAEF. At one point Eisenhower toyed seriously with the idea of giving up Strasbourg, if need be, to stabilize the frontline. It took frantic Gaullist protests and judicious Churchillian rhetoric to avoid that political—if not military—disaster. Plans for a wide sweep to the Rhine began to take concrete shape. First the "Colmar Pocket" was to be cleaned out by the First French Army helped by four American divisions. Then the drive deeper into the Reich would begin.

I returned to France to confer once again with Brig. General Betts, Ike's Deputy G-2, still ensconced in the splendors of Versailles. I reported that during January we had sent one agent overland through Switzerland to Vienna and that B-24s had dropped agents near Stuttgart, Pforzheim, and Karlsruhe. Betts was more interested in rail and road centers leading into the Ruhr and the Frankfurt area, which were to be Montgomery and Bradley's targets after they had cleared the west bank of the Rhine and made the big river crossing. I told Betts that we were ready. Over the next 90 days, the OSS expected to send 100 intelligence observers into the Reich. Our foreign workers could go to almost any center where there were factories. The kind of broad front strategy Eisenhower had adopted—a general sweep rather than one main thrust or selected hammer blows—demanded front-wide intelligence. Betts picked up a pointer and moved it over the map on his wall. Rail and road crossings were of paramount importance so that we could keep tabs on German reinforcements and on how individual divisions were being shifted from one part of the front to another. We developed a list of 20 major cities that ran down a wide crescent from Bremen in the northwest through the Ruhr, and the Rhineland into Bavaria and Saxony, plus points on a north-south line drawn along a Berlin-Leipzig-Munich axis. That would take some refining back in London but it would be our starting point.

I told Betts that the OSS had the men for the job but that we would need SHAEF's help in obtaining the necessary planes. The planes we had were too slow, and the air force refused to drop men north of Stuttgart or east of Munich, thus effectively ruling out penetration of half the targets on Betts's list. Finally, we needed planes equipped with Joan Eleanor systems to make effective use of the men we intended to plant far inside Germany. Betts tended to be noncommittal. If he made binding promises I don't remember them, nor did SHAEF really get into the middle of our intramural squabbles. We had our orders, the G-2 implied, and it was up to us to see that we carried them out.

We did the best we could. For the February moon period that ran from February 18th to March 3rd we had only the lumbering B-24s and our dropping areas were limited to the region east of Munich, south of Stuttgart, and into northeastern Holland. Given the equipment we had and the situation we faced, the restrictions made sense. The B-24 was a solid workhorse but not a craft adaptable to delicate missions. It could not maneuver easily, navigational aids on the plane were limited, and the craft was a sitting duck for heavy flak concentrations. During that moon period we learned—once again—that weather and the equipment to master it were our greatest obstacles. We tried everything. Headquarters were moved to Lyon to cut flying time and distance. We hit seven straight days of bad weather and we simply didn't have the planes or the organization to get the most out of the few good nights the weather gods granted us.

OSS London rustled up transport to take our trained men to Lyon for flights into Germany. Up at the 7th Army front, Hyde decided that Lyon was a better jumping off place for his men as well. As a result of this convergence, agent handlers from London and from the 7th Army base at Lunéville constantly got into each other's way. And there was no one on the spot with the authority needed to resolve disputes as they came up. We only got off six missions. They went into the Frankfurt, Stuttgart, Mainz, and Pforzheim areas. Ten others had to be aborted.

On the first day of March, however, we made a big breakthrough. It came not from Lyon but from London. Steve Simpson had wangled an A-26, a faster, more versatile plane, to take a mission to Berlin. Joe Gould had recruited the men and they carried the Joan Eleanor ground-to-plane wireless telephone equipment. The problems were immense. The plane had to fly through a dense corridor of German flak. The route was long, fuel supply difficult. Simpson solved both brilliantly. The A-26, he decided, would climb up 6,000 feet over the English channel, then dive at 425 miles an hour—fighter speed for those days—through the flak-ringed Dutch coast and then hedgehop along a pre-arranged zig-zag course to Berlin. The fuel question was resolved as ingeniously. First, the plane warmed up, a process that consumed 75 to 100 gallons. Then the tanks were refilled to provide a full load. As an extra safety precaution, arrangements were made to have the plane land in Sweden if necessary. Finally, demolition charges were attached to the top-secret Joan Eleanor equipment. The meticulous planning paid off. On March 2 the A-26 dropped the two native Berliner communists—who made up the team (codenamed Hammer)—about 30 miles from Berlin. Then it swung for home and returned to London with less than 100 gallons in its tanks. Our two agents, meanwhile, had walked to the nearest town and taken a train into Berlin. One had family in the German capital. The agents moved in with them. They were able to get around Berlin freely and to gather useful information on local conditions.

The next moon period was coming up quickly, starting on March 18. It seemed likely that preparations for the jump across the Rhine would be completed before the end of March. We had to go all out and we needed fast assault light bombers, A-26s and A-20s to carry agents far to the east and north. We moved our bases closer to the Reich—at Dijon in France and Namur in Belgium. I gave Cal Bowman, my executive officer, authority to coordinate air operations with Eighth Air Force headquarters in England and our airfield at Harrington from which B-24s could reach into eastern Germany. We set out to squeeze into the March moon period not only the ten missions that had been scrubbed by weather in February, but our missions for March and our whole program for April. Armed with Betts's ambiguous support, John Bross got the air force to assign us two additional A-26s. We arranged to keep four B-24s at Dijon so that several missions could be flown on good nights. General Bradley got Elliot Roosevelt's 155th Photo Recon Squadron to adapt three of their A-20s for our work and fly from Namur in Belgium for shorter drops across the Rhine. Milton Katz went to Namur to establish priorities and direct the dispatching. Hans Tofte took on the same assignment at Dijon. His B-24s were scheduled to make as many as four and five drops on the nightly tours being scheduled for them around southern Germany. The weather remained brutal. Cloud formations moved in from Russia and the Atlantic. On March 5, Bradley had Hodges strike out for Cologne while Patton thrust for Koblenz through the forests of the Eifel. Within two days, resistance on the west bank of the Rhine collapsed. The first white flags hung on houses with all the windows shuttered. Patton was slashing through the Saar Palatinate to line up with the Seventh Army. Although we had snatched the Remagen bridge on March 7, the big effort across the Rhine was still to be made, and Monty was preparing in his massive way.

Monty took nothing for granted. His Rhine journey would equal Siegfried's, in noise level if nothing else. His preparations rivaled and perhaps exceeded those made for the Normandy invasion. All through the dreary March weeks, Allied planes plastered the Ruhr in order to seal off the Reich's industrial basin from the rest of the country. Rail yards, bridges, and canals were bombed systematically.

For three days before Monty's March 24 Rhine D-Day, our aircraft flew 1,000 sorties against barracks, air fields, and communications centers east of the river. On March 23, Allied artillery laid down a deafening barrage that ended abruptly at nine that evening. Men of the Black Watch huddled into landing craft and the boats chugged to the other side in seven minutes flat. Next morning, 3,000 transport planes and gliders ferried 20,000 troops from fields in England and France to the east bank, an operation that lasted precisely from 10 a.m. to 12:30 p.m.

For all the Wagnerian thunder, Monty's operation had lost much of its glamor. The day before, on March 23, a gleeful Patton had sneaked six battalions across the Rhine and told the world that he had arrived before Montgomery had started. At Bradley's headquarters, the G-2 briefer rubbed salt into the British wounds. Poking his pointer at the map, he announced: "Yesterday, without weeks of air attack, without weeks of artillery bombardment, without the help of the Navy, without airborne troops, and without a smoke screen, General Patton crossed the Rhine." Bradley followed up with a radio broadcast in which he needled the British further by concluding that with the First and Third Armies across the river, the Rhine could be breached anywhere with ease.

The intensity of the actions and the massive preparations for them put the heaviest pressures on OSS operations. It mattered little to us or to the generals we served that in retrospect the war seemed almost won. The need for front-line intelligence remained great, as did demands for information on what was really going on inside Hitler's fast crumbling Reich.

By the end of the March moon period, we had dropped 30 teams into Germany. But with the Rhine breached and American armies slashing farther and farther into the Reich, demands for intelligence mounted, and we decided to drop men in the dark of the moon for the first time.

The weeks grew wilder and more hectic as we tried to cope with growing demands. My life was made up of all-day conferences on every imaginable subject: pinpoints, cover, briefing and communications arrangements, keeping intelligence directives up to date, giving final approval to new missions. At night I drove out to Harrington to see off our agents, then back to London for a few hours sleep if I was lucky. Our war room at 70 Grosvenor Street was organized chaos. Battle fronts, bomb lines, field missions, scheduled missions, new intelligence, all were posted day and night, as they came in and as they changed. Our operational map began to look like a slow-motion film, pins outlining Allied lines changed hourly. The decision-making process became a chess game against the clock. Once an OSS pinpoint for a drop or tourist mission was swamped by advancing Allied armies or looked too close to them, operational plans were altered. A new dropping zone had to be selected quickly and the reasons for choosing it factored rapidly into our new strategic equation. We had to consider ultimate mission objectives, and such vital details as new cover stories for agents and data about the location of anti-aircraft batteries and air fields where night fighters might be based. The A-26 could usually outmaneuver ground fire, but a flock of night fighters was another matter for an unprotected craft flying alone. Drops in the dark-moon period complicated site selection. Usually, we had looked for a flat field adjacent to woods and away from houses, main roads, and railway lines. Now we had to add landmarks easily identifiable in the dark, a river or lake for example.

Statistics cemented our progress reports. In a month—from March 17 to April 25—we had sent 58 teams into Germany, 28 from London directly. Hyde and his 7th Army Group had dispatched 15, de Gaulle's French services 9, the 9th Army OSS detachment 7, the 3rd Army 1, while one had gone in from Paris. The work was risky. Everyone knew that and accepted the risk. But in the last two months of the war, chaos and strategic uncertainty became additional factors. Armies moved so swiftly that shifts of team targets by several hundred miles became necessary and were cheerfully accepted. In that vast, milling, disorganized interior of Germany, it was impossible to predict whether a field that looked placid and empty on recent aerial photographs would be crowded with troops by the time a team was dropped. Nearly all our agents leaped into the dark and the unknown. Needless to say, our admiration for this motley crew of Belgians and Frenchmen, German prisoners and deserters, Dutchmen and Poles, deepened as the weeks wore on. They were incredibly brave and tough, none more, perhaps, than the Poles whose morale had sunk close to zero in the wake of the Yalta agreement to recognize the communist Lublin government and not the Polish government-in-exile in London. The Polish soldiers we had trained so carefully began to grumble, while we were criticized for sending them so late in April. But our orders were clear: As long as soldiers fought they were entitled to all the intelligence we could provide. For all their grumbling, therefore, the Poles went, and though none were able to make their radios work inside Germany, most of them were able to give us useful intelligence when they were overrun.

Many of our missions produced valuable target information. On March 29, an A-26 made a Joan Eleanor contact with the Hammer team at Berlin that yielded important air target data on a still-functioning power plant that kept several key factories running. Hammer also detailed the importance of the Berlin transportation net and suggested key spots where bombs could disrupt it.

On April 5, Fred Gercke of our German desk dispatched the Luxe I team into the Reich. Ferdi Lammershirt and Leon Verbach were highly motivated men. They had been promised a chance at U.S. citizenship on their return. Dropped blind near Weilheim in southern Bavaria, Luxe I built up a chain of informants in the town of Rasiting, not far from their dropping point, and in the surrounding countryside. Active until April 29, when they were overrun, Luxe I was a productive team. It located an Me 262 jet fighter plant in an underground tunnel on the Olympia Highway to Munich, pinpointed troop and traffic movements at Weilheim, and spotted defenses set up around Landsberg.

In the early morning hours of April 17, to cite one example of Luxe I in action, Lammershirt took his J/E out to an open field and made contact with a Mosquito circling overhead. During the ground to air conversation, taped on a wire recorder, Lammershirt called for an air strike against the Weilheim railroad junction through which 40 to 50 trains passed each night, and on two airplane factories nearby. The tape was transcribed, sent immediately to air force intelligence in England and relayed to the 15th Air Force in Italy, whose planes could reach Bavaria more easily than those stationed in the west. A little after noon on the next day, formations of 78 P-38 dive bombers streaked across the skies to plaster Weilheim's rail yards and factories.

We put another team, codenamed Pickaxe, into Landshut near Munich. The two agents funneled massive amounts of information about rail and road traffic, communications centers and troop movements—down to shoulder-patch and other marking descriptions—to waiting Mosquitos during no fewer than 9 Joan Eleanor reports. One typical message cited heavy troop movements through the Landshut rail junction. The information was relayed to Air Force HQ the next morning. That night both railroad station and yards were heavily bombed. A follow up report on the damage was radioed up to a Mosquito 24 hours later.

Two Belgians made up the Chauffeur team and were dropped near Regensburg in late March. Their operations were a good example of how porous internal German security had become and how easily an agent could operate in that climate. Good luck, of course, helped.

They were dropped with a regular radio set and with Joan Eleanor equipment. They found at once the right wattage for the wireless. They also found another network—of foreign workers. Jobs were no problem, not when they had our excellent London forgeries as papers. They were employed in a dairy and drove around in milk trucks, so did a dozen other French and Belgian workers. The dairy routes were thus quickly turned into intelligence networks that brought the

Chauffeur team information on troop movements, artillery and anti-aircraft emplacements, and other possible targets for aerial attack. This information was either radioed directly to London or sent up the Joan Eleanor channel. The two Belgians were resourceful men able to draw information from diverse sources. They met two French girls who worked in a German brothel. The girls were amenable to being trained to draw information from clients without arousing their suspicion. Soon customers were talking frankly to the girls about where they had been and where they were going. Even this rather fragile order of battle information found its way back to London.

The pace was beginning to wear us down in London. Simpson's team couldn't keep up with our needs for more Joan Eleanor equipment. I couldn't tighten the screws on him any harder. We didn't have anywhere near enough planes, moreover, to make full use of the Joan Eleanor our 14 teams had in the field. Planes and personnel were pushed to fly missions night after night. High altitude flying adds to the stress on pilot and crew. At times it can be excessive, a fact we realized after one of the navigators broke down and cried like a baby. He had flown eight missions in seven days, all at over 30,000 feet. It was too much.

Yet putting teams into Germany was not our only source of concern in the OSS. The heat never let up, whether it came from SHAEF or from Washington. While we were pouring men into Germany, a storm was brewing in Washington over Allen Dulles's Italian adventure about which I had been hearing fragments during March.

It came to a head on April 12, 1945. The news had just come in over the radio that Franklin Roosevelt had died in Warm Springs, Georgia, when I found a message from Donovan. He was in Paris. Would I fly over and meet him for breakfast at the Ritz the next morning? He listened attentively while I described our successes. The war seemed to be nearing an end, we all sensed that. Yet no one was really sure how long the Germans could keep on fighting. The Battle of the Bulge had left lingering scars. The mood remained one of pouring it on in every possible way.

But Donovan's great interest at that point was in Allen Dulles's negotiations to end the fighting in Italy. Dulles fidgeted in his chair, alternately outraged and embarrassed by the reaction his activities had triggered. Bluntly put, all hell had broken loose at SHAEF. Bedell Smith had called Col. Russ Forgan, who had just replaced Bruce as OSS Chief in Europe, on the carpet in Paris. Back in Washington, an angry Admiral Leahy had summoned Donovan to the White House to demand an explanation of just what Dulles was up to in his dealings with the Germans in Italy and Switzerland. That morning, over coffee and fresh croissants, Dulles told us the whole story with relish and juicy detail.

It had begun in early March when Swiss intelligence and several Italian intermediaries arranged for General Karl Wolff, the ranking SS general and commander of the Rear Military Area in Italy, to make a clandestine visit to Switzerland for discussions with Allen Dulles. The Italians had vouched for Wolff's earnest desire to end the war and avoid unnecessary destruction in northern Italy.

Wolff himself had sent Dulles a set of "references" attesting to his character and purpose, including one from Pope Pius XII. When Dulles demanded a token of good faith as the price for the meeting, Wolff paid that, too. It wasn't easy. He had four days in which to set free and bring to Dulles Ferruccio Parri and Antonio Usmiani, two Italian patriots and underground leaders—Usmiani was an Italian OSS agent—who ranked among the most famous SS prisoners in Italy. That he was able to deliver proved his claim to control SS forces on that front.

On the appointed day, Wolff arrived in Berne—he had taken the Milan express—and was driven straight to Dulles's villa and ushered into his study. His proposals were far-reaching. The war, he told Dulles, was lost, its continuation a crime against the German people. In order to help end it, Wolff would put himself and his troops at the disposal of the Allies. He was acting alone, he assured Dulles, without Hitler or Himmler's knowledge. Wolff pointed to his friendship with Field Marshal Albert Kesselring, the commander of all German forces in Italy. Wolff was sure that he could enlist Kesselring's help for the surrender negotiations. Dulles remained noncommittal throughout and, when Wolff was finished, thanked him and said he would be in touch. The next day, when Dulles was not present, Wolff went further and said he would halt operations against Italian partisans behind German lines, free several hundred Jews held at Bolzano and ship them to Switzerland, and assume personal responsibility for the safety of 350 British and American prisoners-of-war held at Mantua.

Dulles promptly encoded the substance of the conversation and radioed it to Washington and to General Alexander at Caserta. Alexander, in turn, transmitted the report to Moscow and London via the Combined Chiefs of Staff. Then, on his own initiative and without waiting for a reply from on high, Alexander told Dulles that two top aides were on the way to see him—Major General Lyman Lemnitzer, Alexander's Deputy Chief of Staff, and British Major General Terence S. Airey, Alexander's chief intelligence officer. Dulles was to arrange for their crossing into Switzerland from the Lyon area, then set up another meeting with Wolff. Dulles found a secluded villa in Ascona on the Lago Maggiore in Italian Switzerland and on March 19 brought Lemnitzer and Airey together with Wolff. It had only been a short while since the first Dulles-Wolff meeting but already Wolff's plans had gone a little awry. Kesselring had been shifted west to succeed von Rundstedt as commander of the Western Front. That removed a potent friend from the negotiating arena. Still, Wolff believed that he could persuade Kesselring's successor, General Heinrich von Vietinghoff, to stop the fighting. He told the three Allied officers that he would seek a meeting with Kesselring to get his help in turning von Vietinghoff around. General Hans Röttiger, Kesselring's chief of staff, had remained in his Italian job and Wolff was sure Röttiger would help, too. The meeting, Dulles said, had been a little strained but polite enough down to drinks and lunch.

Four days later, on March 23, the day Patton crossed the Rhine, Wolff had met with Kesselring at his new command post at Bad Nauheim, only 15 kilometers from 3rd Army spearheads. The meeting was tense and uncomfortable. Kes-

selring was in an all but untenable position. As commander
of the Western Front he lacked the relative political freedom
he had enjoyed in Italy. He was charged with defending
"holy" German soil and had a couple of SS divisions looking
over his shoulder to make sure he did not shirk his responsibilities. If he did, the SS was ready to take "appropriate"
action and the uncomfortable Field Marshal knew it. Surrender in the West was still out of the question. Nevertheless, he
told Wolff he would "counsel" von Vietinghoff to stop fighting in Italy. But Wolff had to wait more than ten days before
he had an opportunity to work on von Vietinghoff. Himmler
ordered Wolff to Berlin first.

Already apprehensive, the SS general dared not refuse. He
sat in a private compartment of the night train to Berlin and
puffed cigarettes with growing nervousness. It turned out,
however, that he had little to fear. Himmler had heard of
Wolff's visits to Switzerland but had no objections. Intelligence services were supposed to keep lines open to the enemy. But neither Himmler nor his deputy, Ernst
Kaltenbrunner, had an inkling of just how far Wolff had gone
in his talks or the high rank of those he had met. What concerned them in early April was that Wolff might be a com-
petitor. Von Ribbentrop already had peace feelers out in
Stockholm. Himmler was exploring the peace terrain in Sweden and Switzerland. He didn't need or want another "ex-
plorer." His instructions to Wolff, therefore, were clever,
cruel, and appropriate. Wolff was to keep lines of communications to Switzerland open but was forbidden to visit the
country again. And to make sure he did not, Himmler told
Wolff with a very thin smile that he had placed the general's
family under his personal protection. Wolff knew only too
well that such protection meant death to his loved ones if he
were found out.

The threat was dire enough to keep Wolff from returning
to Switzerland but not so severe as to prevent his seeing von
Vietinghoff. Dulles received the results of that meeting in
written communications delivered to him on April 8 by an
Italian intermediary. Clearly, Wolff had turned von Vietinghoff around—but not completely. He was willing to sign an

instrument of unconditional surrender provided some "points of honor" were preserved. In retrospect, they seem halfway between the ridiculous and the pathetic. German soldiers would stand at attention when the Allies arrived to accept their surrender. Internment as prisoners-of-war in England or the U.S. was out, with detention in Italy strictly limited. While in Italy, German soldiers were to be engaged in "useful work of reconstruction" on roads and railways rather than spend time behind barbed wire. After the situation had stabilized, von Vietinghoff's men were to return to Germany with belts and bayonets as proof of an "orderly" surrender. Finally, von Vietinghoff asked for the "maintenance of a modest contingent of Army Group C [his command] as a future instrument of order inside Germany."

Dulles at once cabled the content of the written message to Alexander's headquarters at Caserta. Two days later, on April 10 he received a curt, almost brusque reply. Terms of surrender would be handed von Vietinghoff's emissaries once they arrived at Alexander's HQ—and only if they had complete authority to act in their commander's name. The iron fist of "unconditional surrender" showed clearly underneath the velvet glove Dulles had tried to put over it. Dulles nevertheless remained hopeful.

One of the first things that had to be done was establish better and more assured means of communications with the Germans. Dulles got Henry Hyde to send him a German-speaking radio operator who seemed to fill that particular bill. He was a 26-year-old Czech who had escaped from Dachau in 1940 and lived underground in Germany for three years. Arrested in 1943, he escaped into Switzerland. After the Germans retreated from France, he crossed the border, signed up with Hyde's OSS group and was trained as a wireless operator. Dulles had sent him to Milan with a radio set, a signal plan, and code pads. He was assigned the top floor of a house as his operating base so that he could establish independent and secure communications between Wolff and Dulles. He was known as "Wally."

With the stage thus set for fruitful surrender negotiations, Dulles flew to Paris for his meeting with Donovan. Donovan now provided Dulles with his first inkling of the acrimonious messages that Roosevelt and Churchill had received from Stalin charging that the Allies had agreed to ease their armistice terms. Donovan, nevertheless, told Dulles to keep going. True, the communications had upset the White House and SHAEF. But Donovan was convinced neither the U.S. nor Britain would let such Soviet objections stand in the way of the OSS negotiations. A week later, Dulles discovered how wrong Donovan had been; he was told to break off all contact with the German emissaries. The Joint Chiefs of Staff had decided that the complications with the Russians resulting from Dulles's negotiations weren't worth the candle and the matter was closed.

Fear of such "complications" was grounded in the myth of the Bavarian "redoubt." Allied generals worried that Hitler had built a system of mighty fortifications in the Alps where he could hold out forever. We would need the Russians to grind the Wehrmacht down elsewhere, while the redoubt was reduced. As a result of this belief, battle plans were changed and such vital targets as Prague and Berlin, abandoned. The postwar map of Europe might have looked very different had Dulles been allowed to complete his April negotiations with Wolff, instead of waiting around another two weeks. The Germans would then have allowed the Allies to enter the Alps by the backdoor where they could have exploded the redoubt myth first hand.

Instead, Ike stuck to the strategy shift he had ordered at the end of March when he decided that Berlin had "no military significance"—a decision the Russians were happy to applaud; they knew its political significance. So Ike stalled Monty's drive for the German capital and allowed the Soviet armies to capture it. The British were directed to seize the Baltic ports. Bradley's army group was shifted south and east, toward Leipzig, the Czech frontier, and the Bavarian and Austrian Alpine passes. Eisenhower's decision infuriated everybody. Churchill flayed its blatant political stupidity from London. Montgomery, Bradley, Hodges, and Patton insisted they could easily beat Zhukov to Berlin. But Roosevelt and his advisers supported Eisenhower's policy, and in the spring of 1945 Washington was the last court of appeal. Churchill was left to grumble, Patton shifted his armor toward Prague (which he was never allowed to reach), while Bradley had to worry about closing passes to an Alpine redoubt that never was.

The OSS, too, played a key role in the redoubt myth. We were unable to explode it and we should have, easily. We had a dozen teams in the redoubt area and none of them reported anything justifying belief that enough military strength could be generated in that pastoral, undeveloped country to resist 5 million Allied troops for more than a few weeks. Yet, America had failed to develop the kind of multi-disciplined organization able to coordinate and evaluate all kinds of intelligence—something which Donovan had asked for and Roosevelt had authorized in 1941. But the OSS had never been given full access to the flow of military intelligence. If no one else, the Pentagon's top intelligence officer, General Strong, had seen to that. So fragmentary reports of construction and SS troops in the redoubt area and Goebbels deception and propaganda were blown up and sensationalized in the Allied press to create a myth that changed the shape of the postwar world.

Still, Bill Langer's Research and Analysis Branch had done the intellectual spadework on the redoubt. A long, detailed, solid, scholarly report entitled "An Analysis of the Political and Social Organization, the Communications, Economic Controls, Agricultural and Food Supply, Mineral Resources, Manufacturing and Transportation Facilities of South Germany" had been sent to Europe. Though the report did not focus on the possibility of such a redoubt, anyone who read it would have trouble believing in the German capability or will to build one so late in the war. Unfortunately, Langer's work was too long for any intelligence officer to read, let alone any of the field commanders whose reading time was limited to front-line reports.

It was easier, instead, to believe "diplomatic sources" who speculated that Hitler would make a last ditch stand in Bavaria. The speculation was not based on much factual evidence, no more perhaps than on a series of idle notions: The

Nazis had started in Bavaria, they might want to finish there. The Swiss had built a successful network of mountain fortresses, the Germans might try to emulate them. Perhaps the Nazis had set up underground factories, stored caches of food and ammunition. There were reports of SS schools and organizations in Bavaria. There were stories that prisoners had been moved south as camps were overrun by advancing Allied armies. The Allies themselves contributed to the redoubt hysteria. German agents in Switzerland, for example, got their hands on an American diplomatic report full of such speculation. The Gauleiter of Tyrol-Vorarlberg in the Austrian Alps, Franz Hofer, promptly issued a report of his own, urging creation of an Alpine fortress. Goebbels, whose genius for exploiting propaganda opportunities never left him, even in the darkest days of the Reich, joined the growing chorus. Millions of Germans would wage guerrilla war, he threatened, and take ten Allied soldiers for every German killed. The U.S. and British media smelled a good story and let the lurid imaginations of their best feature writers run amuck. Stories played up Hitler Youth groups organized and trained to hold the Bavarian Alps no matter what the cost. German prisoners-of-war began to manufacture facts for these pieces with accounts of fortifications, supplies, and special caches of arms. Nor was Moscow to be outdone by Goebbels and the Germans. The Soviets issued dire warnings of German power and will to resist in the south. In New York, *The Daily Worker* shrilly echoed the Moscow line.

The real facts, in contrast, were meager. The Germans had begun construction of scattered fortifications. If anyone had analyzed the situation clearly or studied Bill Langer's report with care the conclusion was obvious: No meaningful defensive system could be built in under the two years it took the Swiss to complete their Alpine fortress.

Eisenhower was poorly served by report after report coming from various Allied headquarters that took myths, fears, and lies as coin of the military realm. SHAEF's weekly intelligence summary weighed in with an assessment that German defensive strategy had focused on protecting the Alpine areas. Bradley issued an order entitled "Reorientation of

Strategy.'' It contained appendices that took the redoubt as fact and sketched the outlines of a campaign against the fortress. A Seventh Army intelligence study was even more specific: Himmler had ordered provisions stocked there for 100,000 men. Underground aircraft ordnance factories were already humming. Special armies were on their way to the redoubt, spearheaded by 80 crack units of from 1,000 to 4,000 men each.

All these years later, I still find it difficult to imagine what hard information the study was based on. But it was typical of the obstacles we at the OSS faced in trying to fit sporadic reports into the realities of the military situation. We discussed it among ourselves in London and Paris and none of us could see the Germans mounting anything but a token defense in the mountains against Allied armies that could starve out German troops even if they could not dislodge them. All our information pointed to a castle built on airy propaganda—words out of Berlin that had to be dismissed as trivia.

The Pickaxe team we had dropped into Bavaria in early April toured southern and eastern Bavaria. They sent a complete report via Joan Eleanor that did its best to demolish the myth. Pickaxe had found no evidence pointing to any German ability to mount serious resistance in the Bavarian mountains. The report was at once transcribed and the summary sent to SHAEF, where it had little impact. Other agent reports earlier and later confirmed the more exhaustive Pickaxe study. As early as January, Bert Jolis had sent a tourist team from Switzerland through Innsbruck and the Austrian Alps to Vienna which had reported substantially the same thing.

Of course, agent reports were only one part of the overall intelligence picture. But there were few places in the European Theater where anyone was equipped to understand the complex process of analyzing intelligence. Only Colonel Koch, the Third Army's G-2, did the rigorous analysis required. Fortifications without defenders, he noted, did not represent much risk, and the threat, if there was one, had to come from the elite "Waffen SS," Himmler's front-line army. Koch studied the movement of all SS divisions between January and April and found that not one SS unit had been shifted into the Alpine area from another front. Nor did aerial reconnaissance reveal unusual road or rail movement to signal any buildup in the area. On April 19, Koch issued a report labelling the redoubt a myth. His assessment reexamined a minority position, as did our own.

The problem went beyond analysis. In some ways, it was the most maddening of the many the OSS had faced during its turbulent wartime career. We had the resources to marshall facts into coherent analysis but we found no one who would listen. The U.S. Army in Europe had neither the time nor the trained intelligence manpower. For OSS the myth of the redoubt meant a massive shift toward the south, to Austria and Bavaria, where some of our OSS teams encountered the most bizarre and hair-raising adventures; clear evidence, indeed, if any more was needed, that the German war effort was crumbling.

Take the Belgian team we codenamed Doctor. The two men were loaded on a plane at Dijon in late March and flown over the Austrian Alps, where they jumped onto a mountain slope near Kufstein in the Tyrol. The night was cold, the moon was clear. The parachutes glided down safely and the men landed in five feet of snow. As they gathered the chutes and prepared to hide them they saw three men approach. Their apprehension vanished when they learned that the newcomers were Wehrmacht deserters eager to start an anti-Nazi resistance movement. The night before they had spread a large Austrian flag on the mountain where the Doctor team had landed, hoping to attract the attention of Allied planes and thus get help for their nascent movement.

The Austrians and Doctor moved fast. They found a mountain hut all but secure at this time of year. It proved a safe house from which they could broadcast and build up an intelligence and sabotage network. Doctor's stay lasted 45 days, time enough to get a lot accomplished. Contact had been established with underground groups in Kufstein, Kitzbühel, and the small villages of the region. They had been supplied with arms, ammunition, explosives, incendiaries, binoculars, cigarettes, sugar, and propaganda. Four radio sets had been hooked up in different villages, using local power, a system that allowed fast transmission of spot intelligence. Some of the weapons found quick usage. The Austrians there had grenades to destroy three direction-finding trucks.

Supply missions were flown to Doctor twice, once on April 2, and again on April 24. Doctor, aided by 15 guerrillas, lit the field for the second drop, which included two more London-based Secret Intelligence teams—Virginia and Georgia—that were made up of two Dutchmen each, whom we had recruited from the Dutch secret service. The teams spent a week with Doctor catching up on the local lore before they separated. One team went to live with local resistance leaders in Kufstein, the other in Kitzbühel. From there they sent reports to London and helped direct and expand the activities of Austrian freedom fighters.

The three teams did good work. They sent a total of 66 messages, covering the location and plans of a heavy mountain infantry and training battalion in Kufstein; the new anti-aircraft reinforcements along the Inn river; the headquarters location of the Nazi Werewolf organization in the Tyrol; the oil storage depots around Halle, pinpoint of a trainload of gasoline; and the location of a jet plane base on the Autobahn near Munich. That last nugget was labeled as "of great value" by U.S. air force intelligence. One new element helped greatly—fear. Agents told local villagers that failure to co-operate would result in swift aerial retribution. The flow of information swelled remarkably as a result.

The agents teamed up with guerrillas in counter-sabotage operations, such as removing dynamite charges from bridges and keeping them open for advancing Allied troops. They also put the heat on local Nazi commands in Kitzbühel and Kufstein not to resist the advancing Allied troops. After U.S. troops arrived in their area, the agents helped track down local Nazi leaders and find Nazi arms caches. Later, the commanding generals of the 26th and 42nd Divisions would testify that Kitzbühel had been more thoroughly purged of military and political "undesireables" than any other occupied territory they had seen up to that time.

We had a lot less luck with the missions Howard Chapin

organized and sent north from Bari, near the heel of the Italian boot. More than twenty agents sent on five missions to Austria or Czechoslovakia were either in Gestapo prisons or had already been executed. The one exception and by far the most successful of the operations mounted from Bari took off in February and remained active till the war was over. Codenamed Greenup, the three-man team was to observe traffic passing through the Brenner Pass and to find out what they could about the Alpine redoubt. Greenup was a motley crew. The leader was Frederick Mayer, a GI whose Jewish family had fled Germany before the war and had settled in Brooklyn. Hans Wynberg was his radio operator. The third man in the trio was a Wehrmacht lieutenant named Franz Weber who had been recruited from a POW cage on the Italian front.

Their start was hardly auspicious. They were supposed to land on a frozen lake near Innsbruck. Instead, they floated down on a mountainside 10,000 feet up. Undeterred, they treked to Innsbruck where Weber had two sisters. The women got their brother housed and found him the uniform of a German high Alpine unit. Weber's fiancée found a farmer in the hamlet of Oberperfuss outside Innsbruck to take Wynberg and his radio. In a matter of weeks, Mayer had blossomed into a guerrilla leader. He radioed to Bari that he had a thousand Austrian patriots under his command and demanded explosives and pistols. A chagrined Al Ulmer, who ran the Bari operation, had to tell him in no uncertain terms that he was on an intelligence mission and not acting in an Errol Flynn movie. A chastened Mayer promptly switched to accurate reporting on German convoys heading for the Brenner Pass and the Vorarlberg tunnel.

But Mayer's moment of dramatic triumph came on May 3, when the 103rd U.S. Infantry Division, attached to the 7th Army, bivouacked 18 miles from Innsbruck readying an assault on the Tyrolean capital, long touted as the center of the redoubt. German forces were reported dug in deep and ready to wage a last-ditch defense of the city. The Americans were preparing to pay a high price for its capture. As dusk fell and the Americans brewed coffee and pored over maps, a German "Kübelwagen"—their poor rival to our jeep—drove up. A bed-sheet had been tied to the antenna and flew in the brisk wind, a ludicrous flag of truce. A man leaped out, and in an unmistakable Brooklyn accent, for all the Germanic overlay, introduced himself as Fred Mayer of the OSS. He presented his compliments to the general in command and wondered when it would be convenient for him to accept the surrender of the city he had come to attack. For the last couple of days, Mayer explained, he had unloaded a verbal blitz on Franz Hofer, the Nazi Gauleiter of Tyrol and Vorarlberg, who only weeks earlier had urged the Reich's government to waste no time in building the redoubt. In the last weeks of the war, however, Nazi bravado had begun to melt like wax. He agreed with Mayer that Innsbruck should be given up without a fight. Of course, Mayer's German-Brooklyn eloquence was not the only factor in Hofer's decision. Austrian anti-Nazi resistance was strongest in Tyrol, and patriotic forces had disarmed most Wehrmacht soldiers still willing to fight, not that there had been that many. For the 103rd, none of that mattered. What counted was the occupation of Innsbruck without a drop of blood being shed.

One of the most dramatic stories of our German operations, however, involved a team that never sent a single message back to London, yet made a major contribution to the beginnings of postwar occupational operations in Germany. The team was codenamed Painter, and was made up of two young Belgians, Emil van Dyck, known as Jan, and his partner whom we called Francis. Both had performed brilliantly in occupied Belgium in intelligence as well as in sabotage. They jumped near Munich late in March. Their assignment: find and penetrate any anti-Nazi underground organization that might exist among local Germans. They had an excellent cover story. They were to explain that back in 1943 they had been deported from Belgium to work in Gleiwitz, a Silesian town the Russians had only recently captured. Once in Munich they had the good luck to run into some Frenchmen in a beer hall who had really been to Gleiwitz and had left the town as refugees. The details they learned about living and working conditions there allowed the Painter agents to embellish their cover story to the point where they found work in a Gestapo garage. How they did was symptomatic of the deterioration of the social fabric of the Reich during the last weeks of the war. The Catholic Youth Movement in Belgium had given them the name and Munich address of a young Belgian. Bringing a picture of his mother with them, Jan and Francis contacted the boy cold. He had just the know-how they needed. He showed them how to register with the police using their forged papers, how to obtain food ration stamps, and then got them jobs at the same Gestapo garage where he himself worked.

They gave me a firsthand account of how they lived and worked, and what had happened to them, when I visited Munich in early May. I was led to a small wooden hut in back of the Gestapo garage where they had slept. They had cut a hole in the floor under the double-decker bunk where they hid their radio set. Bringing the wireless to the barracks housing 150 Gestapo officers took guts enough, but asking and getting permission to rig up an aerial for an air raid warning radio required something more.

One day, a German in civilian clothes came to their hut and asked if they were Van Brunt and Schmidt, their cover names, where they had come from, and if they knew Trostberg, the village where they had landed. Clearly, he had the goods on them. When they denied ever hearing of Trostberg, their visitor said bluntly: "I don't believe you."

"Let me tell you a little story that will interest you," he went on. "A few weeks ago we found two parachutes near Trostberg. Two young fellows have been reported in that neighborhood heading north. I'm sure it's just coincidence but the descriptions we've gathered fit you perfectly."

There was no longer any doubt. He was from the Gestapo. But there was something strange in his manner. Why did he hold back?

They fenced for a few minutes, Francis with his hand on his pistol, Jan knowing Francis would never be taken alive, the Gestapo man accusing, Jan evading. Then Francis said sharply: "You know the war will soon be over and the Americans will be here." "Yes, everyone knows that," said the Gestapo man. Jan jumped in: "Do you like South America?"

Startled, a look of crafty interest coming over his face, the Gestapo man replied sharply enough: "What are you driving at?" "Nothing special," said Jan. "Do you have any family?" "Yes, right here in town," was the reply.

With that, Francis reached under the bunk and came up with a roll of 5,000 marks. Tossing it on the little table, he said, "Maybe you need some money. Times are hard." The German, obviously tempted at the size of the roll, shook his head.

"Would you like to go to South America with your family?" Jan pressed on. "Let's talk it over," answered the German, "and I will call my friend in." He went to the door, spoke in rapid German to tell a man waiting outside that the Belgians had made a good offer and beckoned him in.

Seeing the newcomer's eyes widen at the sight of the roll of bills, Francis reached down and threw another roll on the table. Each of them snatched one of the rolls. Jan and Francis now knew they were in control of things. Just to make sure, Francis showed his gun and said there would have to be an understanding if the Gestapo men were to get out of the room alive. Because that was the way they operated, the two Germans believed that the Americans would shoot every high-ranking member of the Gestapo they caught, a belief Himmler had encouraged.

As Jan reported it to us: "Both of these traitors turned out to have important positions in the local Gestapo. Emil, the first chap, was head of the investigating section, and his partner Hans was an administrative official. They had been assigned to our case when children playing in the woods had discovered our chutes. The Nazi garage foreman who had questioned us a few days later had given them a good lead, and a check of new registrations with the Munich police had led directly to us. Evidently they had come with some idea of making a private deal, because they had told their superiors that they had found no trace of us. Of course they assured us that they had never favored Hitler but had been forced into the work. We let that one go by, although we had our own ideas on that score.

"They told us that they could get us complete information

on the Gestapo organization all over Bavaria. They confirmed
that a Werewolf underground organization was already in the
process of formation, and that it was to be built on the frame-
work of the Gestapo and other Nazi security services. Orders
had been coming in over the teletype from Himmler in Berlin. These were top secret and not available to them, but they
said they knew the girl who handled the messages and would
see to it that she was brought to us the minute the American
troops arrived. Having decided to betray their associates to
save their own hides, they were pitifully eager to offer information.

"After they left, Francis and I had to decide whether we
should trust them or escape to new quarters and start all over
again. It was a dangerous game, and we knew that they would
sell us out in a minute. However, the stakes were so unbe-
lievably high that we decided it was worth the risk."

When they met a week later, Hans, the administrative official, brought with him a document that by itself made their
entire mission worthwhile. It was a carbon copy of the payroll
for the whole Gestapo organization throughout Bavaria, complete with real names, false names, and addresses.

And by the time the advance American units arrived in
Munich, Jan and Francis had not only the complete Gestapo
roster, but their plans to go underground. For six weeks, they
led Army counterintelligence forces in rounding up Nazis.
Some of their most spectacular arrests included General
Schmidt Voygt, Commanding Officer of the Secret Police of
all Germany; Haupt-Sturmbannfuhrer Wolf, chief of all the
German agents in Belgium and France; the chief of the Nazi
espionage net in Switzerland; and the head of one of the top
sections of the Bavarian Gestapo. All of the big-time Nazis
were disguised and had false papers, but the Belgians had the
goods on them.

These are but a few of many stories and not necessarily
the most dramatic. Most of our teams had trouble establishing
direct wireless contact with London or other rear-echelon
posts. Sources of power were often difficult to find, direction-
finding vans had to be avoided. Most important, perhaps, the
speed of the Allied advance made constant changes of plans

and instructions normal operating procedure. Bill Grell's plaintive moan that "General Patton is screwing up all my operations" held for most of us. Nevertheless, our teams did deliver valuable intelligence, most often after they were overrun. Many agents acted as guides for Allied troops unfamiliar with local terrain. And those with Joan Eleanor equipment did deliver valuable tactical and strategic information. Only weeks before the German surrender, SHAEF developed a new aerial assault plan. It called for air strikes against rail centers in the Chemnitz-Leipzig-Halle-Gotha area. The rationale was simply that this region had become the hub of Germany and the center of Wehrmacht resistance. Specific targets included 15 marshalling yards in Germany and 13 in Austria. As late as April 19, bombers were ordered to pound yards on the Halle-Leipzig "gate" to the Alpine redoubt. For all the arguments we in the OSS had had with the British forces led by Solly Zuckerman, and for all of the strategic superiority of bombing bridges and cutting isolated rail lines, the Zuckerman marshalling yard theory prevailed. So much so, in fact, that one disgruntled OSSer predicted that the last bomb to fall on Germany would hit the last marshalling yard still in German hands.

In the final weeks of the war, we became embroiled in one other activity—SHAEF concern about Allied prisoners in the hands of a disintegrating government and army command structure. Accordingly, it established SAARF (Special Allied Airborne Reconnaissance Force) to see what could be done to protect prisoners. A POW room was set up at SAARF's forward base. It kept lists of various camps and the estimated number of prisoners held in each. The teams were to provide additional information as it was obtained. They were to use radios but not firearms. Each team had a letter from General Eisenhower asking for continued humane treatment of prisoners (with a subtle but steely "or else" in the missive). Once in enemy territory the team was to approach POW camp commanders to prevent forced marches, massacres, or other mistreatment. Seventeen OSS personnel were involved in the 60-odd SAARF teams (usually made up of two men). Though the first missions met with some success, the idea was not widely implemented.

Six teams jumped on April 25 in the Altengrabow area. Two teams were made up of OSS men in uniform. One team located POW laborers in a field, made contact with a British major and a Russian captain already at work in the area, and together contacted the local stalag commandant. The conversations were difficult but after they had radioed the French base from a prisoner-run wireless set in the camp, the commandant came around. He agreed to disobey his own orders to march his prisoners eastward. Instead, he stayed put and awaited the Allies who overran the camp on May 3.

In the waning days of the war Allen Dulles's Italian saga was completed. Washington's orders to break off talks had infuriated him. He felt the U.S. had been duped by a Soviet ploy that would keep British and American troops mired in the Alps while the Russians cakewalked into Austria, Trieste, and northwest Yugoslavia. But good soldier that he was, he prepared to break off the promising negotiations with General Wolff and von Vietinghoff and to extricate Wally, his Milan-based radio operator, from German hands. He had barely begun the process—Washington's final refusal had come about a week after Dulles, Donovan, and I had met at the Ritz in Paris—when he received word that one of von Vietinghoff's ranking staff officers, Colonel von Schweinitz, was on his way to Switzerland. He carried von Vietinghoff's written authorization to surrender on behalf of the German general commanding in Italy. Two days later, on April 25, Dulles received a letter from General Wolff in which he authorized his chief adjutant to make binding commitments on his behalf.

Dulles's dilemma drove him half mad. He could make a deal for the surrender of all German troops in Italy, regular Wehrmacht and SS, virtually overnight, but was under strict orders not to deal with them. He had radioed to both Washington and to Alexander's headquarters at Caserta about this bind on April 24th. The answer finally came on the 27th. Previous instructions were reversed. He was instructed to bring the German emmissaries to Caserta as swiftly as possible and was told that the Russians had been invited to send a representative. Dulles swiftly made the necessary arrangements for the Caserta meeting, and had Wally moved from Milan to General Wolff's new headquarters at Bolzano in the south Tyrol.

By noon of April 29, an OSS radio at the command post of the SS commander in northern Italy was providing a direct communications link to the German army for both Dulles and Alexander. On April 28, at Caserta, the German emissaries, Major Wenner and Col. von Schweinitz, had signed the surrender document for Wolff and von Vietinghoff and taken it back to Bolzano. The surrender was to take effect on May 1. It did, but not without suspense and drama. When no final word had come from the Germans by May 1, Alexander sent a stiff message through Wally to von Vietinghoff. Early in the morning of May 2, Wally sent a message to Alexander: Kesselring had relieved von Vietinghoff of his command, but Wolff and the commanders of the 10th and 14th German armies had ordered their respective commands to cease hostilities as of 2 p.m. For the next few hours tension mounted. Then, at noon, Wally in Bolzano sent a second message to Alexander. Kesselring had reversed himself and ordered Wolff to agree to both the written and oral conditions of the armistice agreement. Promptly at the 2 p.m. deadline German HQ in Bolzano radioed all Wehrmacht troops to lay down their arms. The war in Italy was over.

Wally had one more contribution to make. On May 3, he tapped out this message:

"Wolff to Alexander by Command of Kesselring—Instruct what Allied headquarters to contact for surrender by commander in chief west."

The next day, Wally received Eisenhower's instructions for Kesselring to contact General Devers 6th Army Group headquarters. The surrender of the German forces in Italy had left the German armies north of them in an impossible position. On May 5, Wally sent a message "To Eisenhower through Alexander from Kesselring" asking Eisenhower to receive Kesselring's Chief of Staff, General Westphal, as a plenipotentiary for the German commander in the west.

One last question posed itself over and over: Would it have been possible to penetrate the Reich as easily and as successfully as we had done in 1945 at some earlier time, say in 1944 or even by late 1943? The British, of course, had insisted that Nazi society was too rigidly structured and too closely controlled to allow successful penetration anytime. For a long time their view prevailed. We had doubted that myth of invincibilty back in the fall of 1944, and a year later we were convinced that we had been right to doubt it. The few agents we had placed inside Germany in 1944 without communications not only survived, but thrived. They established themselves, moved about, and found friends and helpers. The large number we dropped in 1945 did this more easily. They got jobs in the German economy, made friends, found housing.

But why shouldn't they have? The destruction of German city life dated back to 1943. Displaced persons moved through German cities with ease and freedom despite the Gestapo. The conclusion that we should have penetrated Germany earlier seems inescapable. This was largely an American operation. The OSS operated under its own steam in a way it never really had before even during the latter phase of the French campaign, when we had been dependent on the French and on the British. Now, in Germany, the British came to us for help. The painstaking research, and endless assembly and classification of information, had finally paid off. Our work met the acid test of German inspection with flying colors. Only two sets of documents failed to pass inspections and twice the Germans issued warnings that American agents in southern Germany were equipped with papers too good to spot as false.

Donovan's insistence in 1942 and 1943 that the American armies should have their own independent self-sustaining intelligence sources had finally been vindicated in Germany.

19. Aftermaths

As THE fighting drew to a close, a bewildering variety of scientific, industrial, artistic, economic, and financial projects were turning up in my wireless traffic or were brought in by bright-eyed new recruits with orders from Washington.

Preparing for the intelligence activities of an OSS headquarters serving the American commanding general in Occupied Germany was part of my responsibility. I had told both General Donovan and Whitney Shepardson that I did not want to run SI in Germany after the German surrender but wanted to go home and see my family and then serve in the Japanese war until that was concluded. Donovan was fully supportive of this. He told me that he hoped to arrange for me to join an OSS detachment with the Chinese communists in Yenan and that he would like to see me go there with my whole team to conduct operations behind Japanese lines. This seemed an exciting and challenging prospect. I urged Shepardson to get busy in picking my successor and to bring him on the scene as soon as possible so that he could control the preparation for his mission in Occupied Germany. Frank Wisner, a Wall Street lawyer with the rank of Lt. Commander in the Navy, was picked to be chief of SI under Allen Dulles, who was to succeed Forgan as Commanding Officer of the OSS in Occupied Germany. Wisner had served in Cairo and Turkey and was currently in Rumania, so he would not be able to come aboard for several weeks. Fortunately, Dick Helms, who had been an assistant to Shepardson in Washington, and Adolph Schmidt, of the Pittsburg Mellon family, had been assigned to London early in 1945. Both of them knew Germany and the German language and I delegated to them as many OSS projects for Occupied Germany as I could. Nevertheless, it seemed that every week someone would arrive from Washington with a project I would have to accommodate. A fine arts group was charged with finding the valuable works of art Nazi leaders had grabbed for themselves. A host of teams turned up to study German technical achievements and bring samples, drawings, and documents back home.

Some of these activities demanded a fair amount of my attention. One of these was the War Crime Trials. William J. Donovan had accepted the post of Deputy War Crimes Prosecutor to the Chief Prosecutor, Supreme Court Justice Robert Jackson.

I remember vividly having dinner one evening at Claridge's with General Donovan, Justice Jackson, Ed Pauley, who had just been appointed Reparations Commissioner, and Isidor Lubin, Chief of the Bureau of Labor Statistics, who had signed on as Pauley's deputy. Lubin spoke at great length and with considerable vehemence about why it was important to convict the Hitler *Jugend* and other organizations *en masse* so that Russian demands for reparations could be satisfied by German slave labor. Both Donovan and I were appalled at this acceptance of the concept of collective guilt. Donovan was soon disillusioned with the Nuremberg trials and quit.

The most devastating experience of the war for most of us was the first visit to a concentration camp. Rough, tough George Patton tells of retching on seeing a concentration camp for the first time. My first visit was to Dachau a few days after it had been liberated. I'll never understand how, with all we knew about Germany and its military machine, we knew so little about the concentration camps and the magnitude of the holocaust. We knew in a general way that Jews were being persecuted, that they were being rounded up in occupied countries and deported to Germany, that they were brought to camps, and that brutality and murder took place at these camps. But few if any comprehended the appalling magnitude of it. It wasn't sufficiently real to stand out from the general brutality and slaughter which is war. There was little talk in London about the concentration camps except as places to which captured agents and resistants were deported if they were not executed on the spot. And such reports as we did receive were shunted aside because of the official policy in Washington and London to concentrate exclusively on the defeat of the enemy.

As we saw refugees streaming west and heard reports about the behavior of advancing Russian troops, concerns about postwar relations with the Soviets came increasingly to the surface. Donovan, although skeptical about Soviet postwar intentions, played it straight. This seemed to startle the Russians, who had never volunteered any help to us and who had not been responsive to our requests for help on intelligence matters. Of 74 U.S. requests for intelligence, the Soviets granted 21, while we granted 23 out of 24 Soviet requests. Even when the Soviets granted a request made from London or Washington, we didn't always get the intelligence. For example, when the Russians overran the rocket development center the Germans had established at Blizna, in Poland, Churchill had asked Stalin for permission to send some air intelligence officers there. Permission was granted in late July. At the beginning of August, the party was held up in Teheran for almost a week while the Russians issued visas. The party wasn't able to leave Moscow for Poland until five weeks after its departure from London. Once in Poland, the members of the party did find lots of rocket parts and packed them in crates at Blizna, but it took almost a month to get the crates back to Moscow. When the crates were reopened in London, they contained not the rocket components that had been carefully packed at Blizna, but parts of old aircraft engines.

Two days before the German surrender at Reims, I drove from Regensburg to Pilsen, which Patton's 16th Armored Division had just liberated. Reconnaissance elements were already on the outskirts of Prague. An OSS team led by Gene Fodor, who would later produce the famous series of worldwide travel guides, had driven from Pilsen to Prague the day before. The team had passed through the usual stream of German soldiers and Czech civilians marching west in search of an Allied force to protect them from the oncoming Russians, who were still 50 miles to the east of Prague. Fodor and his men entered Prague and were heralded and embraced by Czechs celebrating the liberation of their city. But the Czech patriots had liberated the city at a time when a German army was retreating toward the city, not away from it. Fodor turned around and went racing back to General Huebner's Fifth Corps headquarters at Pilsen to report that the way to Prague was wide open and that the patriots who had liberated the city were likely to face reprisals unless the Americans reached Prague before the German army. Huebner had a spearhead ready to race into the city and Bradley told Patton to get ready to advance to Prague, but when informed of this by Eisenhower, the Russians protested vehemently. Claiming a possible confusion of forces, the Russians—with a German army between them and Prague—persuaded Eisenhower to hold Patton back. Ike's decision went for the OSS as well, and Fodor's little group was yanked back to Pilsen. Moscow's victory in this joust left Patton kicking and screaming in Pilsen and the brave but unarmed Czech patriots in control of the city, but helpless before the shattered but not yet defeated German army retreating toward the Czech capital.

Faced with this predicament, Czech leaders appealed to General Buniachenko. Buniachenko commanded one of three divisions that had been created in January 1945 by a newly proclaimed Russian government-in-exile given the name KNOR or Committee for the Liberation of the Peoples of Russia. His troops were Russians who had previously joined or been forced into the German army.

Buniachenko's division was quartered around Beroun, almost 20 miles west of Prague. On the invitation of the Czech leaders, it promptly smashed its way into the city. This deflected the retreating Germans from Prague but brought two Russian divisions toward the city more rapidly.

Virtually all the KNOR units turned west and raced to surrender to the Americans, as Russian tanks closed in and Russian field commanders assured them that "they would be received back as an erring son is by his father." Of the thousands who accepted this invitation, few escaped almost immediate shipment to a Siberian concentration camp. Most surrendered to the Americans only to be forced to return to the Soviet Union shortly afterwards, where they met the same fate as their brothers who had accepted the blandishments of Soviet field commanders.

Over the next year or so, the Allies handed over to Stalin virtually everyone he demanded—Russians captured by the Germans and forced to work, Russians who put on German uniforms, Russians who refused and went into concentration camps, Russians who fought in the European resistance, Russians who were former Soviet citizens, and Russians who never were Soviet citizens (such as White Russians and others with French and other passports). While the western Allies were forcibly returning more than 2,000,000 Russians to Stalin, only one nation in all of Europe and North America, with a population of 12,000, a police force of 11, and no army, pursued a moral course and gave asylum to 494 Russians. That was Liechtenstein.

After spending six weeks visiting all the OSS bases and outposts from Monaco to Stockholm, recommending decorations and helping agents with their postwar plans, the time to go home arrived in early July. General Donovan had a plane, and Forgan and I flew back to Washington with him, playing gin rummy and talking about the work ahead in the Far East. I immediately went off on a wonderful vacation with my wife and daughter, but expected to set out for China before Labor Day.

Then came the first atomic bomb dropped on Japan on August 6. Three months before the bomb was dropped on Hiroshima, a captain in the Navy had accomplished with Harry Truman what General Eisenhower had failed to accomplish with Franklin Roosevelt. Right after VE day Harry Truman signed a statement spelling out that unconditional surrender meant the end of the war and "the termination of the influence of the military leaders who have brought Japan to the present brink of disaster." It went on to say that unconditional surrender means "provision for the return of soldiers and sailors to their families, their farms, their jobs," and that it "does not mean the extermination or enslavement of the Japanese people." Captain Ellis Zacharias, designated as "official spokesman of the U.S. Government," broadcast this message to the Japanese people in a series of weekly radio talks explaining, in a new twist, that unconditional surrender applied only to the manner in which the war would be terminated, and that after military surrender, the people and the nation would have the benefit of the Atlantic Charter. In early June, the Japanese ambassador to the Kremlin was instructed to ask Marshal Stalin, not yet in the war against Japan, to moderate between Japan and the United States and obtain peace terms. Stalin did nothing. Neither Molotov when he came to Washington in June, nor Stalin when he saw Truman at Potsdam, told us that Japan was ready to quit. Worse still, we either knew or should have known of this perfidy on the part of our Russian allies. American cryptologists, monitoring every outgoing and incoming broadcast in Japan, had picked up and deciphered these messages. Navy Secretary Forrestal recorded in his diary on July 13, 1945, that intercepted messages from Togo to the Japanese ambassador in Moscow, Sato, instructed him to try to see Molotov before Potsdam or immediately thereafter to lay before him the Emperor's strong desire for peace. Togo stated that only the unconditional surrender terms of the Allies prevented termination of the war. At the Potsdam meetings, Stalin told Truman that the Japanese had asked the Soviet Union to mediate an end to the war, but that they had not demonstrated a willingness to accept unconditional surrender and that he had told the Japanese ambassador that he would discuss it with him later. Eleven days after that message, the first bomb dropped on

Hiroshima. Two days later, the second bomb dropped on Nagasaki. The world would never be the same. William Friedman, the man who broke the Japanese code, would say after the war: "If only I had had a channel of communication to the President I would have recommended that he did not drop the bomb—since the war would be over within a week." Whether the bomb should have been held in abeyance while the Japanese were taken at their word and given a chance to accept clearly defined surrender terms, posterity will have to judge.

Certainly Stalin had a conflict of interest at Potsdam in playing down Japan's desire to surrender. When on August 8, Stalin joined in the war against Japan, he did so with intelligence provided him by the Japanese themselves that they were ready to admit defeat. On August 14, Emperor Hirohito surrendered. At the end of August, I resigned from the OSS, and shortly thereafter I received a letter that is still among my most cherished possessions. It says in part:

It has been the policy of the OSS never to hesitate to assign major responsibility to young men who have what it takes. This policy has been, in my opinion, one of our primary sources of strength. It has been vindicated by the outstanding performances of many, but by none more than your own. You took up one of the heaviest loads which any of us had to carry at a time when the going was roughest, and you delivered brilliantly, forcefully and in good time.

It was signed "William J. Donovan, Major-General."

Glossary

A-2. Air Force Intelligence.

AA. Anti-aircraft.

"A" Force. British organization among whose functions was exfiltration of escaped Allied POW's (MedTO).

AAI. Allied Armies in Italy (15th Army Group).

Abwehr. German military foreign intelligence service.

Abwehr II. Sabotage division of the Abwehr.

Abwehr III. Counter-espionage division of the Abwehr.

ACC. Allied Control Commission.

A. C. of S. Assistant Chief of Staff.

AFHQ. Allied Force Headquarters (MedTO).

AGAS. Air Ground Aid Service.

Africa 101. OSS radio direction-finding project in Africa.

AG. Army Group.

"agent provocateur." Agent planted by the controlling authorities of a country to associate with, and thus uncover, foreign agents.

"Agfighters." Air and Ground Forces Resources and Technical Staff (China).

AGFRTS. See "Agfighters."

ALOT. American Liaison Officer Teams (Italian campaign).

AMGOT. Allied Military Government.

AMG. See AMGOT.

ARB. Air-sea rescue boat.

AS. Armée Secrète (French resistance group).

ASF. Army Service Forces.

ASLIB. Association of Libraries and Information Bureaus (British).

ATC. Air Transport Command.

B.A.R. Browning automatic rifle.

BBC. British Broadcasting Corporation.

BCRA. Bureau Centrale de Renseignment et d'Action (de Gaullist secret intelligence agency).

BEW. Board of Economic Warfare (earlier Office of Export Controls, later Office of Economic Warfare and Foreign Economic Administration).

BI. Dutch secret intelligence.

BIS. Bureau of Investigation and Statistics (Chinese National Government's internal security and counter-intelligence service).

"blind." Infiltrated without prearranged reception.

"blow." Reveal or expose.

CAD. Civil Affairs Division (War Department).

CALPO. Comité de l'Allemagne Libre pour l'Ouest (French Office of Free Germany Committee).

CAS. Civil Affairs Section (War Department).

CASA. Civil Affairs Staging Area (California).

CBI. China-Burma-India Theater.

CCC. Chinese Combat Command.

CCS. Combined Chiefs of Staff.

CD. Branch of OSS responsible for camouflage, censorship, and documentation intelligence.

CE. Counter-espionage.

CEA. Controlled enemy agents.

CGT. Confédération Générale du Travail (French labor syndicate).

CI. Counter-intelligence.

CIAA. Coordinator of Inter-American Affairs.

CIB. Counter-Intelligence Branch of SHAEF.

CIC. Counter-Intelligence Corps.

CID. Central Information Division (R&A).

CINCPOA. Commander-in-Chief POA.

CIS. Current Intelligence Staff (R&A).

CIS. Czechoslovak intelligence service.

"City Teams." OSS units dispatched to enter newly liberated cities.

CLN. Comitato di Liberazione Nationale (Italian resistance central committee).

CLNAI. Comitato di Liberazione Nazionale per l'Alta Italia (Resistance Committee for National Liberation for Upper Italy).

C.O. Commanding officer.

COI. Coordinator of Information (predecessor of OSS).

COMINCH. Commander-in-Chief U.S. Fleet.

ComNavEu. Commander, Naval Forces, Europe.

Comm Z. Communications Zone (sector of a theater of operations behind the front).

COSSAC. Chief of Staff, Supreme Allied Command.

C.P. Command post.

CPM. Captured Personnel and Materials Unit (War Department).

CSDIC. Combined Services Detailed Interrogation Center.

CT. China Theater.

counter-scorch. Designed to prevent the destruction of vital installations by a retreating enemy.

cut-out. Intermediary between undercover agents, usually between chief and sub-agents.

CVL. Combattenti Volontari di Liberazione (military branch of CLNAI).

CW. Continuous wave (Morse code, rather than voice, communications).

D/A. C. of S. Deputy Assistant Chief of Staff.

DDOD (I). Deputy Director Operations Division (Irregular), British maritime infiltration service.

Deputy Director—PWO. Deputy Director—Psychological Warfare Operations.

Deputy Director—SSO. Deputy Director—Strategic Services Operations (successor to Deputy Director—PWO).

D/F. Direction finder.

Deuxième Bureau. Intelligence service of the French Army corresponding to G-2.

DF-Section. Unit of British SOE (and later of the joint SFHQ responsible for organizing safe routes of undercover travel in enemy-occupied Europe).

D.G.E.R. Direction Générale des Etudes et Recherches (successor to BCRA).

DIP. Division of Intelligence Procurement (operations section of OSS/ETO as reorganized in late 1944 for the penetration of Germany).

DND. Das Neue Deutschland (''black'' newspaper prepared by MO in MedTo for distribution to German troops).

double agent. An agent who is working on behalf of one intelligence service but actually under the control of another.

DP. Displaced person.

DSI. Division of Special Information (R&A).

DSM. Direction de la Sécurité Militaire (French counter-intelligence agency at the time of French liberation).

EAM. Largest resistance group in Greece, eventually taken over by Communists.

EDES. Anti-Communist Greek resistance group.

EDS. Evaluation & Dissemination Section, SHAEF (established to collate information on Nazi Party).

ELAS. The military arm of EAM.

EMFFI. Etat Major, Forces Françaises de l'Intérieur (London headquarters of the French resistance movement unified under de Gaulle).

EOU. Enemy Objectives Unit (a section of the Economic Warfare Division, ETO).

ETO. European Theater of Operations.

ETOUSA. European Theater of Operations, U. S. Army.

EWD. Economic Warfare Division (a combined unit working under the U.S. Embassy in London, composed of representatives of OSS, BEW, and other U.S. agencies).

FAAA. First Allied Airborne Army.

"The Farm." SI training area (official designation RTU-11).

F-Section. Unit of British SOE (and later of the joint SFHQ) responsible for organizing and exploiting resistance movements in enemy-occupied Europe.

FBI. Federal Bureau of Investigation.

FBQ Co. Inc. Corporation under cover of which OSS conducted radio monitoring activities.

FCC. Federal Communications Commission.

FEA. Foreign Economic Administration (see BEW).

FETO. Far East Theater of Operations.

FEU. Field Experimental Unit (OSS Branch).

FFI. Forces Françaises de l'Intérieur (French resistance groups unified under de Gaulle).

FHA. Federal Housing Authority.

FIC. French Indochina.

FIDES. OSS Field Detachment headquarters in Paris.

Field Photo. Field Photographic Branch of OSS.

FIS. Foreign Information Service (propaganda branch of COI).

FN. Foreign Nationalities Branch of OSS.

FNC. National Liberation Front (Communist-led resistance group in Albania).

Force 136. SOE unit in SEAC.

Force 163. Seventh Army planning staff for invasion of southern France.

FSS. Field Security Service (British counter-intelligence in forward areas of operation).

FTP. Francs Tireurs et Partisans (Communist-controlled resistance group in France).

FUSAG. First U.S. Army Group.

G-2. Military intelligence, U. S. Army.

GBT. Gordon-Bernard-Tan (intelligence chain in Indochina).

GHQ. General Headquarters.

GIS. German intelligence services (counter-intelligence term to cover all German intelligence agencies).

GSI. British Eighth Army intelligence section.

HIS. Hellenic Information Service (Greek intelligence).

IAMM. Independent American Military Mission to Marshal Tito (OSS-staffed delegation to Yugoslav Partisans).

IDC. Inter-Departmental Committee for the Acquisition of Foreign Publications (R&A).

IPDP. Intelligence Photographic Documentation Project (post-liberation joint R&A-Field Photographic project).

IRA. Irish Republican Army.

ISK. Internationaler Socialistischer Kampfbund (German underground political group).

ISLD. Inter-Service Liaison Department (British SIS in MedTO).

ISTD. Inter-Service Topographic Department (a research unit of the British Admiralty).

JANIS. Joint Army-Navy Intelligence Studies.

JCS. Joint U. S. Chiefs of Staff.

J/E. Joan Eleanor (OSS-developed plane-to-ground radio).

JIC. Joint Intelligence Collection Agency.

JICPOA. Joint Intelligence Center Pacific Ocean Areas.

JISPB. Joint Intelligence Studies Publishing Board.

JPS. Joint Planning Staff.

JPWAC. Joint Psychological Warfare Advisory Committee.

JPWC. Joint Psychological Warfare Committee.

JPWSC. Joint Psychological Warfare Sub-Committee.

JSP. Joint Staff Planners.

"K" tablet. A tablet designed to render the subject unconscious for a specified number of hours.

K&L Activities. Early designation of Special (SI and SO) Activities (OSS).

K&L Funds. Early designation of Special Funds Branch (OSS).

"L" tablets. A lethal tablet.

MAAF. Mediterranean Allied Air Force.

MACAF. Mediterranean Allied Coastal Force.

MAS boat. Italian torpedo (PT) boat.

MedTO. Mediterranean Theater of Operations.

METO. Middle East Theater of Operations.

MEW. Ministry of Economic Warfare (British).

M.I.A. Missing in action.

MI-5. British military intelligence unit for home counter-intelligence.

MI-6(V). British military intelligence unit for foreign counter-espionage.

MID. Military Intelligence Division (War Department).

MIS. Military Intelligence Service (War Department).

ML. Military Liaison (British Liaison units dispatched to European resistance groups).

MO. Morale Operations Branch (OSS).

MOI. Ministry of Information (British).

MOPO. MO Operations and Plans Officer.

MRL. Maryland Research Laboratory (R&D).

MS boat. Fast Italian motor gunboat.

MTB. Motor torpedo boat (British).

MU. Maritime Unit of OSS.

NATO. North African Theater of Operations.

NATOUSA. North African Theater of Operations, U. S. Army.

NCAC. Northern Combat Area Command (Burma).

NDRC. National Defense Research Committee.

NEI. Netherlands East Indies.

N.K.V.D. Soviet secret police.

NLRB. National Labor Relations Board.

OCD. Office of Civilian Defense.

OELR. Office of European Labor Research (SI Project of Labor Section, OSS).

OEM. Office of Emergency Management.

OEW. Office of Economic Warfare.

OFF. Office of Facts and Figures.

OG. Operational Groups Branch (OSS).

OGC. Operational Groups Command (OSS).

OI. Oral Intelligence Unit (COI).

OKW. Oberkommando der Wehrmacht (German High Command).

ONI. Office of Naval Intelligence.

O.P. Observation post.

OPA. Office of Price Administration.

OPD. Operations and Plans Division (War Department General Staff).

OPM. Office of Production Management.

OSRD. Office of Scientific Research and Development.

OWI. Office of War Information.

"P" Division. Unit of Mountbatten's staff responsible for coordinating all Allied clandestine operations in SEAC.

POA. Pacific Ocean Areas.

P.Oe.N. Provisional Austrian National Committee.

POW. Prisoner of war.

PPB. Personnel Procurement Branch (OSS).

P.P.F. Parti Populaire Français (French political party of the extreme right).

PT. U. S. patrol torpedo boat.

PW. Psychological Warfare.

PWB. Psychological Warfare Board (AFHQ).

PWD. Psychological Warfare Division (War Department and SHAEF).

PWE. Political Warfare Executive (British).

PWO. Psychological Warfare Operations (OSS; see Deputy Director—PWO).

Q-2. Visual Presentation building planned in 1942 (COI).

Q-Section. Section of SI/Central Europe in Italy (responsible for penetration of Austria through French channels).

Rebecca. A radio beacon device.

"Redoubt." Nazi fortress area in West Austria.

RF-Section. Unit of British SOE (and later of the joint SFHQ) responsible for the training and internal security of European resistance movements.

RSHA. Reichsicherheitshauptamt (Headquarters of German Sicherheitsdienst).

SA. Special Activities Branch (COI).

SA. Sturmabteilung (German pseudomilitary group instrumental in Hitler's rise to power).

SAARF. Special Allied Airborne Reconnaissance Force (formed in 1945 to send agent teams to negotiate with enemy POW camp commanders).

SA/B. Special Activities/Bruce (predecessor of Secret Intelligence Branch of OSS).

SACMED. Supreme Allied Commander, Mediterranean Theater of Operations.

SACO. Sino-American Cooperative Organization.

SACSEA. Supreme Allied Commander, Southeast Asia Command.

"Safe Haven." State Department program for tracing the flight of enemy financial assets.

SA/G. Special Activities/Goodfellow (predecessor of the Special Operations Branch of OSS).

San Marco Battalion. Italian unit for specialized maritime operations.

SAS. Special Airborne Services (British), approximate counterpart of OSS Operational Groups.

SCI. Special Counter-Intelligence (X-2 teams accompanying Allied armies in the invasion of Western Europe).

SCI/Z. Special Counter-Intelligence unit in Italy (X-2).

SD. Sicherheitsdienst: Nazi security police.

SEAC. Southeast Asia Command.

SEC. Securities and Exchange Commission.

SF Detachments. Special Force Detachments, SFHQ (accompanying Allied armies in the invasion of Western Europe).

SFU-4. Special Force Unit-4 (SF Detachment in Southern France invasion).

S-Forces. G-2 units, including OSS representatives, detailed to search newly captured localities for items of intelligence value.

SFE. Survey of Foreign Experts (OSS).

SFHQ. Special Force Headquarters (joint SO/SOE organization in London for the support and exploitation of European resistance movements).

SIM. Italian military intelligence.

SHAEF. Supreme Headquarters Allied Expeditionary Forces.

S-2. Army intelligence units below divisional level.

SI. Secret Intelligence Branch (OSS).

SIS. Secret Intelligence Service (British).

"sleeper" agent. Agent left in territory subsequently to be overrun by the enemy.

SNCF. Société Nationale des Chemins de Fer (French national railroad trust).

SO. Special Operations Branch (OSS).

SOE. Special Operations Executive (British).

SOL. Service d'Ordre de la Légion (militia of "Legion of Veterans of Both Wars"), Vichy-French version of storm troopers.

SOS. Services of Supply (U. S. Army).

SOU. Ship Observer Unit (Project of SI Labor Section, OSS).

Special Ops. G-3 Special Operations Section 15th AG.

SPOC. Special Operations Center (Headquarters in Algiers, subject to SFHQ, responsible for the coordination of the activities of SO, SOE, and French organizations in the support and exploitation of southern French resistance groups).

S-phone. British plane-to-ground communications device.

SR. Service de Renseignement (Intelligence section of Deuxième Bureau, incorporated into the BCRA in 1943).

SS. Schutzstaffel (Nazi elite troops).

SSU. Strategic Services Unit (War Department).

SSTR-1. Agent's suitcase transmitter-receiver. Communications equipment developed and used by OSS.

SSO. Strategic Services Officer (the chief of OSS in a theater of operations).

SSO. Strategic Services Operations (see Deputy Director—SSO).

SSS G-2. Strategic Services Section (G-2) (OSS Seventh Army Detachment).

S&T. Schools and Training Branch of OSS.

Stalag. German POW camp for enlisted personnel.

"stay-behind" agent. (See "sleeper.")

SWPA. South West Pacific Area.

T-Force. ETO units corresponding to MedTO S-Force.

Thaicom. Thai Committee coordinating activities into Siam composed of representatives of OSS/Washington, SI and SO Branches, State Department and other agencies.

T/O. Tables of Organization.

Todt. German Government semi-military labor organization.

UDE. Union Democratica Español ("Popular Front" organization, opposing the Franco Government of Spain).

UNRRA. United Nations Relief and Rehabilitation Administration.

USAFFE. U.S. Army Forces in the Far East.

USAF/IBT. U.S. Army Forces in the India-Burma Theater.

USFA. U.S. Forces in Austria.

USGCC. U.S. Group of the Control Council.

USSTAF. U.S. Strategic Air Force.

V-Forces. Special raiding and reconnaissance groups of NCAC in Burma.

Vet. To check all available counterintelligence files to ascertain whether an individual in question has ever been reported to have unfavorable or potentially dangerous associations.

WDGS. War Department General Staff.

WMC. War Manpower Commission.

W/T. Wireless telegraph.

X-2. Counter-espionage Branch (OSS).

A Letter
To My Daughter

My darling daughter,

   Today is your first birthday, though there is an ocean between us I feel that you and I, thru your mother, are as close together in spirit and soul as I know your mother and I are. There is no material thing that I would not give to bring the three of us together quickly and forever.
   You don't remember, but we'll never forget the quiet happiness and joy we knew when you were just a little bundle of two, three, four, five months. I used to come home and wrestle all around the house with you. You'd squawk and squirm and grunt and groan—just like a wrestler should. Then we'd eat and you'd insist on your mother holding you in one arm while trying to eat with the other. Somehow she always managed. Then we'd roll you out to the roof deck to give you some fresh air and to give the neighbors a chance to admire

278

you. You'd delight all of us by smiling and looking very happy and contented.

As I write now I have a picture of you standing—with the help of a big tree—but still standing. Your mom sent it to me and it must have been taken when you were about 11 months old. Looking down at me from the mantlepiece is a picture of you, your mom and me just before I went overseas. It's hard for me to realize that you've become such a big girl in the 6 months between those two pictures and it will always be a big loss to me not to have seen and helped you grow. But we'll make up for it when we start over again.

I remember so vividly the evenings (there were two) we had the picture of the three of us taken, the Sunday I left you in Bellmore and the morning I left your mom in Washington. I was filled with such a strange mixture of zest for the pending adventure and strong desire to do my part in the nasty job which faced my generation and sadness and apprehension at leaving those I loved so dearly. Now it seems like a bad dream to which I like to return because you & your mother were there.

Today, things seem brighter. This ocean was placed between us by forces you never knew, which the generation before mine failed to control and which mine must stamp out. It is and will be more of a nasty job—but it is a task which must be done if we are to live in peace, freedom and decency. We shrank from the job and the danger grew. And then we found the will to tackle it and now it seems certain that the job will be done and that my generation and yours will get a chance to control the forces of aggression and brutality. So, today, much as I miss being with you, I am glad that I am privileged to do my small part in making our world a decent, peaceful & free one. If I had been with you these 6 months I would always have felt the uneasiness of reaping the benefit of someone else's sacrifice. Now, when we are brought together again, as we all pray daily that we shall be soon, we will know that we have earned the happiness which shall be ours.

And if we remember that whenever the freedom or the dignity of one of us is invaded, the freedom and happiness of all of us is threatened, we may be smart enough to keep this *from happening all over again. If we can do that we'll be free, with God's blessing, to have fun together in our pent-house in New York, on the farm your mother wants, in our suburban home with lots of glass and lots of rolling ground, with all the books we'll get and read, with all the friends we'll have, with trips to England and Ireland and South America & California and the West Indies, where your mom & I had our honeymoon, in talking and swapping ideas and in just being kind to each other & everybody else and in worship of God and in living the way He intended us to live.*

Next time you write don't tell me you have more hair than I have or you'll be over my knee and your dignity will be invaded as soon as I cross that ocean again.

All my love,
Your Dad

Index